Why India Votes?

Mukulika Banerjee

With a Foreword by
Jonathan Spencer

Routledge
Taylor & Francis Group
LONDON NEW YORK NEW DELHI

First published 2014 in India
by Routledge
912 Tolstoy House, 15–17 Tolstoy Marg, Connaught Place, New Delhi 110 001

Simultaneously published in the UK
by Routledge
2 Park Square, Milton Park, Abingdon, Oxon OX14 4RN

Routledge is an imprint of the Taylor & Francis Group, an informa business

© 2014 Mukulika Banerjee

Second impression 2014

This book draws upon data from field reports by Grace Carswell and Geert De Neve, Dolonchampa Chakrabarty, Abhay Datar, Vanita Falcao, Goldy M. George, Mahashweta Jani, Mekhala Krishnamurthy, Satendra Kumar, Badri Narayan, Rosina Nasir, Deepu Sebastian, and Priyadarshini Singh.

Typeset by
Glyph Graphics Private Limited
23, Khosla Complex
Vasundhara Enclave
Delhi 110 096

British Library Cataloguing-in-Publication Data
A catalogue record of this book is available from the British Library

ISBN 978-1-138-01971-3

This book is dedicated to

Aria Gitanjali Banerjee Watts

Contents

Plates

Tables

Abbreviations

ABHM	Akhil Bharat Hindu Mahasabha
AC	Assembly Constituency
ACR	Annual Confidential Report
AD	Apna Dal
AIADMK	All-India Anna Dravida Munnetra Kazhagam
AIJMK	Akhila India Janayaka Makkal Katchi
AITC	All-India Trinamool Congress
AWD	Adarshwadi Dal
BCP	Bhartiya Chaitanya Party
BHBP	Bhartiya Bahujan Party
BHJAP	Bhartiya Jagran Party
BJJD	Bhartiya Jantantrik Janta Dal
BJP	Bharatiya Janata Party
BLD	Bharatiya Lok Dal
BSKP	Bhartiya Sarvoday Kranti Party
BSP	Bahujan Samaj Party
BSP(K)	Bahujan Sangharsh Party (Kanshiram)
CEE	Comparative Electoral Ethnographies
CGVP	Chhattisgarh Vikas Party
CM	Chief Minister
CPI(M)	Communist Party of India (Marxist)
CSDS	Centre for the Study of Developing Societies
CSP	Chhattisgarhi Samaj Party
DMDK	Desiya Murpokku Dravida Kazhagam
DMK	Dravida Munnetra Kazhagam
DTH	Direct to Home
ECI	Election Commission of India
EPIC	Electoral Photo Identity Card
EVM	electronic voting machine
GDP	gross domestic product
GGP	Gondvana Gantantra Party
GMS	Gondwana Mukti Sena
IJP	Indian Justice Party
INC	Indian National Congress

IPL	Indian Premier League
JD(U)	Janata Dal (United)
JGP	Jago Party
JJ	Juggi Jhompadi
JSP	Jansatta Party
KM	Krantisena Maharashtra
KMP	Kongunadu Munnetra Peravai
KNMK	Kongu Nadu Munnetra Kazhagam
LD	Lok Dal
LJP	Lok Jan Shakti Party
LTSD	Loktantrik Samta Dal
MBP	Matra Bhakta Party
MBC	Most Backward Castes
MCC	Model Code of Conduct
MCD	Municipal Corporation of Delhi
MLA	Member of Legislative Assembly
MP	Member of Parliament
NDA	National Democratic Alliance
NELU	Nelopa (United)
NES	National Election Study
NLHP	National Lokhind Party
NREGA	National Rural Employment Guarantee Act
NREGS	National Rural Employment Guarantee Scheme
OBC	Other Backward Class
PA	public announcement
PAP	Parambikulam Aliyar Project
PC	Parliamentary Constituency
PDS	Public Distribution System
PECP	Peace Party
PMK	Pattali Makkal Katchi
PO	polling official
PPOI	Pyramid Party of India
PRCP	Prabuddha Republican Party
PRO	presiding officer
RDMP	Rashtriya Dehat Morcha Party
RJD	Rashtriya Janata Dal
RJVP	Rajasthan Vikas Party
RLD	Rashtriya Lok Dal
RPI(A)	Republican Party of India (A)
RPIE	Republican Party of India Ektawadi

RPP	Rashtriya Pragati Party
RSBP	Rashtriya Swabhimaan Party
RWS	Rashtrawadi Sena
SC	Scheduled Caste
SHS	Shiv Sena
SM	Sector Magistrate
SP	Samajwadi Party
ST	Scheduled Tribe
SWJP	Samajwadi Jan Parishad
UID	Unique Identification Number
UP	Uttar Pradesh
UPA	United Progressive Alliance
VHP	Vishwa Hindu Parishad
YVP	Yuva Vikas Party

Glossary

aam ras	mango juice
aandhi	storm
aashirvaad	blessings
adhikar	right; also *odhikar*
adivasi	indigenous people
anaj-pani	bread and butter
andolan	agitation
annadan	gift of food
arasiyal	politics
astitva	self-worth
atti-samvedansheel	sensitive
baaraat	bridegroom's party
bachhe	children
bahu	bride; daughter-in-law
bhandara	a soup kitchen to feed any passerby, held as an act of charity and virtue
Bharat Mata	Mother India
bhavai	a dance
bhitti	basis
bhudan	gift of land
burkha	veil
chadar	sheet
chamchagiri	currying favour
chaniya choli	clothing for girls and women; skirt and top
chapatti	unleavened bread
charkha	spinning wheel for making homespun yarn, popularised by Gandhi during India's anti-colonial struggle
chunav samagri	papers and materials relating to elections
chunavi mahaparv	great festival of elections
cinnam	symbol
daldal	quicksand

dan	The concept of a gift that is given without expectation of material return and is used variously to describe the gift of alms to a beggar or the prestations that are made to a priest. It is a word that is widely used across the country and in very many different Indian languages.
darsan	to see; catch a glimpse of
dehdan	gift of one's body
desh	country
desh seva	serving the nation
desi daru	country liquor
dhol	drum
dhoti	men's garment, fashioned by draping and tucking a long piece of cloth around the waist and between the legs
Eid ka chand	the moon sighted at the end of Ramzan to mark the festival of Eid
ek din ka sultan	sovereign for a day
English *daru*	bottled liquor (foreign)
fayada	advantage
garba grha	sanctum sanctorum
gautiagiri	nepotism
ghodi	mare on which bridegrooms arrive for their weddings in some parts of India
goudan	gift of cattle
haath ka nishan	thumbprint
harijan tolla	neighbourhood where Dalits live
hawa	wind
irettalai	two-leaf
izzat	honour, prestige
Jai Shri Ram	commonly used greeting by Hindus; 'Praise the Lord'
jameen	land
jan sabhas	congregations
jananayakam	democracy
jar	wealth
jonogono tantra	democratic republic
joru	wife
kadamai	duty
kajkarta	worker

kamal	lotus
kanyadan	gift of daughter
katchi	party
kartavya	duty; also *kartobbo*
khadi	cloth made from handspun yarn
Khudai Khidmatgar	Servants of God
kisan parivar	solidarity of farmers
kudimagan	citizen; drunkard
kurta	long tunic
kuttani dharmam	alliance loyalty/duty
lakshman rekha	The reference is to the Ramayana story in which Lakshman, the hero Ram's brother, drew a line of protection around Sita, when entrusted to look after her safety.
leher	wave
log	people
lokniti	politics of the people
maha michil	large procession
majboori	without choice
makkal atchi	democracy
mandi	agricultural market
manmanapan	whims and fancies
matdan	In the electoral context, the word is adapted such that 'giving/casting one's vote' — i.e., the act of voting — is called 'matdan' (mat=opinion; dan=to give).
mazdoor	worker
mazdoori	labour
mosadi	cheat
nagarik	citizen; also *nagorik*
naye neta	new leaders
neta	leader
nishkam	self-less
nukkad	street corner
paan	mildly addictive parcel made with betel leaf and spices; chewed after meals and otherwise
padyatras	campaigning on foot
paise	money
palki	palanquin; litter

panjo	palm
pativrata	virtuous woman who is loyal to her husband
patwari	revenue officer
phul	flower
pilkhan	Police
prachar	campaign
pracharam	campaign
pradhan	head of the village council
pukka	cooked; baked
punya	virtue
raj	rule
rajniti	politics
sabha	meeting
sakkadai	drain
samagri vitaran	distribution of materials
samaj	society
samikaran	equation
sampradik sadhbhav	communal harmony
sarkar	government
sahukars	upper-caste Kshatriyas
salwar kamiz	common three-piece dress for women consisting of trousers, long tunic and scarf
shrikhand	yoghurt-based dessert
shrmdan	gift of labour
sneh	love
supatra	son
theerthal	election
urimai	right
uzhal illaame katchi	corruption-free party
vakku	vote
vakku chavadi	election booth
vasi	inhabitants
veetpaalar	candidate
veshti	sarong
vote *bahiskar*	vote boycott
Yuva Sammelan	meeting for young people

Foreword

I love elections. I have voted in 10 general elections, four elections to the Scottish parliament, countless local elections, and two referendums. On occasions when I have been unable to go to the polls myself I have used a postal vote or arranged a proxy vote. Not only do I vote frequently and enthusiastically, in my youth I would attend election meetings, canvass from door to door, address envelopes to potential voters, and deliver messages from the candidate of my choice to his or her potential electors. In 1992 I even shed blood in pursuit of a Labour victory, when a large dog sank its teeth into the hand that was pushing an electoral address through a hostile letter-box. When I am away from Britain I particularly enjoy a chance to observe other people's elections. I have watched, more or less for pleasure, elections in Canada, the United States and Sri Lanka. Once, in a particularly blissful coincidence, I found myself in Italy in the month in which not one, but two, popes were elected.

I have just been quoting a paper I wrote 20 years ago in an effort to persuade anthropologists to think more creatively about elections, and about the cultural implications of the institutions of representative democracy. On the whole, they have been somewhat slow to respond. Anthropologists are well used to talking about other people's rituals; they are rarely so comfortable when asked to talk about their own rituals. How many topics are there in the study of ritual in which it is fair to assume that virtually every member of an audience of anthropologists will have not only witnessed several different examples of the ritual in question, but almost certainly participated in at least some of them? With participation comes familiarity and with familiarity comes, if not contempt, at least a certain taken-for-granted indifference to the sheer oddity of the experience.

'Scientifically', elections tend to be apprehended as statistical events, and the bulk of academic study consists of tables and calculations and mountains of figures. But elections are also cultural, and therefore moral, events. The analysis of elections is usually profoundly teleological; who won, and by how much, is taken to be the only really interesting question. But in rushing to the end of the story, analysts miss so much that is just possibly of even greater interest: the effervescence of the crowds at political rallies, the uncertainty that consumes even the most confident participant, the oratory, the spectacle. Elections can be funny and they can be tragic, they can be peaceful and they can be extremely violent. For the real enthusiast they can be beautiful, but they are also often rather ugly. What they are not, is a particularly sensible or straightforward way to get something done. The instrumental value of an individual vote is immeasurably small, yet every voter participates with the conviction that his or her vote matters. Without that conviction, there would really be no point at all.

Nowhere are these questions more pressing than in the world's largest parliamentary democracy. The national turnout in India has been over 60 per cent in 10 of the last 15 elections. In the US, the last time more than 60 per cent of the electorate voted for a President was in 1968. With over 700 million registered voters, India is not only the largest, but also one of the most enthusiastic and engaged of democracies. Indeed, on grounds of scale and enthusiasm, it is surely time to abandon the dreary assumption that Western politics are the taken-for-granted norm, and instead start to treat India as our proper exemplar of 21st-century democracy.

Asking 'Why India Votes?', as Mukulika Banerjee does in this wonderfully lucid book, is hardly a trivial question. Nor is it an easy one. To construct an answer, Banerjee has to make the case for an ethnographic approach to democracy, in the face of an ocean of statistical data, and an academic apparatus usually only oriented towards understanding elections in statistical terms. She also has to persuade her fellow anthropologists to accept two potentially transgressive moves (transgressive for anthropologists, that is). One is to enter into a constructive dialogue with survey data, and the researchers who collect and analyse that data. The other is to construct a properly comparative approach to a huge and complex ethnographic phenomenon. The comparison is internal to the phenomenon, and between fieldsites in radically different parts of the country. In each site an experienced fieldworker has contributed insights and evidence, which Banerjee has in turn had to filter, interpret, and synthesise. Unlike most examples of 'multi-sited ethnography', there is no watering down of context as a single ethnographer flits from site to site. Rather there is the daunting task of embracing complexity and somehow rendering it intelligible, without simplifying or reducing it in any way.

The results of Banerjee's inquiries are always interesting and illuminating, sometimes startling, and they are laid out here with great skill and no little clarity. This is a rare thing: a modest book on an immodest topic, but the modesty is merely a polite facade. There are huge questions being addressed here, with something fresh and compelling on every page. It would be nice to pretend that books on anthropology are always like this, but they are not. The reader will not find any unnecessary recycling of the latest theoretical idiolect. The language is accessible rather than hermetic. Through each chapter, our author reminds us of a central anthropological truth, that people are always much more surprising than we safely assume. 'Why India Votes' is a very good question indeed. Mukulika Banerjee has started to provide her readers with some equally good answers in this excellent book.

Jonathan Spencer
Professor of the Anthropology of South Asia and
Head of School of Social and Political Science
University of Edinburgh

Acknowledgements

This book is a result of many collaborations and it is a pleasure and privilege to thank those who made it possible.

First and foremost, my thanks goes out to the Economic and Social Research Council, UK who provided the funding for the research project 'Comparative Electoral Ethnographies During 2009 Lok Sabha Elections in India' [RES-000-22-3376] on which this book is based. My thanks to the Research Division at University College London for managing the grant and to Mekhala for helping me kickstart the application process.

This project attempted a methodological innovation of simultaneously conducting ethnographic research in different locations across a country. This is a fairly untested path in anthropology and was much dependent on the rigour of each individual study and so my biggest thanks therefore is to the researchers who conducted the individual studies: Priyadarshini Singh (Bihar), Dolonchampa Chakrabarty (West Bengal), Geert De Neve and Grace Carswell (Tamil Nadu), Deepu Sebastian (Kerala), Abhay Datar (Maharashtra), Mekhala Krishnamurthy (Madhya Pradesh), Goldy M. George (Chhattisgarh), Vanita Falcao (Rajasthan), Mahashweta Jani (Gujarat), Rosina Nasir (Delhi), Satendra Kumar (Uttar Pradesh), and Badri Narayan (Uttar Pradesh). Each researcher brought their own perspective to the study while also sticking faithfully to the aim of the project. This allowed for a coherent set of data to be generated in order to create a national picture that was larger than merely the sum of the parts — for this I am very grateful. Sophie Haines was an efficient editor of each individual report and made up the Appendices included in this book and the team at Routledge, New Delhi, were most helpful in providing editorial support for the book as a whole. Oroon Das, as always, provided another striking jacket design.

We were also able to disseminate the results of the research to a large audience during the 2009 elections through a documentary made for BBC Radio4. Mukti Jain Campion of CultureWise was the producer of this programme and it was a pleasure and education to travel with her to various research sites to collect material for the programme.

Benjamin Dix travelled with us, capturing the elections through his camera and some of his wonderful photographs are included in this volume.

The team of Lokniti based at the Centre for the Study of Developing Societies (CSDS) were our academic collaborators during the course of this project. Various members of the Lokniti team were involved in the different stages of the project — the initial training workshop for the researchers, during the elections when the study was being conducted, and at the de-brief conference held in Shimla. My thanks to Suhas Palshikar and Sanjay Kumar, the Directors of Lokniti for their interest and support; to Banasmita Bora for facilitating this collaboration in so many ways; and to Peter deSouza who agreed for us to hold the de-brief conference at the Indian Institute of Advanced Study, Shimla.

Two exemplary civil servants — Manish Gupta provided invaluable early logistical support for my research in West Bengal and thereafter provided helpful insight with his own growing political career; and Dr S. Y. Quraishi in his role as Chief Election Commissioner in 2009 was a great interlocutor and facilitator as the ideas for this research grew.

For my understanding of the meaning that elections hold in people's lives I am entirely indebted to those who live in the villages of Madanpur and Chishti in West Bengal, India. For the past 14 years that I have visited and lived with them they have continued to educate and enlighten me. Two people have shaped my analytical thinking about elections fundamentally. Jonathan Spencer's early paper on elections as social dramas helped me make sense of my own experience of elections in India and conversations with him over the years have helped me sharpen my understanding. Yogendra Yadav persuaded me that ethnographic work was essential to explain India's counter-intuitive trends in voting behaviour that surveys conducted in the 1990s revealed. In the ensuing years I have had the privilege of innumerable conversations about my findings with him and his inexhaustible knowledge of Indian politics and clarity of analysis have helped me hone my explanations of elections and democracy.

I was based at University College London when the research for this book was conducted. My thanks to colleagues there, in particular Michael Rowlands, Paolo Favero, Daniel Miller, David Wengrow, Michael Stewart, and Murray Last — who provided collegial support and ideas as I navigated through uncharted waters of comparative ethnography. Chris Fuller provided limitless wisdom and good counsel during the planning and writing of this book. My students both at UCL and the LSE challenged and discussed previous drafts of this book and their questions forced me to bring greater clarity to my analysis. Maurice Bloch has been inspirational through conversation and his writings in recognising how a study of elections can be developed for anthropological analysis. Craig Calhoun's writings on Chinese democracy movements were crucial in clarifying the meaning of elections in India. John Dunn was an important early supporter of the importance of ethnographic work on elections and provided encouragement at a crucial moment.

I had the privilege of being able to share some of the findings of this study and the innovation in methodology at universities across the world. In particular my thanks go to the following friends and colleagues for their interest and generosity with ideas: K. Sivaramakrishnan, Ramachandra Guha, Steve Wilkinson, Akhil Gupta, Anirudh Krishna, David Gilmartin, D. L. Sheth, John Dunn, Paul Brass, James Manor, Ashis Nandy, Thomas Blom Hansen, Phil Oldenberg, Sanjay Ruparelia, Christophe Jaffrelot, Oliver Heath, Devesh Kapur, Nate Roberts, Rupa Vishwanath, Lisa Björkman, Wendy James, Jit Uberoi, John Davis, David Gellner, Sudipta Kaviraj, Lucia Michelutti, Dipesh Chakravarty, Roger Jeffery, Patricia Jeffery, Bhikhu Parekh, Alpa Shah, Jonathan Parry, Joya Chatterji, Anil Seal, Chris Bayly, James Laidlaw, Meghnad Desai, Julia Paley, Arild Ruud, Kenneth Bo Nielsen, Pamela Price, Kumkum and Ranjit Bhattacharya, John Harriss, Craig Jeffrey, Marc Abeles, James Scott, and Stuart Corbridge.

My friends Sangeeta Datta, Soumilya Datta, Soumik and Souvid Datta, Nilanjan Sarkar, Chris Banfield, Nasser Munjee, Manisha Priyam, Gopa Sabharwal, Alex Aisher, Laura Bear, Jeremy Blackham, Kathryn Earle, Graham Farrant, Geeta Gopalan, Surina Narula, Susan Manly, Jawhar Sircar, Partha Mukhopadhyay, Swaminathan, Katriana Hazell, Adrienne Loftus Perkins, Samya and Arnab Goswami — they have all sustained me in fundamental ways. Special thanks to Clive but for whom the book might have been done sooner but life would have been a lot less interesting. I would particularly like to thank my friends Vayu Naidu, Subur Munjee, Dixie, Oroon Das, and Safina Uberoi without whom I would not have got through 2012.

As always, my family continues to remain the bedrock on which I exist. M. K. Sen provided me a welcoming home and an ever-ready audience during all my visits to 'the field'. Margaret and John Watts, Bethan Watts and Joyal Masih, Elliott and Alexander have kept spirits light and convivial. Prema continues to help run my household, without which it would have been impossible to write. My parents Roma and Akshay Banerjee continue to nourish me with their interest and unwavering faith in all I do. It is always of great solace to know that my sisters Krittika Banerjee and Madhulika Banerjee are always there for me despite the severe demands on their own time; their respective husbands Elliot Stechman and Yogendra Yadav and the wonderful children in the family — Mihi Aumiya and Sufi and Sahej — are a reminder of all things good and valuable in life. Nothing I accomplish is ever possible without the unstinting support of my husband Julian Watts whose wit lights up my life everyday and with whom I continually discover what integrity, love and companionship are about.

To all of the above, my deep and heartfelt thanks. I dedicate this book to my wonderful daughter Aria for she, above all else, provides the best reason to carry on.

As mentioned at the start of these Acknowledgements, the researchers submitted reports from their respective field sites; the Appendices in this volume are abridged versions of these reports. The field research was focused on four questions framed by me for the larger project, and was conducted over one month before and during the 2009 general elections in the 12 sites. I have integrated material from the original reports throughout this book according to my analytical framework and arguments, and alongside material from my own fieldwork. It should be taken as understood that wherever references to individual sites appear, the information is taken from the respective field report (FR). However, I draw the reader's particular attention to the following pages, where I have paraphrased or taken extracts at length from the original reports — cited in the text as 'Researcher FR: page number' with reference to these reports — submitted by the researchers to me, material which may or not may not appear in the abridged Appendices: Carswell and De Neve (Tamil Nadu) 49, 52–53, 58, 63, 66, 77–80, 85, 91–92, 106, 108, 123, 125, 126–27, 129–30, 133, 140, 149–50, 159, 160, 162; Chakrabarty (West Bengal) 102–4; Datar (Maharashtra) 153–54; Falcao (Rajasthan) 57, 83, 97, 107, 110, 133; George (Chhattisgarh) 108, 152–53, 161–62, 163–64; Jani (Gujarat) 46–47, 60–61, 71, 96, 104, 146, 147, 160; Krishnamurthy (Madhya Pradesh) 58, 64, 73, 94, 130–32, 165; Kumar (Uttar Pradesh) 64–65, 66, 70, 126, 145, 148; Narayan (Uttar Pradesh) 27, 85, 127–28; Nasir (Delhi) 44–45, 59; Singh (Bihar) 61–62, 68–69, 81–82, 94, 97, 154.

I
Introduction

Vignette 1

One afternoon in March, I stopped to collect my customary *paan* from the little kiosk, a box balanced on four poles, by the highway that ran through my research villages. Not many people were around, most people having retired indoors for some quiet time after lunch. I chatted with Dukhai Dom as he put my *paan* together deftly — betel leaf, a few betel nuts, a lick of shiny golden gloop and a clove. I knew him well, having learnt a lot about paddy farming from talking to him out in the farmlands that surrounded the village. He worked as 'labour', earning about ₹80 a day, on the days that his emaciated body allowed him to work. The rest of the time he earned a few paise from selling cigarettes and *paan* on the rare occasion that anyone who could actually afford one stopped at his kiosk. I asked him today, as I asked everyone I knew at some point, whether he would vote in the next elections. He looked up quickly, his hands stopping for a second, and asked me 'Why wouldn't I? Of course I will!' I wondered if he knew that it was becoming mandatory to produce a photo identity in order to vote. He smiled and replied he had. I asked if I could see it the next time I was in his home. His smile got broader and conspiratorial. 'It's not at home' he said and handed my *paan* to me and as I tucked it into my mouth, he rummage among a mass of worn plastic bags, some matchboxes and empty jam bottles behind him. From this assortment he produced a plastic bag that looked stronger than the others, the sort that you would get from one of the bigger shops in a town. From within it he produced a beaten old tin, its latch firmly closed. Inside lay more plastic bags and an envelope, each of which he unwrapped carefully as if handling rods in a nuclear reactor. I waited patiently, wondering if he was looking for cigarettes, a new ingredient for *paan* or his spectacles. Instead, he produced the unmistakable laminated card, bearing the words 'Electoral Photo Identity Card' along with Dukhai's photograph, his age and father's name on it.

The broad smile on his face as he held it up for me to see told a story that this book will try to recount.[1]

Vignette 2

One morning in May, when the agricultural grain market was winding down from a busy season of wheat sales, we found Rukmini Bai, an elderly woman who worked in the trading yard, wiping away tears with the end of her sari. She was inconsolable, and explained that the day before she had been unable to vote at the elections because she did not have the correct identification. She had produced other pieces of paper with no success, so in the end, she had to wait outside the polling booth and watch everyone else emerge with newly-inked fingers proving that they had cast their vote, while her own remained bare. When we asked why this made her so sad she explained that she always wanted to vote because every vote was important and she did not want to waste hers. When we tried to console her saying that it was after all, only one vote, and that she should not feel so bad about affecting the outcome, she paused amidst her tears and said, 'You see me? My work is to sweep up all the grain that falls from the sacks and the weighing scales on the floor. At the end of the day, I sell what I have collected and I am allowed to keep half the money. That is my income. So you see, I understand the value of each grain of wheat. On the floor they look insignificant, just one isolated grain of wheat, but each grain that is added to the heap determines what I earn. My vote is like those grains of wheat'.[2]

'Why India Votes' is a big question in two senses. First, Indian voters make up one-sixth of the world's electorate, so their attitudes to elections really do matter to the political future of the planet, and their experience may prove helpful to understanding democracies, old and new, elsewhere. Second, in a polity that faces so many challenges to its own social and political cohesion, what the masses think about voting seems a vital indicator of how India may survive and evolve in the future. Sceptics are right to say that elections alone do not make a true democracy, but India's problems will surely be still

---

[1] All unaccredited quotes in this book are from interviews conducted by different members of the research team in their respective field sites.
[2] Thanks to Mekhala Krishnamurty for this story from her research site in Harda, Madhya Pradesh.

greater if its people lose faith in the electoral process.[3] As the opening vignettes show, elections mean a great deal to Indian voters, and has more significance for them, I would suggest, than for many voters in established democracies elsewhere. This book will show in detail that for many Indian voters, and especially the poor, voting is not just a means to elect governments. Rather, the very act of voting is seen by them as meaningful, as an end in itself, which expresses the virtues of citizenship, accountability and civility that they wish to see in ordinary life, but rarely can. For these voters, Election Day creates a time out of time, a carnival space, where the everyday reality of inequality and injustice is suspended, and popular sovereignty asserted for a day.

Why should people bother to vote? The importance of this question has dogged public discussions for at least 50 years. Influenced by certain kinds of economist thinking, some rationalist scholars have considered the value of voting in terms of the payoff for the individual, with the assumption that people will vote only if they get something out of it. Given that voting is a large group activity, the problem of the 'free rider' — a person who believes that his individual contribution doesn't make any difference to a collective activity and so decides to ride the wave rather than make an effort himself — has complicated matters further. It poses the question why anyone should bother to vote at all, given that a single vote rarely makes a difference to an election result, and it is easy to excuse one's apathy behind others' participation. This is a sentiment that most readers will recognise from their own thoughts on voting day. Voting has thus emerged as 'the paradigmatic case of the problem of the worthlessness of individual contributions to the actions of large groups' (Runciman 2008). And yet, as Rukmini Bai explained in 'Vignette 2', some people might believe in exactly the opposite proposition.

In India, the question of why one should bother to vote at all has particular salience. The size of the electorate here is vast (larger than North America and Europe combined) so each constituency has millions of voters where one vote is a proverbial drop in the ocean. The motivation to free ride would be very tempting given how easily one

---

[3] The novel *Seeing* (2007) provides an engaging satirical account by the Nobel Prize winning writer Jose Saramago of what happens when on National Election Day disillusionment among voters leads to 83 per cent of the ballot being cast as blank votes, rendering the entire democratic system useless.

person's absence could be missed. Furthermore, the instances of corruption in the political class are regularly exposed, thereby damaging the credibility of elected representatives severely. And finally, despite India's famed economic growth rates and high gross domestic product (GDP), per capita income levels remain low while poverty, disease and illiteracy remain alarmingly high, making disenchantment with the state and the electoral process understandable among this section of the electorate.

Despite these factors, research from India shows that the Indian electorate behaves in unexpected, indeed baffling, ways. Despite voting not being compulsory, and the prevalence of high degrees of illiteracy and poverty — which are regarded elsewhere as an obstacle to voting — turnout has been consistently high for 60 years, and has even risen in recent decades. Moreover, among the most enthusiastic are the poorest and most disadvantaged. Furthermore, unlike many other countries, turnout is higher the more local the election. And women do not, despite their greater distance from public discussions about politics, lag behind in commitment to the voting process (NES data).[4] We may ask, therefore, whether these trends make for a certain 'Indianness' in Indian elections, and whether this distinctiveness is likely to continue in the future.

By asking 'why India votes' this study examines the motivations and opinions of ordinary voters, without assuming, as many might do, that poor people vote with enthusiasm because they can simply be bought off or coerced into voting for particular parties. This study introduces three major innovations. First, it focuses on ordinary Indians' *experience* of elections, and on what elections *mean* to them. Above all, it explores what they *think* they are doing when they vote. Second, it explores the meaning of elections through the ethnographic method in 12 different locations across India to provide a genuinely national picture — something that is fairly unprecedented. Third, the research is continually informed and engaged with survey research through constant dialogue and discussion with political scientists who study Indian elections. Using these new approaches, this study hopes to present a fresh look at elections — one that lets the questions

---

[4] The National Election Study (NES) series based on post-poll surveys conducted by Lokniti, Programme for the Study of Comparative Democracy at the Centre for the Study of Developing Societies, is the 'largest and the most comprehensive social scientific survey of Indian General Elections and perhaps of any election in the world' (Kumar and Rai 2013).

determine the choice of methodology rather than letting the methods dictate the questions.

These three innovations are an attempt to capture the reasons why the relatively 'new' idea of elections has to come to acquire such force in India. How does the novel philosophical concept of universal suffrage in an otherwise unequal setting resonate with what Charles Taylor calls the 'social imaginaries' of Indian society? Taylor uses the concept of the social imaginary to explore why democracies take root in some places but not others. He does this by examining why democracy sprouted in India but not in Pakistan, even though both achieved independence from the British Raj at the same time. In this, earlier post-war assumptions that democratic development correlates with economic development have been proven to be wide off the mark. Thus, rather than asking what the conditions for democracy are, Taylor proposes that we consider different cultures of democracy in the plural, in the same way that we now speak of multiple modernities. And again, Taylor evokes the existence of the Indian Republic, the world's biggest democracy, to make his point. Indian democracy is robustly healthy, particularly in its rising or steady voter turnouts, which are in sharp contrast to the declining turnouts in older democratic regimes of the North Atlantic world. This forces us to recognise that what we might be witnessing is not the same form of government in different regions, but rather the particularity of Indian democracy's dynamic mode of operation, which is very different from what we see in northern societies. Therefore, Taylor proposes a comparative study of democracies that does not look for general laws (such as the American development theory of the post-war period) but instead turns to an older tradition originating with Montesquieu, where comparison 'does not aim at general truths but at enlightening contrasts where the particular features stand out in their differences' (Taylor 2007: 119).

The 'social imaginary' is one such dimension of comparison proposed by Taylor. Through the use of this term, Taylor attempts to get to 'the ways in which people imagine their social existence — how they fit together with others and how things go on between them and their fellows, the expectations that are normally met and the deeper normative notions and images that underlie these expectations' (ibid.). The distinction that Taylor draws between social imaginary and social theory is of particular interest in the context of this book and my larger argument about popular perceptions of democracy in India, given my interest in probing the distinctions and overlap between popular understandings and philosophical concepts. Taylor outlines three major differences:

1. Social imaginary is about the way ordinary people imagine their social surroundings, which is often not expressed in theoretical terms but is, instead, carried in images, stories, legends and so on;
2. social imaginary is shared by large groups of people, if not the whole society, while theory is often the possession of small minority; and
3. social imaginary is the common understanding that makes possible common practices and a widely shared sense of legitimacy, while theory can circulate only among elites (2007: 19).

The social imaginaries of democracy can therefore be both the democratic vision for the future and the pre-democratic repertoires that are transformed and adapted to fit the new understandings and practices to achieve the ideal. Both of these shape the variable successes with democracy that we witness in different settings. In each case, the existing pre-democratic repertoires vary and shape the pathways to the democratic goal.

As an anthropologist, I would argue that the ethnographic method is the ideal way in which to gain access to social imaginaries, because it privileges people's ideas over social theories and pays close attention to the popular practices and popular imagination that Taylor argues is the characteristic of social imaginaries. Ethnographers pay close attention to 'images, stories, legends' and such material provides an understanding of how people share and perpetuate ideas of everyday philosophical importance. It is for this reason that this book presents this kind of material in abundance and we have deliberately tried to keep our mediations as social scientists to a minimum, as that invariably brings about the kind of mediation through social theory that Taylor warns against.

I realised the importance of an ethnographic perspective on elections based on a number of observations, both as an Indian citizen and from my work as a social anthropologist. Three things struck me:

(a) *Quantity*: An Indian national election is the largest humanly organised event in the world, with over 728 million voters, 11 million election officials, over 1 million voting machines, more than 7 million polling booths and 543 constituencies. Despite this mind-boggling scale of operations, they are run with an

exemplary efficiency rarely seen in other areas of state (or indeed private-sector) delivery, and this in itself marks elections out as an area of distinctive experience.
(*b*) *Quality*: India's elections are noisy, colourful and rambunctious. Election hoardings loom large on city skylines, murals and posters appear on building walls, and any advertisement, from soap to scooters, incorporates election-related themes and motifs in its copy. Colourful bunting and banners festoon lanes, tea stalls and highways, and dead trees burst into colour with flags. Loud hailers parade the streets, dust is churned by thousands of public meetings and tempers run high as traffic is stalled by processions of canvassing supporters. In the media and in conversation at home and work, elections generate endless passionate discussion, and for a while at least, comparison of politicians displaces that of film stars, and voting receives as much attention as cricket scores. Indian elections are thus a distinctive social and sensory experience and it is evident that most people in India actually enjoy an election and throw themselves into the experience in a big way.
(*c*) *Mystery*: Judging by trends elsewhere, especially in the West, and the political science orthodoxy that explains them, the data from India seems to defy predictions about how its elections should fare.

Commentators with various methodological leanings have sought to explain these unusual trends, but most tend to reduce the question of why Indians vote to a simple co-efficient of whom they vote for. Traditionally, scholarly perspectives on elections have been mainly institutional — looking at the statutes and arrangements — or psephological, assessing who votes for whom and why.[5] These approaches ignore the early warning by influential political scientists that political participation is a multi-dimensional rather than a unitary phenomenon, which includes voting, campaigning, cooperative activities,

---

[5] The NES surveys conducted by Lokniti, Centre for the Study of Developing Societies (CSDS) based in Delhi are a notable exception to this trend. Much of my own work has been conducted in dialogue with them and the reader will see the evidence of this exchange throughout this book.

and citizen-initiated contacts, and also that 'voting can be about the gratification of the act itself and not necessarily some expected outcome' (Verba et al. 1971: 16). Focusing too narrowly on the issue of 'who voted for whom' runs the danger of being limited and patronising. Explanations of who the masses vote for typically portray the average voter as an uneducated or illiterate person who is essentially passive; who doesn't know better; and who can be variously coerced or swayed by incentives, landlords, higher castes, priests and *mullah*s or political brokers. To the extent that voters are seen as active and thinking, their motivations are explained either in the narrowly rational terms of self-interest — using votes to seek better roads and schools — or as the irrational expression of primordial loyalty to a particular community. Though there is clearly much truth in all of this, particularly in people's decisions about who to vote for, my instinct was that this approach was ultimately reductionist and did not capture the whole story about popular participation.[6] The question of whom people vote for has, without doubt, increasingly begun to generate complex and nuanced answers, not least because of the diversity of political parties and of the political landscape.[7] The need to explain why certain parties and candidates won popular support in certain elections and not in others has motivated a wide range of scholars to provide sophisticated analyses of voting behaviour (Ahuja and Chhibber 2009; Chandra 2007; Varshney 2002; Wilkinson 2007; among others). But analysis also showed that despite the growing number of political parties, there has also been an increasing 'flattening of political choices', whereby despite their differing vote constituencies and ideologies, political parties have come to resemble each other when in power (Yadav and Palshikar 2009). Their performance in terms of governance and delivery of development programmes has often been poor, and marked by the hubris and corruption that power brings. For the common voter, therefore, the expectation that voting for 'their' party could bring about improvement has often been a

---

[6] Ahuja and Chhibber (2009) outline different motivations for voting according to social classification and I will engage with their arguments in Chapter 5.

[7] For a comprehensive review of the literature that shows how formal democracy has also led to substantive democratisation see Corbidge, Harriss and Jeffrey (2013: 149–57).

tarnished hope and could understandably cause disillusionment with the whole political system. And yet, enthusiasm about voting seems to have persisted and increased among large sections of the electorate, despite the fact that their elected representatives bring most of them negligible improvements in living standards. Surely you cannot fool all of the people all the time? Why *do* they vote?

However, my skepticism about reductive explanations of higher voter turnout mainly stemmed from my specific experiences as a social anthropologist and ethnographer. My first book was a reassessment, based on oral histories and archival research, of the nonviolent Khudai Khidmatgar anti-colonial movement in the North-West Frontier during the 1930s and 1940s (Banerjee 2001). Where the British, and even the Indian National Congress, had largely seen the mass of participants as an unthinking rabble hoodwinked by a charismatic leader (Khan Abdul Gaffar Khan), my conversations with participants, now in their 80s and 90s, revealed a remarkably sophisticated and nuanced understanding of the aims, doctrine and methods of the movement, and its place in the wider nationalist struggle (Banerjee 2001).

Inspired by this 'subaltern' view, I began to probe the contemporary political awareness in two villages in rural West Bengal for my next project in 1999 — a state where democratic forms blended distinctively with the two-decade-long one-party hegemony of the Communist Party of India (Marxist) (CPI[M] or CPM), lately overturned by a reforming opposition (Trinamool Congress). Thus, for more than 10 years of drama and change, I have talked politics with the villagers, both between and during elections, following conversations wherever they led, but always mindful of the pivotal question of 'why do you vote?' and always seeking to record and privilege the villagers' perspectives over my own.

They talked, of course, about their material needs and hope for a better future, and the importance of voting in trying to secure this. But these discussions would often take a more philosophical turn as they variously described, often very articulately:

- the importance of voting for generating a feeling of citizenship, and for signalling the values of that citizenship;
- voting as an expression of their identity as Indians;
- the duty they felt to exercise what they saw as the most precious of rights;

- the sense of gratitude and obligation they felt towards the Election Commission of India (hereafter ECI) for organising free and fair elections; and
- the importance they attached to the fact that 'each and every vote' was important to any election.

They placed far more weight on these 'expressive' aspects of voting, than political scientists' accounts of participation are wont to do. Given such sentiments, most people expressed surprise when I asked why they voted, as for them, it was unthinkable *not* to vote in elections, just as it would be not to talk or sing in everyday life. It implied something one just did as part of living. In fact, more often than not, when I have asked people why they vote, their riposte is the counter-question: 'Why would you not vote?!'

Elections as Carnivals

Being among such people on election day also made it clear how the actual casting of one's vote stood out as a unique experience for the villagers. On this one day, the inequality of wealth and status that dominated normal life in the village was briefly set aside, as rich and poor alike had to queue to vote under the election officials' watchful eyes, each of them able to cast but one vote of equal worth. For a short while, therefore, the truly competitive nature of the contest, along with the rigorous umpiring of the Election Commission, moved the country into a special time and momentum. While no one in authority would normally pay ordinary people any heed, during campaigns, the candidates would come to listen to the villagers with ostentatious concern, having to stand in the sun and drink the proffered tea as they conversed with their prospective supporters.

Thus, elections in India are carnivalesque, in their noise and colour and in the way in which the normal rules of life are turned upside down. Yet, it is an unusual carnival, for rather than creating anarchy, it brings about a far *more* orderly and structured manner of living than the normal unruly conditions outside the campaign. The election is thus a liminal period with a new ethic, but one in which 'hyper-structure', not 'anti-structure', prevails.

On the basis of these observations, I published a paper entitled 'Sacred Elections' (Banerjee 2007), which argued that India's elections

provide in the lives of the masses such a unique moment of procedural fairness, equality, rule of law, efficiency, unity of enterprise,
citizenship, meaningfulness and festivity, that they have taken on the
mantle of ritual in the deepest sense, transcending quotidian experience, and have come to be regarded as sacrosanct in modern Indian
public life (ibid.).

My fieldwork, which included trailing Mamata Banerjee herself
in the early years of her assault on the Left front, also taught me that
reading about an Indian election campaign in English language dailies
or watching television debates, is a world apart from experiencing it
from the vantage of the voter in a small town or village. The earnest,
engaged and often profound ways in which my informants discussed
politicians, campaign styles or the work of the ECI were in stark
contrast to the cynicism, sensationalism and superficiality in much of
the media. And attending a public rally in the press enclosure gives a
different and attenuated understanding of what these rallies achieve,
as compared to sitting on the fringes of the crowd, in the sun without
an awning, listening to the chanting of slogans and the discussion of
the speeches afterwards. As Yogendra Yadav has put it, basing the
analysis of popular political understandings solely on media accounts
of reported speeches would be like trying to 'understand the social
meaning of an Indian wedding by restricting one's attention to the
priest's utterances' (2007: 361).

Many of the villagers I interacted with over the course of my fieldwork talked about politics all the time, and their everyday language
had the creativity and plasticity to describe the politics unfolding
around them. They modified official English words to describe local
events, and used local idioms to explain philosophical notions of
citizenship and participation. Entirely new words were coined to
describe unprecedented events, and in general their discourse had a
liveliness and accuracy that the official language of social science and
political commentary simply does not capture.

These fieldwork experiences and findings impressed on me the
value and importance of pursuing an ethnographic approach to the
experience and discourse of ordinary voters, without whom elections
would be meaningless affairs. Thus, in a forthcoming monograph,
I will expand on that analysis, and through 'thick description' situate
the political and electoral experience more organically within the life
of the village and its other cycles of cultivation, kinship and ritual.

However, I was also conscious of the need to avoid the common shortfall of ethnographic fieldwork, i.e., the issue of representativeness or an inability to speak for any unit other than a particular field site. I wished, therefore, to propose an explanation for all of India's voters rather than only the few who lived in two particular villages in West Bengal. Therefore, ahead of the 2009 National Lok Sabha Elections, I resolved to marry the key benefits of the ethnographic approach with a comparative multi-site approach so as to provide a broader assessment of my Bengal-based characterisation of Indian elections through the Comparative Electoral Ethnographies (CEE) study. In order to do this, I took my main findings from the West Bengal data and tested them in different parts of the country in varying cultural, social and electoral settings. In this way, the nature of the CEE was genuinely inductive since the questions that were investigated were the results of prior long-term ethnographic research and had emerged as important themes from my own village-based research. Taken together, these questions were intended to help us understand exactly what goes on during an Indian general election, what people imagine is going on and why they do what they do. Accordingly, the four principal research questions of the CEE study were:

(a) What did an election campaign look like from the vantage of the voter?

(b) How plastic was the language of politics — what new words were coined, what local metaphors were used to describe the processes of electoral democracy, etc.?

(c) What happened on Polling Day? How did people experience the act of voting itself? What were the culture of the polling booth and the attitudes of polling officials towards voters like?

(d) What were the reasons that people gave for voting when they were asked 'Why do you vote?'

The 2009 elections were fairly typical and there were no unusual factors affecting it.[8] The 15th since 1950, it was held on schedule and

---

[8] It should be noted that national-level elections are relatively low-key events when compared to more local elections. State Assembly elections, conducted at the level of each of the individual 28 states, are more engaged and colourful affairs and Panchayat elections held in the village are the

the result was genuinely uncertain with no obvious extraordinary factors affecting the outcome. The United Progressive Alliance (UPA) government, led by the Congress had served a full term and the country waited to see if an anti- or pro-incumbency sentiment would prevail. Furthermore, the campaign coincided with both the hysteria of the Indian Premier League (a new cult within the national religion of cricket), and the astrologically auspicious wedding season (in many regions), making for an especially carnivalesque atmosphere and presenting particular challenges of transport and accommodation to election officials and wedding guests alike!

During the CEE study, we also paid special attention to the workings of the ECI, especially at the ground level. An important statutory body, the ECI is one of India's public 'institutions of restraint', which, alongside the judiciary and police, is entrusted with the responsibility of creating a level playing field for electoral competition for individuals and political parties alike. This fairness

---

most boisterous of them all. As someone in Uttar Pradesh (UP) put it: 'If you want to see real fireworks then you should visit during the Panchayat elections when the turnout is 98 per cent' (*Aji agar asli jalve dekhne hai to* Panchayat vote *ke time aiyey, tub to* 98 per cent vote *hoga*). People often referred to these intensely local contests as the *saap* and *nevla* (snake and mongoose) faceoffs. There are a number of reasons for this, but it mainly has to do with arithmetic. For a Panchayat seat, votes are cast in their thousands, sometimes, in their hundreds, thereby making every vote count. Candidates and campaigners, therefore, make an effort to personally reach out to every voter through a variety of means, urging voters to show up to vote; everyone has at least second-hand knowledge of all candidates; and counting is a tense affair. In India, therefore, the levels of excitement and visibility of a campaign increase the more local an election and this distinguishes elections in India from its older Western counterparts.

In Madhya Pradesh, some women party workers all agreed that this is the least taxing election from their perspective: the Vidhan Sabha election and especially the Nagar Pallika elections take up much more of their time and bring heightened responsibility. 'The Lok Sabha elections are fought only on the basis of the symbol whereas Vidhan Sabha elections are fought on the basis of individuals'. Campaign strategies are also quite different. In the Vidhan Sabha elections, there is much more emphasis on neighbourhood meetings and on reaching out to each and every voter as personally as possible; this time because of the huge size of the constituency there was much less home-to-home canvassing.

is an essential requirement for the ultimate realisation of the ideal of equality that democracy enshrines (Kapur and Mehta 2005: 10). As André Béteille puts it, it is 'within the framework of the institution that the contradiction [between the ideal of equality and the practice of inequality] could be observed, described and analysed' (2012: 3). When an election is announced, the first act of the ECI is to introduce what is known as the 'Model Code of Conduct' (MCC) for all political parties and incumbent governments to create an atmosphere of equality and fairness (see Gilmartin [forthcoming] for a discussion of the Code). Thus, the period when nominations are filed, names of the contesting candidates confirmed and the election campaign conducted is governed by the conventions of the Code. Under its stipulations, all parties are expected to behave in moderation and are laid open to close and constant scrutiny by the millions of officials who are drafted to work for the Commission across the country. (These officials are usually on the payroll of the Government of India the rest of the year in different capacities, such as schoolteachers, administrative officers, accountants, etc.) Once elections are declared, incumbent governments are forbidden from offering schemes and loans that might act as electoral incentives, and the power of the ECI supersedes the powers of all institutions of government.[9] The constitutional backing of the ECI's sphere of jurisdiction implies that it can function above political or State interference. Thus, all political parties, including those that form the incumbent government, have to defer to its authority, as do all levels of the state's administration. As a result, candidates can be disqualified, partisan bureaucrats and police officers transferred away from their domains of influence, and parties fined for violating the norms of the MCC. Elections thus present the unusual sight of nervous and vigilant political parties, an efficient administration and otherwise lowly clerks empowered in their role as ECI officials. By 2009, we had come to expect such institutional proficiency on the part of the ECI that it was indeed one of the most taken-for-granted features of Indian elections.

Despite the vast scale and logistics of a national election in India, the results are declared within less than 12 hours of the final vote being cast with negligible instances of recounts. In a country where

---

[9] See Macmillan (2010) for a detailed account of the ECI and Kumar (2009) for an exhaustive account of electoral reforms.

much smaller events are often tainted with scandal and inefficiency, it is extraordinary that the ECI delivers such an exceptional performance every time. Indian citizens rank it highest among all public institutions (NES data). At least part of this credibility reflects its creative and innovative approach, developed over several decades. The introduction of electronic voting machines (EVMs), the use of party symbols corresponding with the name of each party, the location of the EVM away from the gaze of polling officials, and the marking of fingers with indelible ink to avoid voter fraud have all made the voting process attractive for illiterate and literate voters alike.

The ECI makes adjustments to its arrangements from one election to the next in light of past experiences. In the 2009 election there were three big changes. First, constituencies (including our sites) were re-drawn in all but six states of the country, to reflect demographic changes.[10] As a result, most voters were effectively voting in a brand new constituency. In some sites included in our study, a 'regular' constituency now became a 'reserved' one for Scheduled Tribes (STs) or Scheduled Castes (SCs) seats and this had a significant impact on how much people knew about the contest and the leaders involved. The second change was the introduction of Electoral Photo Identity Cards (EPICs) in all but 21 of the 543 constituencies. Officially, cards had been issued to 82 per cent of the electorate but a significant proportion of voters who did not vote complained that could not because they had not been given their EPICs (10 per cent in NES data). They had been either unaware of the change, or had tried but failed to acquire the new cards and had not reckoned with the impossibility of voting without having it in their possession. Finally,

---

[10] In India, this is called the Delimitation Exercise. 'Delimitation' literally means the act or process of fixing limits or boundaries of territorial constituencies in a country or a province with a legislative body. The Delimitation Commission in India is a powerful body whose orders have the force of law and cannot be called in question before any court. These orders come into force on a date to be specified by the President of India on this behalf. The copies of its orders are laid before the House of the People and the State Legislative Assembly concerned, but no modifications are permissible therein by them. In India, Delimitation Commissions have been constituted 4 times — in 1952 under the Delimitation Commission Act, 1952; in 1963 under Delimitation Commission Act, 1963; in 1973 under Delimitation Act, 1972; and in 2002 under Delimitation Act, 2002 (ECI).

the ECI decided to impose a stricter and more intense implementation of the 'Model Code of Conduct' for election campaigns. This has been one of the ways in which the ECI has increasingly tried to impose control over election expenditure by limiting the money candidates and parties spend on campaign materials. By prohibiting the use of public spaces for displaying posters and murals, it has also tried to control the cleanup costs of the detritus from a four-week campaign. The ECI has said this was also done to send campaigners back to the doorstep, forcing them to interact with voters one-on-one rather than merely broadcasting their messages *en masse*. The NES data shows that political parties did indeed contact more people in 2009 than in the previous two elections and that the trend was rising. This might also explain why fewer people attended rallies (19 per cent) than in the previous election, with parties taking more initiative to reach out to them, while the proportion of people who said they had an interest in the election campaigns (39 per cent) increased.

In a world where election results in the most advanced countries are compromised because of faulty technology (US federal elections in Florida in 2001 was one example), neither the importance of the Commission's innovations, nor the significance of an enduringly independent and efficient ECI for the future of Indian democracy should be underestimated. Furthermore, its constant vigilance over its own functioning and the corresponding vigilance of the officials acting in its name has perhaps been one of the reasons behind its reputation as one of the most respected public institutions in the country. Despite the onerous task of having to conduct free and fair elections in a large and unruly country, it has been able to 'adhere to the norms of *self*-restraint', a truly crucial factor in the effectiveness of such an institution (Kapur and Mehta 2005: 10; emphasis added).

Are Elections a Key Indicator of Democracy?

It has been argued that attaching too much significance to these brief intervals of institutional efficiency and voter enthusiasm runs the risk of neglecting the many wider substantive problems that undermine India's democracy: the growing inequality alongside the introduction of economic reforms; the prolonged failure to translate growing GDP into social development (more poor people live in India than in sub-Saharan Africa); the inability to provide better education and living standards for the poorest (a third of the poorest remain illiterate and many remain underfed); the growing gap between rich and poor; the persistence of religious conflict; the widespread human rights abuses by the army and police; the everyday corruption at all levels; a growing 'economy of influence' in which corporations, politicians and the press collude to bolster entrenched private interests and further weaken public institutions and ethics; and political parties and parliamentary seats which are becoming ever more dynastic. Such problems have led ideologues to disavow the hypocrisies of the democratic state and commence pervasive armed insurgency movements, which the state has responded to with its own brutalities.

Given this litany of failures, and the testing to near destruction of the assumption of the founding fathers that democracy and the assignation of rights and responsibilities to all citizens would ensure fair and responsive governments and lead India to a social democratic prosperity, is there any sense in discussing India's excellent record of free and fair elections? Are elections a true or even partial indicator of a democratic record? Can voter enthusiasm be seen as anything more than a tragic victory of hope over experience?

Though there is indeed much to worry about in India's future, commentators on the nature of the Indian state have also pointed out a curious feature of contemporary India, namely that while economic liberalisation measures are designed to achieve a retreat of the State from economic life, they also have simultaneously led to a continuing enchantment with the state among the poorest in India. The reasons for this are historical, as Kaviraj has pointed out, for the colonial state set the model of putting the state at the centre of all social initiatives thereby creating 'a political culture of dependence on the state' (2011b: 44). This culture continued into post-colonial democratic India and was exacerbated further by capitalist growth whose benefits failed to trickle down and therefore deepened rather than removed the enchantment with the state. 'In any case, the great legitimation of the new state stemmed from its promise of social justice, the promise of the state to interfere in market processes sufficiently to produce outcomes more favourable to the lower classes than the unhindered operations of the free market. It is impossible for the Indian state to escape from that aspiration of its own making' (ibid.: 45). It has therefore had to respond to populist pressures and increase its public expenditure to enable people who have been displaced from their lands and their livelihoods by the rapacious demands of industrial capitalism to meet basic needs. This paradoxical response of a neo-liberal government, as noted by commentators, is determined by political compulsions (Chatterjee 2008). As a result, Akhil Gupta and S. Sivaramakrishnan have gone on to argue that this feature itself is a 'peculiar outcome of Indian democracy because voter participation for poor, subaltern, and rural populations is often higher than for urban, middle-class people, and numerically poor and rural groups form a preponderant part of the electorate' (2011: 5). Thus India provides an example of how popular pressure exerted through participation in elections can directly influence public expenditure and force governments to revise the practice of neo-liberal ideology. As Pranab Bardhan notes, 'The radical promise of democracy continues to be subscribed to precisely by those who appear to have got little substantive outcomes' (2005).

While free elections may not be sufficient for a healthy democracy, few today would deny that they are at least a necessary mechanism to continually renew the understanding and practice of citizenship among ordinary people. Moreover, as several scholars have pointed out, even a traditionally 'minimalist' definition of 'democracy' as a form of government made of elected representatives who have to face electoral competition after finite terms requires a certain set of laws and governance to be in place to ensure that such a system can work. The presence of an independent and efficient administration to conduct elections, an impartial judiciary, non-partisan military forces, an autonomous and articulate media, and a regulatory body such as an electoral commission are all essential elements of this system. On closer examination, therefore, 'this definition is actually not so minimal, for these conditions cannot exist without there being a certain regime of freedom, rights and rule of law' (Yadav forthcoming). Despite the armed Maoist insurgency in large parts of India, the 2009 election was successfully conducted in all but 15 of the 640 districts in the country.

Yadav further argues that as contemporary observers, we cannot reasonably share the founding fathers' hopes and assumptions. As he puts it, 'the conceptual trick of equating democracy with social democracy may have its rhetorical value, but it comes with huge analytical costs' (ibid.). So we cannot simply define democracy as something that produces good social outcomes, nor assume that it has benign social consequences. Whatever our wishes, the failure of a functioning electoral system to generate healthy social and economic ends cannot subvert its status as a genuine political democracy.

In fact, I would go further and argue that India's many difficulties and injustices *increase* the centrality and significance of elections. This is because amidst the extant reality of inequality, injustice and irresponsible governments, elections are able to provide a glimpse of a transcendent reality of fairness and prosperity for all that can be imagined for the future, but is yet to be realised in the present. When asked about the significance of elections, voters across India emphasise this quality of the time of elections, when the transcendent utopia of equality supersedes the immanent reality of inequality. By exploring what significance elections hold for people we are drawn to the real-isation that they mean much more than multi-party politics, a game of numbers or politicians playing musical chairs. Instead, elections provide a glimpse of a political vision that democracy promises but never realises. As Bhikhu Parekh (forthcoming) points out, if elec-tions, public deliberation and (peaceful) protest are three important components of a democratic system, then in India today, elections are the only one of the three to have survived in good health. This is because 'the standard of public debate in the legislature has fallen sharply in parliament and public protests have largely degenerated into explosions of anger rather than the sustained and disciplined campaigns of the anti-colonial struggles'. As a result, the 'burden of deliberation and protest have transferred to the institution of elec-tions alone, [which] remain largely free and fair and exceptionally well organized' (ibid.).

India's elections are thus a special time and place, briefly blos-soming oases of civil society and reasoned public discourse, and the only occasion for real challenge to venal politicians and the injustice of the status quo. As such, they fully warrant detailed study by as many methodologies as we can muster, including the ethnographic approach used here.

Election Studies — In India and Elsewhere

In designing this study, I was very aware of the rich legacy of Indian election studies that we have inherited and it is worth recalling a few milestones here.[11] In the 1960s and 1970s, Myron Weiner and Rajni Kothari conducted the leading studies in the field, followed by Paul Brass, who developed the case study method. In his discussion of Indian election studies, Brass examined the relative merits of different methodologies to study elections and principally to explain voter choices. This field has been dominated by the methodology of the survey method, though, as all the reviewers of election studies have pointed out, there has been the occasional exception, such as Myron Weiner's landmark study of the 1977 elections. On the whole, the merits of election studies, however, are measured according to their explanatory value for 'who voted for whom and why'. While this has limited utility for the present study, Brass's discussion of the merits of an 'ecological analysis' is worth recalling. Such an approach prefigured the NES of today, and in the absence of such opinion surveys at that point in time, the ecological analyses attempted to correlate available demographic and socio-economic aggregate data from censuses with election results in order to identify patterns and variations in turnout, inter-party competition and party support. In the 1980s, election surveys made a comeback through the renewed energy of notable psephologists such as David Butler and Prannoy Roy, who also were able to disseminate the results through the relatively new medium of television. This important innovation took election analysis into people's homes and to the general public for the first time, making discussions of elections among people not only about their local contests, but also about how local results could be situated within a much wider electoral arena. The attractive graphics and reports to camera from field reporters gave elections the combined excitement of cricket and war reportage. The charisma of the programme anchor and the palpable passion that he and the experts invited to the studio had for election-related data successfully made the otherwise esoteric jargon of election analysis comprehensible and even attractive to a wider public. From then on, elections became a national hobby in India. However, when those studies were published, the authors were careful to point out what their studies did *not* deal with. In the book based on their research called *How India Votes*,

---

[11] Recent articles by Palshikar (2007), Lama-Rewal (2009) and Kumar and Rai (2013) provide comprehensive summaries of election studies in India. Older reviews include Narain et al. (1978) and Brass (1985).

they presented the proviso: 'This book . . . offers the "What?" of the electoral record; it does not deal with the "Why?"' (Butler et al. 1995: 4, in Lama-Rewal 2009: 6). This book fills that gap by exploring the hitherto missing 'why' behind India's voting patterns.

The legacy of the popularisation of election analysis in the 1980s was most effectively demonstrated by the ambitious and innovative programme of the Lokniti network of scholars, who designed and set up the NES in the 1990s. Building on the work of the previous generation of political scientists, Lokniti has conducted in-depth surveys of voter attitudes and opinions at every state-level and national election since 1996. Among other survey questions about political attitudes, respondents were also asked who they would vote for. These answers provided the eagerly awaited data for 'predicting' election results on widely watched programmes on television. These election programmes have been so popular that television stations have been happy to fund the surveys that are expensive to conduct — even more so when conducted nationally in a vast country like India. As a result, the Lokniti network has been able to fund an expensive research technique while generating data not just on election results, but a whole lot more. A look at some of the key findings of the NES survey results in 2009 reveals the kind of data it is able to produce on macro trends in the political behaviour of the electorate. In 2009, overall voter turnout remained high, at about 60 per cent, the same as it had been for the past seven national elections. The average was dragged down by lower turnout in the metropolitan cities (which non-voters there attributed to their 'lack of interest'). Small-town voters emerged (for the first time) as the most enthusiastic voters, outstripping their rural counterparts, though many rural non-voters attributed this result to their lack of the newly mandatory photo identity card (Kumar 2009). *Adivasi* voters, despite being the most disadvantaged and least educated of groups, nonetheless had a higher turnout than the national average. Conversely, the idea of larger turnout from caste-based vote banks was undermined by the fact that despite the gathering momentum of Other Backward Caste (OBC) politics, there was no discernible upward trend in turnout among OBC voters. Lower class turnouts were substantially higher than upper class ones in states like Tamil Nadu, West Bengal, Andhra Pradesh, and Assam. Looking across generations, young people voted less than the national average by about 4 per cent, though they voted more than the average in the odd state like Madhya Pradesh. Dalits (as always) voted higher than the average in most states except for Bihar, Delhi and Maharashtra. Muslim OBCs on the whole voted in larger numbers in 2009 than before. Each of these findings is interesting in itself, and like all good surveys, this one also throws up as many useful questions as it does answers and members of the Lokniti network have provided several insightful analyses.[12]

But on the whole, as a sub-discipline of political science, election studies have tended to concentrate on 'the "formal" sector' of politics (national political parties, manifestos, electoral outcomes) rather than the substance of politics, the meaning of the vote, shaping of the agenda and party political platforms, the back calculus of politics and the role of money and crime in shaping and restricting political choice' (Yadav 2010: 350).[13] One important reason for the neglect is that the research methods at one's disposal tend to shape the questions that can be asked. Thus, quantitative methods are by definition better suited for collecting electoral outcomes than, for example, gathering data on the role of money in politics. Furthermore, institutions and election results provide a more accessible and finite subject of study than social life. And a study of social life and of those social processes that underpin political institutions and elections has to perforce confront the unpredictability and chaos of the data generated. This 'messiness' of social life, as Yadav puts it, not only poses a challenge to the researcher but is also an embarrassment to the idea of free and fair elections and its resistance to easy theorisation (ibid.: 309).

Anthropology and Elections

The discipline of anthropology, on the other hand, strives and thrives precisely on making sense of the messiness of social life and pursues meaning in seeming chaos. The study of elections pose a tempting challenge for the anthropologist for they are complex social dramas, encoding a complexity of meaning and counter-intuitive findings about ordinary people and their views about politics. But despite this, anthropologists have curiously ignored the study of elections

---

[12] See the Special Issue of *EPW* October 2009 for a collection of articles by members of the network.

[13] A striking exception is Hauser and Singer (2001) that provides some excellent details on the period between nomination and results in an Indian election.

leaving them to other social sciences, thereby implicitly buying into the formalist approach to the study of elections. Elections have been treated largely as part of a formal set of political institutions of a country rather than something to do with real people and therefore left to political scientists and others who study institutional politics. Thus, even when anthropologists work in places that are part of a system of electoral democracy (and this includes large parts of the world in the 21st century) they have resisted paying them the same empathetic and theoretical attention that they would to other more traditional rituals and institutions in the same society. Anthropologists who are interested in politics have trained their ethnographic and theoretical attention to themes of patronage, big men, violence and trauma, the everyday state, and local politics, all of which influence elections, but rarely the election itself. The anthropology of democracy, however, is a small but growing interest within the discipline (see Paley 2002 for an overview). In an early study, Frederic Schaffer raised the question whether what his Wolof-speaking Senegalese speakers call *demokaraasi* is the same as what we might understand by democracy (1998). In other words, can we assume that we know what the word 'democracy' means in the various contexts in which it is used — that is to say, is there a given set of institutional arrangements and philosophical ideas that is associated with democracy? Given the enormous variation of institutional arrangements across the democracies of the Western world itself, for instance, between France, the United States, the United Kingdom, and Sweden, could we assume a universality of its manifestation across the globe? Schaffer concluded that,

> it is risky to equate democracy with what Chinese speakers call *minzhu*, what Luganda speakers call *eddembe ery'obuntu* or what Wolof speakers call *demokaraasi* for the ideals and practices that infuse American institutions are not universal. Even when democratic ideas are diffused throughout the world, local communities assimilate imported ideas selectively and transform them to fit their own life conditions. Social scientists thus need to take culture and cultural differences seriously. That is, they need to make explicit the presuppositions of their own behaviour as well as those of the Chinese, Ugandas and Senegalese — an undertaking to which a close attention to language and translation has much to contribute (ibid.: 146).

The importance of taking into consideration the context and specific histories of the settings in which democracy flourishes as a concept was highlighted by the contributors to the first anthropological anthology on the subject. In her Introduction to *Democracy: Anthropological Approaches*, Julia Paley highlighted the 'analytic openness' in how anthropologists approached the study of democracy. Such an approach, she argued, moved 'away from a core definition of democracy and closer, instead, to an awareness of democracy's open-ended construction' (2008: 4). Thus, rather than treating democracy as a rigid checklist of attributes, anthropologists who contributed to that volume demonstrated how local histories, social imaginaries and relations of power among political actors shaped the manifested local form of the democratic idea. Such openness in the imagining of the concept of democracy itself was possible because as ethnographers each scholar was mindful of the importance of continual dialogue and engagement with informants in field sites whose ideas forced anthropologists to re-frame the terms of their enquiry. Akhil Gupta questions whether political literacy is dependent on formal literacy as a precondition and shows through his material on India that 'arguments positing literacy as a requirement for democracy operate with a notion of democracy that is largely formal instead of substantive' (2008: 180).

Compared to the growing field of anthropology of democracy, there have been fewer studies of those events that are the basic common denominator of any democracy — elections. But even this small body of work indicates the rich insights that anthropologists have provided when they *have* taken elections itself as serious social events worthy of attention. Jonathan Spencer's work in Sri Lanka (2007) demonstrates that elections are much more than a game of winning and losing seats and characterises them instead as 'moral dramas' through which one can gain an understanding of how ethical and political issues are addressed and resolved in society. Kimberly Coles's work (2007) on elections in Bosnia-Herzegovina shows the importance of collecting fine-grained data on the technology of the elections to understand how dominant ideologies such as that of democracy are put into practice in new settings. In her book *Democratic Designs* she analyses the practices of international intervention and democracy building, examining both the lives of internationals and the 'democratic work' they perform. Lucia Michelutti's work (2008) in north India demonstrates how the new ideas of democratic practices are 'vernacularised' successfully by communities by reinterpreting traditional myths and genealogies to suit a new electoral idiom. It is, therefore, clearly worth paying ethnographic attention to elections because one of anthropology's strengths as a discipline has been to demonstrate how big concepts such as capitalism, socialism, liberalism, and development are refracted and instantiated in particular settings (Miller and Taussig on capitalism, Ong and Bear on liberalism, Gupta, James and Ferguson on development, to cite a small sample). The same no doubt would hold true for the concept of elections, and I would contend that what Paley (2008) argues for the term 'democracy' is just as true as for 'elections'. While 'free and fair' elections might ultimately boil down to a basic list of transparent and well-designed procedures, what these procedures mean to the people participating in them might be unexpected and even counter-intuitive. As with the term 'democracy', so too with elections, we have tended to assume we know what they mean to people anywhere and everywhere on the basis of research conducted in some parts of the Western world. Within a decade of India's inception as a democratic republic, perceptive scholars of Indian politics such as the American political scientist Myron Weiner observed: 'too many of our current generalizations in the field of politics (and in other social sciences as well) are made solely on the basis of Western political experience. And if "general" theories are too elusive, further studies in non-Western areas may at least call our attention to the limitations of many of our existing concepts' (1957: 3). Subsequent scholarship on India's colonial encounter and post-coloniality has highlighted this provincial nature of European ideas and institutions when applied to the rest of the world (Chakravarty 2000). An alternative reading of Indian elections, i.e., one that takes the substance and meaning of elections, highlights the gap between a parochial democratic theory developed on the basis of a particular history of the Western world and its success in very different contexts such as India. Unlike the outcomes that were seen in European democracies — a two-party system, voter choice being determined by ideology, elections as a time of effective accountability, and so on — Indian elections have produced wholly different results. In the Indian case, we already know from the writings of the more insightful political theorists that the local meanings and messiness are precisely what makes the story of democracy in the world's largest electorate a paradoxical and therefore challenging one. The question to ask is whether the 'messiness' of Indian society is particularly Indian or the characteristic of all societies. One answer is that it

> is not the result of any essential cultural difference or Indian exceptionalism; it is simply the outcome of the historically unique circumstances

in which the game of adult franchise was instituted in India. The challenge therefore is to capture the specificity of this encounter between the modern structure of political choice and the historically constituted public sphere with its own definition of politics and its pattern of organization of political interest (Yadav 2010: 352).

The strength of an anthropological study of democracy and elections is that it is well-equipped to capture this specificity by its ability to capture both the emic view of concepts while being aware of its etic provenance. Furthermore, as a discipline, social anthropology attempts to grasp the holism (and the accompanying messiness) of social life rather than compartmentalise it into the political, economic, philosophical, and religious spheres of society. An anthropological approach recognises that individuals simultaneously inhabit and interact with these varied aspects of social life, and so to isolate any of them for investigation is to lose the bigger picture. As I will argue in the next section, when elections are studied using this ethnographic holism, it is possible to capture some of the specificity of the encounter between the social dynamics of Indian society and the political structures of liberal democracy.

What is an Ethnographic Study of Elections?

It is important to clarify at this stage what I mean by an ethnographic method and why it is essential in order to understand Indian elections in all their complexity.[14] To my mind, three elements are key. First, in contrast to surveys or opinion polls, the ethnographic method involves observing actions, not just asking people questions. This is vital, as what people say is often different from what they do. The burden of expectation on a person who has been asked a survey question is enormous — they want to be seen as saying the right thing,

---

[14] Over the past few decades, an easy congruence has occurred between 'fieldwork' and 'doing ethnography'. Social scientists from various disciplines have increasingly recognised the importance of 'going to the field' and gathering data about events and opinions in the contexts in which they occur. As a result, a number of them can be said to conducting 'fieldwork'. In light of this, it is important to highlight the finer distinctions between research carried out in the field and the specificity of the ethnographic approach.

are worried about what others may hear, and will wish to sound intelligent to the educated researcher. Let me provide one small illustration from the north Indian state of Uttar Pradesh. On the day of voting, our researcher (Narayan FR: 15) found a young woman cleaning some silver bangles at the village well, with a heap of washed clothes next to her. As she worked, he struck up a conversation about the elections and whether she would be voting. Her response was a tirade against politicians' corruption and cynicism and their failure to do anything for poor people like her. On the basis of her speech, she appeared a sceptic who was unlikely to vote. Yet, later that day we spotted her at the polling station patiently waiting her turn in the queue, dressed in her best sari. She had clearly been able to make the trip to vote only after completing her household chores and making herself presentable for the occasion. It dawned on us only then that all the time that she had been railing against politicians' uselessness, she had continued to polish her bangles just so that she could wear them to the polling station! Had we spoken with her only at home it likely that we would have seen her as a non-voter, and if only at the polling station, we may have assumed that rural women like her silently and submissively turned up to vote as required. It is only because we had heard her out and then lingered long enough to see what she did that we could gain a more nuanced understanding of her attitude and behaviour.

The second key feature of the ethnographic method is putting the conceptions and vocabulary of the informant at the heart of the study, and privileging their point of view rather than our own analytic preconceptions, pursuing this through open-ended conversations, observation and complete submersion in the life world of the informants. As Kaviraj notes, 'It is not always appreciated how difficult it is to . . . dredge up from the ruins of everyday life pieces of subaltern experience, then to find a language to express them, and finally to theorize on the basis of the distinctiveness of that angle of vision' (2010: 4). This process is an enormously complex one and anthropologists have been acutely aware of the ethical and moral dilemmas of conveying the views of their informants through their own analytical lenses. By privileging the point of view of the informant, we are also aware that we are just as implicated in what is expressed because each opinion that is voiced is a unique statement that is created in the inter-subjective space between the researcher and the informant. As ethnographers, we choose to ask certain questions over others and these are shaped as much by our analytical frames as they are by the expediencies of the occasion. In turn, our interlocutors respond within their own frames and constraints and how they feel at the time. The inter-subjective space is one in which differing ontologies, epistemologies, emotions, and energies interact in complex ways. Through this process, the ethnographer makes an attempt to gain enough insight so as to represent the perspective of their informants with as much veracity as possible.

It may be argued that there appears a contradiction between these two features, in saying both that informants' actions can betray or subvert their speech, and that informants' speech and ideas are key to understanding them and the events they join in. But the resolution of this lies in the third feature of the ethnographic method, namely that it casts its net wide and aims for a holistic account. Privileging folk ideas does not mean simply taking informants' statements at face value, but rather seeking to understand their significance and allusiveness by reference to everything else we know about them and see them do. As I had learnt from my own research in West Bengal, it was impossible to understand what people thought about politics without examining their ideas about other aspects of life — ritual, kinship, work, labour, inequality, spirituality, and so on. This is because of the obvious fact, worth restating simply because it is so often ignored in political analysis — that the voter is also a mother, friend, labourer, believer, or employer. The 'voter' who shows up to vote is a complex individual holding multiple motivations and beliefs. It was therefore possible to understand why the woman with the silver bangles voted, and to some extent, even whom she voted for, only by fully understanding the rest of her life in the round. It is the pursuit of this holism that leads ethnographers, and social anthropologists in particular, to prolonged and participatory immersion in local culture and social life, where they pay as much attention to mundane daily life as to conflicts and carnivals. A small illustration of the importance of this kind of broad understanding of a society in order to understand its political behaviour is provided by a small but significant observation during my own fieldwork. As an anthropologist, I had attempted to be present in my research village for every significant ritual and festival while also being there for quieter times. Thus, over a period of years, I had been present for Id, Qurbani, weddings, circumcisions, Ramzan, harvests, and elections. I also learnt that most women in the village owned two saris made of milled cotton, whose colour and texture withstood daily washing and drying in the sun. In addition, they also usually possessed a third sari, their 'best sari', which they saved for special occasions. This was usually made of more fragile handloom cotton and was therefore worn sparingly and saved for special occasions. Over time, I got to know everyone's 'best saris' as they were worn on each of the important celebrations mentioned above. It is only when I saw women dress in the same 'best' saris to visit the polling booth on Election Day that I realised the importance they attributed to the rite of voting. From there emerged an insight about the sacrosanct nature of voting, which I developed in my argument 'Sacred Elections' and which formed the basis of the all-India CEE study. Such long-term pursuit of this holism in turn allows us to see patterns in seeming messiness and leads to an understanding of the rationale underlying seemingly contradictory perceptions among people.

An apposite illustration of this kind of 'thick' description can be seen through a discussion of the concept of *dan*. In the Indian context, *dan* stands for the concept of a gift that is given without expectation of material return and is used variously to describe the gift of alms to a beggar or the prestations that are made to a priest. It is a word that is widely used across the country and in many different Indian languages. In the electoral context, the word is adapted such that giving/casting one's vote, i.e., the act of voting is called *matdan* (*mat* = opinion; *dan* = to give). But instead of treating it only as an official word with a limited electoral significance, our informants as well as the politicians and political workers in the various field sites constantly played on the notion of 'giving without an expectation of return' when they talked about voting. They also compared the act of voting to older patterns of *dan* such *annadan* (gift of food), *goudan* (gift of cattle), *shramdan* (gift of labour), *kanyadan* (giving away a daughter in marriage) to compare and contrast them. In doing so, they were able to assimilate a relatively new act of voting brought in only in 1952 with much older modes of action. But in the process they demonstrated how voting has been thoroughly incorporated into a pre-existing social repertoire. As ethnographers, it is by paying attention to such organically generated comparisons and metaphors that we are able to represent how voters themselves make sense of the act of voting, and by being aware of the significance of the other notions of *dan*, we are able to assess the relative significance of voting.

Organically situating villagers' political views and voting within a wider ethnography of their villages' life across a decade is the ambition of my forthcoming monograph. Clearly, however, we could not achieve such specific and prolonged immersion in the present multi-site study despite the researchers' broad familiarity with the locales. So are our various accounts too limited in perspective and therefore not really ethnographic at all? I do not think so. Elections are certainly not the whole of life, but they are, in India at least, peculiarly intense, distilling an enormous range of messages and actions which in quieter times are hidden from view. Where in ordinary times questions about politics might generate only desultory answers, amidst the drama of an election in full swing, people were more confident and relaxed about adding their own voices to the surrounding hubbub and talking about politicians, events and scandals, and what they got out of living in a democracy. And they were also curiously more philosophical in their assessment of their own roles in this drama. It was as if the thousands of messages directed at voters galvanised them into articulating their own responses, often contradicting the perceptions held of them by the power elite.

Elections are also important and revealing times because it is then that democratic participation is most forcefully and physically enacted, in the practical activities of queuing, inking fingers, and pressing the EVM button. Such matters are omitted from most discussions of elections. But it is the meticulous conduct of these processes, regularly reenacted and reactivated, which help to create a democratic sensibility among ordinary people and a 'moment of identification' with the wider democratic vision (Norval 2006: 248). So while our studies were snapshots, and somewhat divorced from the album of their wider ethnographic setting, I would argue that they are still of great value and richly descriptive because of the great breadth of characters and depth of feeling which elections pack into that single vivid frame. As John Dunn puts it,

> To treat elections as a privileged focus of investigation, it is necessary to treat then as holistic narratives of development over time of a skein of political relations which extend across a sovereign territorial unit — as readings of the shaping and outcome of national electoral campaigns (1993).

Thus, by advocating the ethnographic approach, we are in dialogue with political scientists whose expectations are: 'a study of the political beliefs of ordinary citizens; a study of the making and unmaking of social blocs operating in politics; thick description of the local context of electoral choice' (Yadav 2007, in Shah 2007: 366). This book hopes to provide at least some measure of this kind of data. In turn, as anthropologists faced with the findings of the 2009 NES study (whose results have been discussed previously), many questions remain. For instance, *why* we may ask, are indigenous *adivasi* communities more enthusiastic about voting than the rest of India? Does their enthusiasm have anything to do with the Maoist challenge to the Indian state being fought in their name or are these two phenomena unrelated? Similarly, we may wonder whether young people in Madhya Pradesh have specific reasons for participating more enthusiastically. What made members of the Muslim OBCs vote in larger numbers in 2009 than other OBC communities? And so on. In each case, the macro trends that teach us valuable lessons about the nature of the Indian electorate also inevitably raise the question 'why'. It is the ambition of future collaborations that we be able to coordinate even more closely between survey and ethnographic research, and this book is the first step in this direction. What we were able to do as a part of the CEE was to review our fieldwork findings subsequently in light of the NES survey results for the election. These did not throw up anything that undermined the insights gained from our study; if anything, we were able to compare our results and in some cases deepen our understanding of some key findings of the survey results. The product of collaboration among the ethnographers themselves and the political scientists of the Lokniti network provides, perhaps for the first time, a more comprehensive picture of the popular experience and meaning of Indian elections than we have had before.

The 2009 Comparative Electoral Ethnographies (CEE) Project

In the final section of this chapter, we present the key features of the CEE study — the research questions, the methodology adopted, who the researchers were, and finally a summary of the main findings of the study.

The key features of this study were as follows:

(*a*) There were 12 fieldwork sites in a balanced representation of big cities, small towns and rural sites across the country (see Map 1.1).

Map 1.1
India: Map of Election 2009

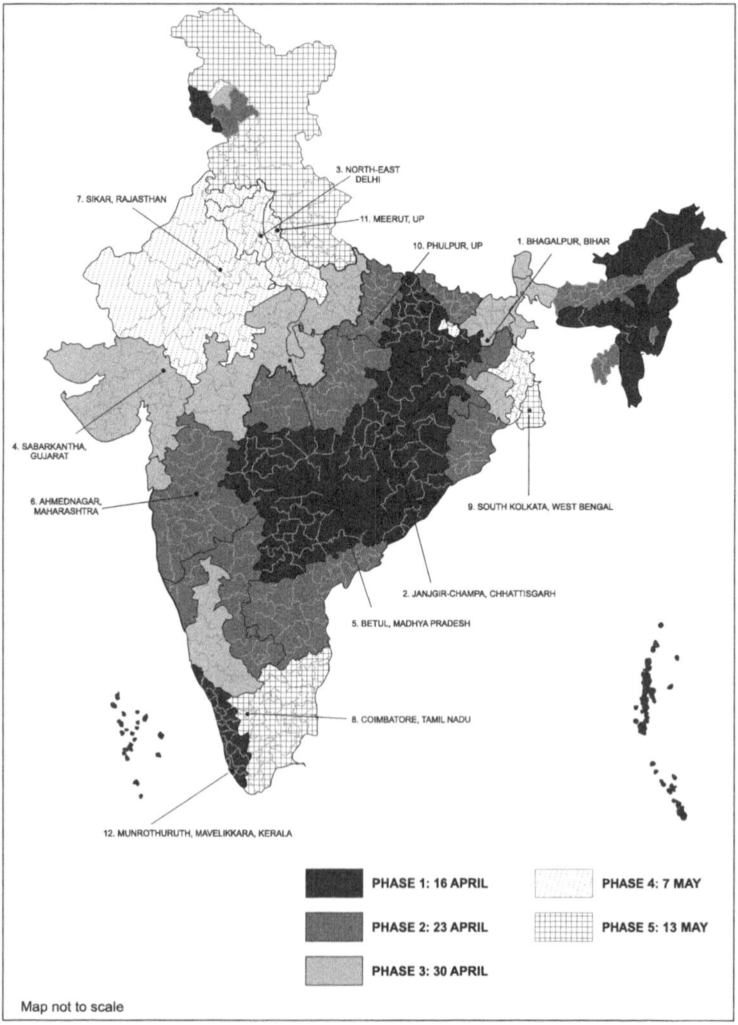

3. NORTH-EAST DELHI
7. SIKAR, RAJASTHAN
11. MEERUT, UP
10. PHULPUR, UP
1. BHAGALPUR, BIHAR
4. SABARKANTHA, GUJARAT
6. AHMEDNAGAR, MAHARASHTRA
9. SOUTH KOLKATA, WEST BENGAL
2. JANJGIR-CHAMPA, CHHATTISGARH
5. BETUL, MADHYA PRADESH
8. COIMBATORE, TAMIL NADU
12. MUNROTHURUTH, MAVELIKKARA, KERALA

PHASE 1: 16 APRIL
PHASE 2: 23 APRIL
PHASE 3: 30 APRIL
PHASE 4: 7 MAY
PHASE 5: 13 MAY

Map not to scale

Source: Prepared by the author.

(*b*) Of the 12 researchers, most were experienced ethnographers who had lived and worked in those places before and were thoroughly familiar with the local people, institutions, ideas, and idioms. As a result, they could capture the shift in the register of discussions and mood that the elections brought.

(c) By pursuing the same set of four principal research questions across all the sites, we attempted to build the comparison into the research design in order to generate data that could be aggregated to provide a national picture.

(d) The methodology was a combination of ethnographic research and use of data generated by surveys and other quantitative methods. The researchers spent a month in the field site, culminating in the day of polling, and used a variety of traditional anthropological methods. These included informal conversations, formal and partially structured interviews, shadowing candidates on the campaign trail, attending political rallies and street corner meetings, accompanying party workers on door-to-door campaigns, and above all, being present at all times at the field site to absorb and watch life as it unfolded around them.

The 12 researchers who carried out the electoral ethnographies were in most of the cases, established ethnographers in those sites and were thoroughly familiar with the local setting — Grace Carswell and Geert De Neve in Tamil Nadu, Satendra Kumar in western UP, Badri Narayan in eastern UP, Mekhala Krishnamurthy in Madhya Pradesh, Rosina Nasir in Delhi, Mahashweta Jani in Gujarat, Goldy M. George in Chhattisgarh, Deepu Sebastian in Kerala, Vanita Falcao in Rajasthan, Abhay Datar in Maharashtra, Priyadarshini Singh in Bihar, and Dolonchampa Chakrabarty in West Bengal. In over half these cases, the researchers had lived and worked in these sites prior to the election and they were, therefore, thoroughly familiar with the local people, institutions, ideas, and the idioms. As a result, it was possible for them to capture the shift in the register of discussions and mood that the elections brought with them, and compare it with non-electoral times. Each research site was the catchment area of a polling booth that on an average accommodates 1,000–1,500 voters, a manageable number of people to get to know in depth if one was already familiar with the setting.[15] Furthermore, all of the researchers attended a three-day workshop that provided training in doing ethnographic research specifically designed for the study of elections

---

[15] The polling booth was also the unit of study for Myron Weiner and Rajni Kothari's studies (Brass 1985).

and received a briefing from members of the Lokniti team on the NES findings for each of the states where our studies would be located. A common website was created for researchers to upload their data and to exchange findings. Taking advantage of the multiple phases in which the elections were held, some researchers travelled to other sites to work alongside the ethnographer located there. In this, we also drew inspiration from the findings of the NES surveys that captured a nation-wide picture of political opinions and attitudes during Indian elections. In April 2009, I undertook to make a radio documentary for BBC Radio 4 on voter perceptions of the elections and travelled to a number of the sites personally, thereby gaining valuable first-hand awareness of the nature of the sites and attended the first day of polling in the state of Kerala.[16] In June 2009, the team met for the last time to exchange and compare their findings before submitting their final reports. Some members of the Lokniti network attended these discussions. The findings presented in this volume are, therefore, the result of teamwork between political scientists of the Lokniti network and anthropologists, as well as exchange and collaboration among the ethnographers themselves.

In sociology/social anthropology, the recent volume edited by A. M. Shah, *The Grassroots of Democracy*, was the closest parallel to this study. Published in 2007, it presented studies carried out during elections held in the 1960s and 1970s by a number of different sociologists from the Delhi School of Economics under the leadership of M. N. Srinivas and A. M. Shah. It was an admirable attempt given that sociologists then, as also now, did not normally pay attention to elections and left it to political scientists. But this project consciously sought to critique existing quantitative methods to show what the field method could reveal and argued in the end for its inarguable superiority over the survey method in the understanding of elections. The reasonableness of this claim is arguable especially because the essays in the volume did not bear this claim out and were extremely uneven. However, this volume (many of the contributors were my professors while I was a graduate student at the Delhi School of Economics) provided useful lessons for the study of elections in the future and we kept them in mind while designing the CEE study. The first was the issue of methodology and the turf war that usually accompanied it.

---

[16] The 40-minute documentary was produced for Radio 4 by CultureWise.

As Suhas Palshikar put it in a thought-provoking review essay of the book, '[the] study of elections is often caught in the crossfire between the proponents of quantitative studies and the supporters of the field study' (2007: 24). By collaborating with the Lokniti network we sought to address this issue. But we were also mindful of the problems that arise when multiplicities of methodologies are used to study electoral politics. For instance, Shah (2007) was criticised for its use of 'surveys' that did not yield meaningful results because they were, in effect, questionnaires administered to non-randomised focus groups of people. This also raised the genuine problem of how survey and ethnography could be combined in the same study for, by definition, ethnographic methods were well suited to a small unit of study and survey results got stronger as the sample grew bigger. It is for this reason that we did not attempt to conduct any surveys of our own during the CEE survey. Further, it raised the question of what the ideal unit for election studies should be. Palshikar advocates the Assembly constituency as the ideal unit of study because it allows us to 'make sense of the play of power politics' (ibid.: 24). The reason for this is that even though an assembly constituency forms only one part of a Lok Sabha constituency, it provides a unit in which significant electoral contests can be observed and compared to data from previous elections. An urban neighbourhood or village, on the other hand, despite being the preferred unit of ethnographers, is too small for comparison. Shah (2007) shows that if the electoral story is too local, it makes generalisation impossible on the basis of the data. Consequently, *The Grassroots of Democracy* fails to provide any sense of the overall atmosphere of the landmark elections of 1967 and 1971 and is instead a mere collection of 18 disparate electoral stories.[17] As a result, we took this issue of the unit of study seriously and considered carefully whether or not to take an Assembly constituency as our unit of study. In the end we settled for the polling booth because our unit of study had to reflect its emphasis. Given that our main task was to study people and their context closely, we could only achieve this at a scale where it would be possible to get to know them very well. An Assembly constituency is a vast region with a correspondingly vast

---

[17] In 1971, Indira Gandhi delinked the state- and national-level elections, so the election focussed the electorate on exclusively national issues that were economic ones for the first time.

average number of voters, a scale impossible for the sort of in-depth ethnographic study we had in mind. By using the polling booth as a unit instead, we were able to observe the various local processes that went on during an election: the social dynamics between groups variously defined by caste, class, gender, age, and proximity to power. Contrary to general perception, we were able to see how different factors came into play at different points in the campaign period in influencing people's voting decisions. As we were concerned with capturing the nuances of how people talked about politics, this was possible only when we were able to spend enough time among them to listen carefully. Also, rather than cover a campaign as it unfolded across a vast constituency, we tried to capture how a campaign arrived and was received in one setting. Thus, while the CEE study might not throw any fresh light on electoral politics per se, it provides new insights into what goes into making electoral politics possible.

The final lesson to be learnt from Shah (2007) was the importance of a common framework of questions without which findings from different research sites fail to come together to reveal insights into general questions applicable to India as a whole. This prompted Yogendra Yadav's comment in the Epilogue of the book, 'Interesting answers, but what exactly was the question?' (ibid.: 345). Learning our lessons from the contributors to that volume, I was mindful of the need for a common theoretical framework for a study of elections in India, using a range of methods, and for a well-defined research design. Further, given that it was a comparative project, it was also of crucial importance to design a common framework of questions to be examined by all the researchers involved in the study in order to enable a coherent discussion afterwards. The aim of the CEE project was to study politics in India and to understand the meaning of elections in public life. As a result, I was willing to be catholic about my choice of methodologies to serve this purpose, rather than the other way round. This book, among other things, responds therefore to Palshikar's complaint about the 'lack of dialogue between the two methods and a process of learning from each other's strengths' (2007: 27).

The 12 sites studied during the CEE project were in different states of India, each with its own electoral histories, diverse caste dynamics and social composition. However, despite this enormous variation, some findings emerged that were common to all the different settings. These can be grouped under four themes: the importance of the EC's work in popular imagination, the importance of the election campaign in creating a sense of *communitas* in the country, the flexibility and vigour of the language that Indians use while discussing politics, and the various meanings that people attach to the act of voting. Let us look at each of these in turn. Elections usher in a special period of time in India, marked institutionally by the imposition of the 'Model Code of Conduct' by the ECI People have a great deal of confidence in the ECI which is seen as a public body that performs its function with a unique efficiency and probity otherwise missing in other Indian institutions. People are able to see its functioning for themselves at the grassroots level in voter education campaigns and in the millions of polling booths across the country and express a sense of gratitude and admiration for the Commission's massive efforts. Election campaigns from the viewpoint of the ordinary voter look very different from that portrayed in media reports. The ways in which ordinary people assess politicians, discuss party ideologies, or evaluate campaign tactics show that voters deeply appreciate the levelling effect that election campaigns have on the powerful when, in a period of role-reversal, however temporary, politicians have to beg for votes and get their spotless clothes soiled in the heat and dust of the campaign battle. For at least 40 per cent of the Indian population who officially still live below the poverty line, such humbling of the powerful, however temporary, carries deep significance. Further, the assessments that people offered of the importance of voting show that illiteracy and poverty are clearly not impediments to understanding, and the practice of voting regularly in Indian elections over 60 years has allowed the masses to develop a sophisticated understanding of the ideas of democracy and citizenship in India. As much of this study was based on open-ended conversations and mingling among voters day in and out over several weeks, we were able to capture some of the characteristics of the language of common usage in India. Dozens of neologisms in various languages were coined across the country to capture and describe the rapidly changing political landscape, to make jokes and to create awareness of ideas. It is possible, therefore, to analyse the plasticity of this language to see how everyday conversations are more nimble than the categories and concepts of political philosophy in capturing the essence of the Indian political experience. People offered various explanations for their enthusiasm for voting and stressed, most of all, that the act of voting was *an end in itself* and not just an instrumental means to achieve certain ends. The reasons for this belief were various but perhaps the most important one was that voting allowed people, if only for one day, to be counted as equal citizens according to the principle of 'one person one vote', which for otherwise marginalised communities was particularly significant and valuable. Voting was an opportunity to exercise a fundamental right that was freely and fairly available unlike others that could be severely threatened. Voting also provided an opportunity to discharge an inviolate duty of a citizen and to reciprocate the efficiency of the ECI in holding well-conducted elections. For all of the above reasons and many more that are provided in this volume, voting in elections is considered sacrosanct by a large majority of Indians.

That the findings can be accurately summarised in this way, without needing regional caveats, is itself a vindication of the project's hypothesis that in much, if not all of India, there is a distinctive and recognisable popular perception of sacrosanct elections grounded in a strong sense of citizenship, duty and rights. The findings are also a vindication of the strength of the ethnographic method and proof that sustained long-term research in one setting can yield insights that are profound and accurate. It is undeniable, of course, that Bengal politics has a very specific set of characteristics — the longest engagement with colonial rule, a legacy of partition at independence, the unique experience of the longest elected Communist government in the world (1977–2011), and a history of land reforms that at least partially altered social dynamics. These factors and others have created a fairly unique political culture in Bengal that doesn't share many of the characteristics of politics in other Indian states. For instance, the two party contests that have been the hallmark of electoral contests in most other states have been notably missing in West Bengal due to overwhelming dominance of the Left parties and the moribund nature of the Congress until the relatively recent inception of its newer avatar, the Trinamool Congress. Furthermore, West Bengal did not display the characteristics of the third democratic upsurge and the mobilisation of other backward castes that dominated the politics of the 1990s in the neighbouring states. In fact, caste, while all pervasive as social practice, has had less electoral valence in Bengal politics when compared to other states. The state also escaped the rise of Hindutva politics and issues of religious nationalism witnessed elsewhere. Yet despite these distinguishing features West Bengal continues very much to be part of the Indian polity and its political parties and electorate continue to inhabit the same landscape as all others. It has had a very particular political history that makes it distinct from other Indian states, especially being ruled by the Communist parties from 1977–2011. Yet, as evidence from across India showed, on the more generic issues of democratic politics such as the meaning of the vote, notions of citizenship and so on, Bengali voters were not much different from other India voters.

Whatever the imperfections of this study compared to an ideal ethnographic method, I believe that our multi-site comparative approach was essential. Ethnographic work is subjective, and anthropologists studying the same locality have notoriously differed in interpretations and judgements of what was significant and what was not. Intensely individual research agendas, immersion only in 'their' village or neighbourhood, and caution about the 'representativeness' of the particular fieldwork site all lead to a reluctance to generalise conclusions or aggregate findings with those of others to draw a larger-scale picture.[18] Too often, Clifford Geertz's assertion that 'an anthropologist speaks from a village rather than for it' is ignored. Regional or national-level conclusions are thus typically left to other more quantitative methodologies.[19] When I did venture such larger scale propositions, as I did for India as a whole in 'Sacred Elections' (Banerjee 2007), the doubt remained whether West Bengal was too much of an exception, resulting from three decades of Communist agitprop. However, my own hunch from conducting research in other parts of India was that West Bengal was not an exception and that the sophistication and pro-vote attitudes of Bengali rural voters was likely to be shared by Indians elsewhere. But the only way to test this conjecture was by pursuing mini-ethnographies across multiple sites in order to produce hard evidence. Whether we have succeeded I leave to the reader to judge from the rest of this book.

---

[18] For a thoughtful discussion by one of the most respected ethnographers of India about the limits of generalisation possible from an anthropologist's 'my village' perspective, see the section on 'method and meaning of village studies' in Breman (2007: 6–11).

[19] Weiner (1957) was an early experiment in political science in state-level comparison, but this set a trend in the discipline with Kohli (1988) and Jenkins (2004), among others, building on this tradition.

Plan of the Book

The four chapters that follow present the findings of each of the four research questions in greater detail. Each question is addressed with data that has been collected from across the different sites, thereby providing a genuinely national picture in our findings. Chapter 1 presents a vivid description of a country in the grip of an election campaign, with all the accompanying cacophony and effervescence. We look at all the stages that make up a campaign from the 'nomination *sabhas*' when political parties announce their candidates — the various ways in which candidates outmanoeuvre each other to gain the coveted 'ticket', the multiplicity of techniques deployed in reaching out to voters, and the diverse scales of political meetings that are held — and we examine in some detail how party workers do political work during a campaign. In all of these descriptions, we privilege the point of view of the voters themselves to present a campaign as it appears from their standpoint. The data collected by the researchers for the CEE project on this issue is particularly rich and the reader will find a wide range of examples and scenarios from across the country presented here. In Chapter 2, we look at the issue of political language, a relatively understudied aspect of Indian politics. In this, we take our lead from Kaviraj, who pointed out the need to pay attention to everyday language that is able to capture better the constantly evolving nature of Indian politics through its own plasticity. We found that in all the different languages spoken in different parts of India, people were remarkably inventive in how they used it, combining their own with English, coining new terms, using metaphors imaginatively, and reinterpreting held concepts to describe new phenomena as and when they unfolded around them. For instance, given that the auspicious wedding season coincided with the elections in 2009, election officials and voters alike used the various concepts associated with an Indian wedding to describe the electoral process. The play on the word *dan* was another instance in which people explored the Hindu notion of *dan* as giving without expectation to ponder on why voting is called *matdan* in Hindi. This chapter also examines in detail the deeply held popular idea that politics is ultimately a demonic and corrupting realm through the various metaphors and analogies they used to describe their ideas. Chapter 3 presents information on another unexplored dimension of the electoral process in India — the culture of the polling booth. In looking at this issue closely, we examine whether there is anything special about the environment in which votes are actually cast that could affect how voters view the electoral process. Polling day is a holiday in India and our sense as ethnographers was that it brought with it a shift in register in people's daily routine through the sense of excitement about going to vote and the relaxed conviviality afterwards. To this end, we look carefully at the numerous processes through which thousands of school buildings across the country are transformed into polling booths, at how polling officials conduct themselves in front of the voters, how voters view the process, and so on. In all our sites, we spoke to voters as they emerged from polling stations, and it was evident that they found the experience transformatory in some way and were affected by an altered state for at least the duration of the day before they returned to the normality of life. 'The polling booth is like a *garba grha* [sanctum sanctorum]', said one person, as he came out blinking into the summer heat. As stated before, it is my contention that elections have come to hold a sacrosanct place in Indian public life. By giving due attention to the manner in which people consume political messages during an election campaign, talk about politics and experience the process of voting itself, we can hope to recover the ways in which meaning is created in the electoral process. A final test of this meaning was therefore to ask people directly what voting meant to them. By posing the question 'why do you vote?', we received a variety of explanations and we present these in Chapter 4. As the reader will see, people cover a whole gamut of possible reasons for voting — from naked instrumentality ('I vote for X so that he will protect me from the police') to bureaucratic existentialism ('I vote to prove that I exist'). In the Conclusion, I engage with more theoretical debates on the basis of the data generated by the CEE study. The appendices at the end of the book contain details about particular 2009 'electoral stories' — the contest, the political parties involved and key local events.

II
The Campaign

An average Lok Sabha parliamentary constituency has 2 million voters (about 20 times the average British constituency) and some are spread across hundreds of miles, encompassing a wide variety of rural and urban populations from different social strata. Much of this vast and varied electorate is savvy about politics in general and acutely aware of its own interests. Yet people are unlikely to recognise the names of all the individual candidates, and even the incumbent may remain unfamiliar to most voters. Parties' campaign strategies take this scale and diversity of audience, awareness and setting into account, and so deploy a wide range of media and campaigning techniques. These are expensive and labour-intensive, and have to be carried out within established electoral conventions under the watchful eye of 11 million ECI officials. Thus, like a military campaign, an effective election campaign in an Indian constituency relies on discipline, shrewd strategy, intelligence, optimum deployment of personnel, and a judicious amount of 'shock and awe'.

For all the plans of the party high command, however, it is ultimately the millions of rank-and-file party workers who play the key role in winning voters' hearts and minds. The election campaign facilitates a rare contact between voters and their representatives. These two worlds remain largely separated during the business-as-usual tenure of a parliament, but during the campaign, politicians need to go to the voters to show them what they have done, to promise more in the future and to ask for their votes. The voters, in turn, see this as an opportunity to rate the performance of the powerful and register complaints about their poor performance. Since modern Indian politicians are widely reviled as, at best, ineffectual and, at worst, corrupt, these periodic encounters of rulers and ruled are potentially explosive and need to be carefully managed (see Chapter 3 for a description of how people talk about politicians). Party workers play this crucial role of mediation by performing what I call 'political work' (see Banerjee 2010b). In Bengal, for example, someone involved in the Communist Party's work, particularly at the local level, was never described as merely 'belonging to' or 'supporting' it, but rather as *doing* it — 'he *does* Party' (*o Party korey*). This is also true of many of the cadre-based parties in India. Their political work continues in the interim period between elections for the three tiers of democratic government, but in a low-key way often hidden from view, done at the margins and as much through casual conversations and meetings as through formal institutions. To that extent, the election campaign is less a military matter than the overt harvest that follows quiet and prolonged sowing and cultivation. Years of alliance-building and discussions around political ideology are placed in the limelight and drawn on by the party workers as they deliver votes to the polling station.[1]

This chapter discusses the key stages in the campaign cycle across our fieldwork sites in 2009, and what it reveals about such political work and its reception by voters.

Pre-Nomination Work

In some constituencies, parties followed the traditional path of informally announcing their intended candidates well before the official election dates, which gave them a headstart with the groundwork of preparation and strategy for the local campaign. On the whole, incumbent Members of Parliament (MPs) were seen as an obvious choice for candidacy in a Lok Sabha election, as were sitting Members of Legislative Assembly (MLAs), especially those who had 'done their time' over several terms. The next best candidates were those who had money to fund their campaigns. For instance, it was said of Bharat Singh Tanwar, a successful businessman from Mumbai who was standing for election as a Bahujan Samaj Party (BSP) candidate in faraway Rajasthan, that he was a 'readymade politician'. That he was also a high-caste Rajput and had links to an equally rich high-caste 'god man' made his BSP credentials even stronger as the largely low-caste Chamar BSP tried to widen its electoral net to include higher castes.

---

[1] See Harriss (1986) for an account of how political parties create their networks through *manram* or 'party room' in the south Indian city of Coimbatore.

In other cases, however, there was a prolonged debate about whom to nominate that continued right up to the eve of the campaign. A recent development in this process has been the growth of private detective agencies whose services are hired to do background checks on potential candidates. 'The major ground work services provided by us include pre-election, constituency-based socio-economic research, background check of prospective candidates seeking [a] ticket, their socio-political status, reputation check' said Kunwar Vikram Singh, who runs Lancer Network, one of the oldest detective agencies in the country. He added that their work also includes providing information about '[w]in-ability factors and dissention levels among prominent workers and local leaders and . . . to check on the anti-party activity of those who were denied [a] ticket' he added (cited in Raza 2012). In 2009, there was the added complication of there being more than the usual number of late nominees because of the significant redrawing of constituent boundaries by the ECI (known in India as a delimitation exercise). This significantly altered the socio-demographic composition of many constituencies and forced parties to reconsider the suitability of their incumbents. The considerations and manouevres that resulted were illustrated by the following saga from a North-East Delhi constituency.

Drama in Delhi

The delimitation exercise had created a constituency that now had a one-third Muslim population — the highest proportion of any constituency in the state. The two major parties, Congress and Bharatiya Janata Party (BJP) had announced their respective candidates, Jagdish Tytler and B. L. Sharma (aka 'Prem'), well in advance. Tytler was a seasoned politician and Congress heavyweight, who had been a Union Minister several times. Though the newly-drawn constituency was three times larger than his previous seat (Sadar), he used the energy of the Youth Wing of the Congress and the networks of the Congress MLAs to organise street corner (*nukkad*) meetings and together, they managed to conduct an efficient initial reconnaissance of the new constituency in just seven days. The BJP organisation, meanwhile, began 'mapping' the non-Muslim areas in order to concentrate campaigning efforts there, knowing that its ideological appeal to Muslim voters was limited. Also in the fray were the BSP who were already dominant in the neighbouring state of Uttar Pradesh and were looking to establish a stronger presence in Delhi. They had put forward a Muslim candidate, Haji Dilshad Ali, who was reputed to have paid the BSP ₹30 lakh for the privilege of the 'ticket'.

These orderly intentions and preparations were suddenly thrown up in the air, however, when, at a press conference, a Sikh journalist threw a shoe at the Home Minister. He was protesting the fact that the recently released Congress report into the anti-Sikh riots of 1984 had cleared Tytler of any wrongdoing, whereas many others judged him to have played an instrumental and incendiary role. The Congress Party now decided that continuing to support Tytler's candidature after this furore might harm its chances in Punjab and other areas with a significant Sikh population, and so decided to withdraw his ticket. This led to a fresh round of speculation about who the new Congress candidate would be. Two potential replacements emerged: Matin Ahmed, the incumbent MLA from the Muslim-dominated seat of Seelampur Assembly Constituency (AC), or J. P. Aggrawal, a senior Congressman who was Chief of the Delhi Committee and a Rajya Sabha member. This gave the BJP fresh hope, since if the Congress chose Ahmed, the substantial Muslim vote would likely be split between the BSP and Congress's Muslim candidates. As a local journalist observed, 'The public was not impressed with the "only shoes, no issues!" manner in which the campaigns were run'.

Just a few days before the final official nomination date, however, a fourth candidate suddenly announced his intention to stand, namely Shoaib Iqbal, also a Muslim, representing the small Janshakti party. This threatened to split the Muslim vote still more. But then, he just as suddenly withdrew, and rumours abounded that Aggrawal, one of the two Congress hopefuls, had offered Iqbal ₹3 crore' to do so! With tongues firmly in their cheek, people punned on the alleged pay off, saying that Iqbal had found the 'glue' to hold together the anti-communal forces (*ab unhe fevicol jo mil gaya he haath mazboot karne ko*). This tactical coup impressed the Congress Party and helped Aggrawal win its ticket. This upset his rival, Ahmed, who, as the sitting MLA, felt he knew the area much better. While he dutifully accompanied Aggrawal on his neighbourhood *padyatra*s, he also began a negative campaign against him behind his back, and accused the Congress of never supporting a Muslim candidate if another option was available.

Despite Aggrawal's selection, in the following weeks, the BJP ran their Hindu-focused campaign energetically, in the hope that the Muslim vote would be split among the other two parties. But just three days before polling, the BSP candidate Dilshad Ali also withdrew, saying he did not want to split the 'secular vote'. The rumour was that he too had been paid off handsomely by Congress. At the end of what was belatedly a two-horse race, Aggrawal was further bolstered by a visit by Rahul Gandhi on the last day of the campaign, whereas none of the national BJP leaders visited the constituency, and won the election (Nasir FR: 8–9).

Nomination *Sabha*

Once the political parties had made up their mind about their candidates, the campaign officially kicked off with what was called a 'nomination *sabha*'. This was the designated event for the candidate to file his nomination papers with the ECI, thus make his intention to stand for election official. In some places, as in western Uttar Pradesh, this event was conducted with much fanfare, as the candidate was carried out of the party offices on the shoulders of his supporters and taken to the local election office to file his papers. Party workers and young men were often paid to swell the numbers accompanying the candidate before and after his filing, cheering and shouting slogans. This show of strength at the outset was important to set the tone of the campaign and manifest the potential of the candidate to win. Vast numbers of unemployed young men jockeyed to attach themselves in this way to a campaign, in the hope of becoming a modest retainer or at least indulging in some novel 'time-pass' (see Jeffrey 2009). It is they who continued to create much of the buzz and crowds in the weeks following the campaign. Lacking other prospects, the campaign also provided an opportunity for such young men to get noticed and show commitment and discipline in the hope of acquiring a career as a party worker in the future. As one youth remarked in Bihar, 'If I can't make it good now then when else can I manage it?!' (*abhaun na chalni te kabhaun chalni*) (Singh FR: 7).

In one Gujarat constituency, we saw two particularly colourful and rival nomination sabhas in close proximity:

(*a*) The Congress chose to start their parade from a statue of B. R. Ambedkar, the famous Dalit leader and architect of the Indian constitution. The members of this parade were mostly from the rural working classes, dressed in traditional *chaniya choli* and silver ornaments, making their own music with a large *dhol* and performing their traditional dances. Women from the forest of Poshina, who performed their indigenous dance styles in the procession and musicians, who played a variety of instruments otherwise reserved for rituals and weddings, joined the candidate, who had his base in the tribal areas of Sabarkantha.

(*b*) The BJP's procession, on the other hand, consisting of the candidate Mahendrasinh and his family members, started from the Ramji Temple where the candidate offered his prayers and was honoured by a turban and sword in recognition of his warrior Rajput caste. His next stop was to offer flowers at the statue of Sardar Vallabhbhai Patel, the great Indian nationalist leader from Gujarat, where other BJP leaders also joined him. As they made their way to the election offices, a crowd of about

4,000 people travelled with them, dressed in the party's saffron hue. The participants were mainly middle class. The women were dressed like stars from TV soap operas in synthetic saris, *sindur* in their parting and *mangalsutra*s around their necks, and the workers carried flags with the party's symbol of the lotus and danced to songs from Bollywood songs from a public announcement (PA) system ('Namak Ishque Ka', 'Kanta Laga', 'Hare Ram Hara Krishna', 'Deva Ho Deva Ganpati Deva') as they went along. Everyone was given lunch at the party office. On reaching the local election offices, only a couple of people were allowed to accompany the candidate inside as he filed his papers but after he emerged, he addressed his supporters. This was the first of the many political speeches to follow, and as such, was keenly discussed in detail by onlookers and cadres (Jani FR: 14).

Party Workers and Political Work

After the filing of nomination papers, the ECI takes two weeks to scrutinise the candidates' eligibility before formally confirming them. During this interim period, the more established political parties began organising their campaign work in earnest. Here are three examples:

(*a*) To tackle the size of a large parliamentary constituency, the BSP divided up its work according to the different Assembly segments within it. In our site in eastern Uttar Pradesh, for example, the Nawabganj Vidhan Sabha was divided into 28 sectors, each containing 10 polling booths. Each sector was allocated 53 party workers (three overseers plus five workers for each booth). They were all given 10 days of training on how to go among the Dalits and explain to them that the BSP was working towards bringing about social change and helping them achieve economic independence.

(*b*) In West Bengal, the famed CPI(M) election machine rolled into action as the Party began its work with its own process of 'scrutiny' of each constituency. This work involved all the members of the party organisation from the lowly Booth Committee to the Politburo, and involved duties such as checking electoral rolls, assessing the strength of the constituency and, most importantly, identifying undecided voters who would need special attention.[2] The Booth Committee members carried out door-to-door campaigning, the Local Committee members organised the campaign at the local level and the Zonal Committee were responsible for a cluster of localities. The leaders were asked to visit the various localities to address the people whenever needed in the campaign process. The district and state committees oversaw the entire campaign in the districts and the state respectively.

(c) The BJP mounted a strong campaign for the north-east Delhi seat discussed earlier. At the initial planning meeting with its workers, in the main control room of their party headquarters, they proceeded to 'map' the constituency in two senses: first by tallying the names and serial numbers of houses in the constituency with those provided by the Election Commission, and second, by determining the different demands and needs of the various neighbourhoods (for example, for better infrastructure or amenities) and thus their likely susceptibility to particular promises and messages, based on the experience of previous elections.

The quality and granularity of such mapping is often what distinguished one political party from another. Those with strong grassroots organisation and experienced party workers in an area were able to draw up a fairly astute picture of the social and demographic composition and political leanings of practically every street and household. On this basis, party workers then decided the routes of door-to-door campaigns and allotted canvassing teams of four to five people. Other workers engaged in preparing the literature for speeches and pamphlets, which could be similarly tailored to particular neighbourhoods. The parties would also often set up a makeshift sort of field office in the heart of the constituency, which for the following weeks would serve as a busy hub for campaign materials, news and gossip, and the to-and-fro of workers manning smaller satellite offices further afield. This style of operation was true of most of the cadre-based parties we observed in Tamil Nadu, Uttar Pradesh, West Bengal, and Gujarat.

---

[2] See Banerjee (2010a) and Chatterjee et al. (1997) for detailed accounts of the Left Front machinery.

We could distinguish four main modes of campaigning activity across the country and among the various political parties.

Producing and Distributing Promotional Material

(*a*) *Flags, Pamphlets, Handbills, and Posters*: These were printed, and the flow was usually from the state capital to the district headquarters. There, the candidate often took personal charge of the material and distributed it to the local party leaders, who, in turn, passed it on to the rank-and-file party workers. The symbols of the parties, so crucial to the dissemination of their platforms, began to appear in all available spaces. Some of these spaces included walls on which murals were painted, street crossings across which bunting was strung and posters plastered on every lamp-post and pillar.

(*b*) *Murals*: Murals or wall paintings represent another aspect of promotional material for campaigns. 'Professional sign writers were usually employed in the weeks before the election and, together with a local activist, would travel around the region painting advertisements on walls, which consisted mainly of the candidate's name, the alliance parties' names and the alliance symbol. Because of the concern that many All-India Anna Dravida Munnetra Kazhagam (AIADMK) supporters would not recognise the alliance party symbol (CPM's sickle and hammer), this aspect of the campaign was very important for the AIADMK-led alliance. Therefore, we found many sickle and hammers, painted in the AIADMK colours of red and black with "Amma cinnam" written around it' (Carswell and De Neve FR: 38). (In line with ECI rules the party workers removed all flags, banners and wall paintings within a 100-metre radius of the polling booth a few days before the election.) This method of painting slogans and logos on walls was called 'Walling' in West Bengal.

(*c*) *Street Theatre*: Street theatre has always been a popular tool to disseminate political messages. In several states, we saw performances by established groups of performers who were commissioned by political parties to perform plays dramatising their achievements.

(*d*) *Vans with Loud-Hailers*: Vans with loud-hailers roamed the streets throughout the day with noisy pithy messages. In Kerala we heard one that repeatedly asked people to vote for the 'clock' (symbol of the Nationalist Congress Party [NCP]) and in Rajasthan, one that merely repeated the phrase, 'the sign of the hand', over and over again (*haath ka nishan, haath ka nishan, haath ka nishan, haath ka nishan!*). In Gujarat there were announcements of the timings of Narendra Modi's TV appearances: 'Because Modiji is now on tour of the country, we Gujaratis have not been able to listen to him speak for days, so let's meet our popular (*Lokladila*) leader on India TV at 8.30 tonight and tomorrow on Star News at 9 pm'.

(*e*) *Giant Cutouts*: Giant cutouts were used in some states — for instance, of Jayalalithaa in Tamil Nadu and Chiranjeevi in Andhra Pradesh, and, seemingly inspired by them, of Mamata Banerjee of the Trinamool Congress in West Bengal.

(*f*) *Bottles of Liquor*: Free bottles of liquor were distributed among men in some areas, typically in the dead of the night before polling. Parties tried to find the funds for bottled liquor (English *daru*), always more appreciated than country liquor (*desi daru*).

While the activities described here took place as in previous years, in 2009 with the more stringent interpretation of the Model Code of Conduct (MCC), such liberal use of public spaces was curtailed. While publicity materials could be put up for a political meeting they had to be taken down within an hour of its conclusion. Before the ECI imposed its stricter interpretation of the MCC, elections were seen as cultural events as much as political ones. The tradition of painting street murals with political messages and cartoons also provided employment to hundreds of otherwise impoverished painters. But now, such organic forms have given way to more synthetic ones. On the whole, in 2009, we found that the MCC was more strictly enforced in the north of the country than the south, and in urban areas more than rural ones. Paintings on privately-owned houses and walls in villages were still to be seen in most parts of the country. Permanent displays had to be confined to the private property of supporters with their permission or by making a payment to the property owner. 'Look at this small flag that they have hung outside our shop' a trader in Harda, Madhya Pradesh, said to us, 'It costs the party ₹18 to display it here. And observers have already come around asking whether it has been put up with our permission'.

(g) *Merchandise*: These ECI strictures led to greater innovation in creating merchandise to display the party's symbols. Given the heat of the summer, caps made from paper and cloth were widely used, each in the colours of the political party and with its symbol printed on them, and some even had pictures of their leaders. Across the country, we found baseball caps, small flags, umbrellas, balloons, stickers, badges, buttons, masks, and even saris made and distributed in the colours of the different political parties. Parties with greater resources, like the BJP in Gujarat, produced pens and cloth bags with Modi's picture on them. These were reserved for party workers and journalists, as were packets of mints (a novelty) for the children of the workers.

(h) *Campaign Vehicles*: These also provided ideal sites for constant and wide dissemination of party paraphernalia. For instance, in Gujarat, the main BJP campaign car (a Toyota) was plastered with the photographs of Atal Bihari Vajpayee, L. K. Advani, Rajnath Singh, Narendra Modi, Purshottam Rupala, and the candidate Mahendrasinh printed on it. It also bore BJP's slogan of *Majboot Neta Nirnayak Sarkar* ('A strong leader and a decisive government'), the party's symbol of lotus, and a picture of Tata's newly launched low-price Nano car, which was meant for the masses and was being manufactured in Gujarat. This campaign car was seen by thousands of people as it toured the state. Similarly, the Congress used a more modest Jeep covered with the photographs of Madhusudan Mistry, the Congress candidate, and Manmohan Singh and Sonia Gandhi. There was also a huge picture of a farmer saying 'My vote for Congress', a long list of Mistry's achievements as Member of Parliament (MP) and statements like 'press the button and give your vote to Congress'.

(i) *Paid News*: Another unintended consequence of stronger strictures against campaign materials was the phenomenon of paid news. This was one in which newspapers and television stations provided coverage of particular political parties and candidates in return for money, rather than the news they usually distributed. Party workers, especially those that controlled funds, remarked dismissively that most reporters would print any story in exchange for a few bottles of liquor. Conversely, those who did not pay the necessary tariff courted the danger of unfavourable stories being printed about them in the press. In Rajasthan, while on the Congress campaign trail, we saw the candidate's aides make phone calls to a dozen reporters to relay a negative story about a rival candidate that one of his workers had just reported to him. In fact, he made it a point to mention the story for days even when he was asked about something completely different. Each political party put out advertisements to extol its virtues. In Gujarat, the BJP advertisement on television revolved around their main slogan — *Mazboot Neta Nirnayak Sarkar* — and focused on the issues of price rise, terrorism and powerful leadership. The rival Congress raised issues of the gang rape of a girl in Patan, rape of a girl from the Koli community and suicides of farmers and diamond workers, and showed how many schemes like the 108 Ambulance service and the *Sarva Shiksha Abhiyan* primary education drive, which the Modi government had claimed credit for, were, in reality, Central government schemes provided by the Congress-led UPA government. In Chhattisgarh, we found a cable operator who aired one party's advertisement for several days before switching to its rival's advertisements when offered a better deal by them. Sometimes this caused people to unsubscribe from a particular cable network and at other times the cable operator remained committed to a single party. Either way, political parties often entered a cable war as a result.

(*j*) *Text Messages*: We also found campaigns conducted through the aggressive use of text messages on mobile phones everywhere. In the Bilaspur constituency we found the use of fake messages using the doctored voices of the opposition that showed them in a bad light! 'In Tamil Nadu, one such message went viral within a few hours of it being sent out and people received it on their phones several times. The message merely listed the former Dravida Munnetra Kazhagam (DMK) Chief Minister (CM) M. Karunanidhi's assets and properties that he had come to own since he first came into power:

> TN C.M Dr Karunandid Family Property: 4th millionaire in ASIA in 2001. Now 2nd. 1) 1951 – a house; 2) 1992 – 80cr 3) 2006 17,000cr, 60,000cr in black 4) SUN Net19 channels 5) Aircel 6) Poongi Textile 7) Sheshayee papermills 8) Dinakaran450cr 9) Vigadan 100cr 10) Tamil murasu 280cr 11) kungumam 150cr 12) Mursoli 90cr 13) Many cinema theatres all over TN 14) 30% of shares in TATA group etc. In 2009 he'll be 1st in Asia. Thanks to TN voters! PLZ FRWD 2 ALL.

The message did not need to say much more; the list itself was a statement about his enrichment while in power and that was a message enough, especially as the DMK was considered a cadre-based pro-worker party. By prompting the recipient to "forward to all", it ensured that as many people as possible would see it and was the perfect ammunition for local AIADMK workers who needed to convince voters to not vote for the DMK. Another message provided details of black money of rich Indians stacked away in Swiss banks. It read as follows:

> Black money in Swiss banks — Swiss Banking Association Report, 2006, details bank deposits in the territory of Switzerland by nationals of the following countries: Top five: India — $1456 billion; Russia — $470 billion; UK — $390 billion; Ukraine — $100 billion; China — $96 billion.

This was particularly discussed by the activists of a small party, the Kongunadu Munnetra Peravai (KMP), who could use the statistics to emphasise their own genuine efforts for better irrigation and infrastructure initiatives and to criticise all the big parties that had enriched themselves and allowed their cronies to stack away money in foreign banks, thus escaping tax duties in India' (Carswell and De Neve FR: 39).

The Effect of the MCC

As noted in Chapter 1, an important element of the ECI's strategy in conducting free and fair elections and, in its own words, 'creating a level playing field', is its enforcement of what is called the 'Model Code of Conduct' to mark the start of the election period. This is an interesting phenomenon in itself as it is more a convention than a legality, which was initially drafted by an officer of the Indian Police Service of the Tamil Nadu cadre in the 1950s. The Model Code, also known as the *Aachar Samhita* in Hindi, is a set of rules about what is permissible behaviour on the part of politicians and political parties during the campaign period. It has evolved over the past five decades and the rules have been further elaborated to include limits on expenses on campaign materials, the hours during which loud-hailers can be used, the restraint on the use of public spaces for any campaign materials and the price of each if used, and so on. The use of public resources in general, specially by incumbent governments, the impartiality of serving civil servants, the disbursements of public

Elections and Music

'Political music' has been a notable feature of Indian elections and has evolved, over time, to reflect changing needs. People used to display their creativity by composing songs that highlighted the strong qualities of candidates they supported and the negative qualities of the rival candidates through interesting satires and metaphors. In eastern UP, for instance, traditional folksongs like *birha* and *kajari* with election messages had given way to film songs modified to reflect political messages. [For the 2009 elections] the Congress party hired the services of an advertising agency, Percept, which composed a song in support of the party based on the song 'Jai Ho' from the film *Slumdog Millionaire* (2008), which was recorded by the music company T-Series. The BJP composed a song with the lyrics *Saathi saath nibhana ab ke bhaiya phir se tum kamal par batan dabana* ('let's stick together; this time again, press the button next to the the lotus' [BJP symbol]), which was played in all the vehicles used by the party for campaigning, while the Samajwadi Party (SP) composed a song whose lyrics were *Suno suno Phulpur walon, sun lo bhaiya dhyaan lagaai, ye saikil hai apna saathi, phir se bhaiya diyo jitae* ('listen, listen carefully, the cycle [Samajwadi Party symbol] is your friend, help your elder brother [i.e., the SP candidate] win'). In West Bengal too, there used to be a strong tradition of *Gana Sangeet* (chorus singing), which was an important feature of the campaign trail of CPI(M). In the 1970s and the 1980s, many of these songs were linked to the Tebhaga movement, food movement and other struggles. These songs were a way to reach out to a wide cross-section of society but in 2009 this medium was rejected by the CPI(M). Interestingly, however, this tradition was enthusiastically embraced by its rivals, the Trinamool Congress. At a meeting in UP, before the arrival of the leaders, local musicians held the crowds together, which also witnessed a performance by a band led by Ghanshyam Singh 'Premi'. Premi is not only a singer but also a radical poet who has composed a couple of revolutionary and radical songs. He sang these at the meeting along with *ragani*s (local form of songs) that are based on Hindu mythical characters. He also narrated jokes and anecdotes.

works, and the use of hate speech in political speeches are all significantly curtailed during this period in order to create a level playing field for all political parties in the election battle. While the MCC has been in existence for many decades, the ECI has chosen to apply its rules more stringently than before over the course of the last two general elections. In its efforts to address the issues of 'booth capture' and 'rigging' in some 'problem states', the ECI also introduced a number of innovations in how it conducted elections. Among them were holding the election in several phases to allow for the movement of observers, deployment of observers from outside the state and a close monitoring of election expenditure. Election officials, acting on behalf of the ECI were granted powers that allowed them to impose the Code without impunity and charge fines for the smallest breach of guidelines. This led to a greater awareness of the ECI's role in Indian public life and also of its powers over politicians and parties alike. As a result, during elections, a palpable sense of nervousness and tension prevailed among party workers, local officials, civil servants, and the police, as they constantly looked over their shoulders for fear of being caught breaching rules. 'This is Model Code of Conduct time, we cannot do this' was an oft-repeated phrase across the country during the elections.

On the whole, this austere interpretation of the Code largely facilitated the desired objective. Elections were, as a result cleaner, quieter and a bit more transparent than they had been before. Election campaigns no longer left behind a detritus of pamphlets, flags and banners in streets and public grounds the way they had before and political parties became more vigilant about the language they deployed and the tactics they generally used in their campaigns. However, the stricter imposition of the MCC also had a number of unintended consequences, as we shall see in the discussion in this chapter. It drove a great deal of campaign expenditure underground, and most importantly, it took away some of the magic that elections used to bring in the past. Prior to the 2009 elections, the abundant use of resources used to transform the landscape into one of colourful festivity. Everywhere in India, and especially in the northern states, everyone commented on how in 2009, campaigning lacked much of the colour and drama generally associated with elections. As many of the voters, party workers, and journalists themselves remarked, 'Elections don't have their usual colour this time; it doesn't feel like an election' (*Chunav mein voh rang nahin raha*; *Lagta hi nahin chunav hai*). Conversations that began by describing changes in elections, politics and politicians today would often turn towards the nostalgia of elections of an older time. As one senior journalist in Bihar recalled, 'In the past, there was palpable excitement over elections, women dressed in fine clothes, huddled in groups on bullock carts, singing festive songs would make their way to the polling station (*Aurateein kajri, teej gaati hui jaati thi*). When they came back from voting they would admire their freshly inked fingers and indulge in friendly banter. But now all this has disappeared'. As this quote shows, in some places, some of the excitement and festivity of elections was also swept away along with the bunting and banners. There were no party flags flying over households declaring the political allegiances of the family nor street children, as one person remarked, being paid to sing and shout

out the party slogans, the frequency of which were often enough to deduce which party was winning. Makeshift party offices, especially in rural areas, wore a deserted look and it was difficult to distinguish them from the often drab shops surrounding them, because, as I was often told, the ECI had given strict instructions that all publicity material be taken off in an hour's time after political rallies and meetings. Candidates were careful not to cross what became an administrative *lakshman rekha*.[3] After inaugurating the makeshift party offices on their campaign trails, they would often sternly tell party workers to remove festoons and decorations immediately. Without the props, the work of campaigning had therefore also become harder as target audiences had become more difficult to reach and resources had been limited.

Face-to-Face Contact with Individual Voters

As in previous elections, committed party workers spent most of their time among the voters, talking endlessly at tea stalls, factory gates, *jan sabha*s (congregations), *biradari* (community) panchayats, hukka sessions, card games, weekly markets, weddings, buses, fields, intersections, and the doorsteps of homes and shops. All day one heard gossip, discussions and judgements about different candidates, their performances as incumbent MPs or MLAs, their assets and liabilities, their characters, personalities and skills. These conversations were usually emotionally charged and politically acute, yet also courteous for the most part, often oscillating between hope and despair.

Door-to-door campaigning largely took place in the evenings, and the conversations followed a fairly standard pattern. Unlike the party leaders, local activists could not make any specific promises or policy announcements and were thus limited in what they could tell the people, but they emphasised what their party had done in the past and then asked people to vote for them. In the week or so before polling day, activists visited houses of known supporters, giving out flags and banners to be displayed. In the past, activists also campaigned in neighbouring villages, but because of recent restrictions by the ECI on the use of cars, in the 2009 elections they campaigned mainly in their own village or neighbourhoods.

---

[3] *Lakshman rekha* refers to the Ramayana story in which Lakshman, the hero Ram's brother, drew a line of protection around Sita when entrusted to look after her safety.

Campaigning on the Hoof

In Rajasthan, on the margins of a political rally, we witnessed a conversation at a tea stall between Mahavir Singh, the candidate's right-hand man, and an ordinary, bored-looking bystander. This man was extremely downhearted about politicians and described his aversion to politics as an 'allergy'. Mahavir asked the man if he voted and he replied in the negative, and then declined repeated invitations to explain why. Mahavir aggressively called the man a fool for not participating in the political system, since as a poor man, voting was the only way he could influence the system. But he softened his tone when he realised that it wasn't helping, and enquired if the man was educated. The man replied that he was, so Mahavir then attempted to convince him that, as an educated citizen who is aware of his rights and duties, he must vote. The man would still not budge. Next, Mahavir tried to sell the Congress candidate to him as a pro-development and non-corrupt leader. When this failed as well, he resorted to appealing to caste identity, saying the man should vote for his fellow Jat and thereby raise the stature of their kind! Party workers carry out countless such conversations during the campaign, at all hours of day and night, thinking on their feet as they endlessly change their messages to appease and appeal to the unpredictable reactions of the varied voters, saying almost anything to get their vote, and honing their canvassing skills in the process (Falcao FR: 18).

In UP, we found that BSP workers had been trained to highlight some issues more than others. Given that their main achievement had been to increase self-respect among Dalits, they were told to stress on social equality rather than talk about general things like *bamba-khamba*, i.e., water (*bamba*) and electricity (*khamba*). They also talked about the social change that the BSP government had brought about and discussed the transformed relations between upper castes and Dalits — an issue that everyone recognised immediately; so radical had been the changes. And they also talked about having raised the labour wage to ₹100 and granting lease of land to Dalit sharecroppers. All these changes had made the Brahmins take them more seriously and their parties were now inviting Mayawati, the BSP leader, for electoral alliances.

In Gujarat, at the level of a Lok Sabha election, door-to-door campaigns principally consisted of party workers or little boys who were paid ₹200 to go around the houses handing out small labels and stickers. The BJP ones said 'Strong Leader, Decisive Government' (*Majboot Neta Nirnayak Sarkar*) and had a picture of the Gujarat CM Narendra Modi and the local candidate next to it. The Congress had their own with pictures of Sonia Gandhi, Manmohan Singh and the local candidate.

Dummy EVMs

Many candidates tried to familiarise the voters with EVMs, given they were still a novelty in 2009 and also used door-to-door campaigning.

Dummy machines were produced for people to handle and press the buttons on although in some cases this backfired badly. In Madhya Pradesh, BJP workers had advised voters to press the first button on the machine during the state-level elections held six months ago, as their name was listed on top. They had sold the idea by saying that in order to start the EVM the voter needs to press the first button. After that, the machine begins to work and you can vote for whichever candidate you want by pressing any button! In 2009 however, the BJP was listed second after the Congress and so special effort had to be made to erase the memory of their prior advice so as not to lose their votes to the Congress! (Krishnamurthy FR: 13)

As far as voters were concerned, they expected visits by door-to-door campaigners and played their part by talking to them. Sometimes they asked questions or grumbled about broken promises, but generally, they just told the activists that they would vote for them, although they often had no intention of doing so. 'Gayathri explained that the activists "all come to our house asking for our vote and we'll just say to all of them 'Yes, we'll vote for you' and let them go. As we are already on bad terms with some of them in the village, we don't want to make things worse."[4] The final part of the door-to-door campaigning was the distribution of "voter's slips" to voters the night before the election' (Carswell and De Neve FR: 38).

While much in these exchanges was traditional, there were also new developments in the 2009 election. An important rationale for being stricter with the MCC was to impose control on election expenditure among candidates and parties in order to create a more level playing field among candidates. ECI officials explained that by curtailing the display of posters and other media, they hoped to motivate the parties to reach out to the electorate more directly through door-to-door campaigning.

However, while the MCC did have the positive effect of putting a stop to the open display of power and wealth of the candidates, it also had unintended consequences. A new breed of agents and middlemen

---

[4] Gayathri's opinion is not dissimilar to Sir James Ferguson writing in the 19th century about election campaigns: 'I have heard many arguments that have influenced my opinion, but never one which influenced my vote' (Snelling 2002: 48).

promised parties they would do their door-to-door campaigning for them, at a fixed fee per village. However, few actually went to the villages, and as we witnessed at a number of our rural sites, their cavalcades of jeeps and SUVs often just drove through without stopping or visiting any households. The term 'door-to-door' thus often became more of an empty electoral mantra than a reality. This had repercussions on the morale among voters in these areas because visits by local leaders were greatly missed by the people as they helped to build up a festive and interactive environment in the village. As Nirmala Devi, a resident, said, 'Earlier the election campaigns used to be like people meeting at celebrations during festivals. This time no candidate came to meet us personally so how could the election environment be created?'

Public Meetings

The NES surveys show both that a large number of people in India attend political rallies and meetings, and that those who do are more likely to vote. Our fieldwork showed that not only did what attendees see and hear at these meetings play a crucial role in how they thought about politicians and voting, but also that they also typically described their visits, and the discussion and debate that ensued, to non-attendees, thereby influencing them. Political parties thus considered the management of political meetings as being of crucial importance and invested a lot of effort into facilitating and arranging them.

For whatever the volume of other campaign material displayed, it was ultimately face-to-face meetings and mass rallies that connected a candidate with his audience. As some people at our Delhi site remarked, 'politicians were like the elusive moon whose sighting marks the commencement of Id festivities to begin (*Id ka chand*) and so for candidates it was important to be visible during the campaign, especially to compensate for their absence at other times. But, as a worker pointed out in Delhi, if the politicians were the elusive moon, and Election Day was the festival of Id, then the campaign period was definitely like the month of Ramadan, of fasting and fervent prayers for success' (Nasir FR: 12). For the few weeks of their campaigns, it was important that candidates be able to convey the impression of being everywhere at once, of not neglecting any corner of their constituencies and of willingness to listen to all manner of complaints and demands. Depending on their resources and organisational strength, parties planned to hold political meetings of varying magnitude. As polling day approached, candidates could be seen visiting 20 villages in a single day to cover maximum ground.

In an average constituency, political meetings were of varying size. Along with door-to-door canvassing and individual conversation, smaller gatherings were held for collective canvassing, usually in the evenings to capture attention as people returned home from work. Typically, these smaller-scale gatherings, variously known as Khatla Parishad, were more usual for the local-level elections. *Jan sabha*s (congregations), *nukkad* (street corner) meetings, and *padyatra*s (campaigning on foot) were held in the more residential areas of urban neighbourhoods, where people could attend with minimum travel or simply stay indoors and listen as loudspeakers carried the speeches into people's homes. *Padyatra*s were specifically routed to cover most by-lanes between houses so that as many voters as possible could catch a glimpse of the candidate and supporters from their doorways and balconies.

Slightly Bigger Venues/Events

Party workers were constantly on the lookout for appropriate canvassing venues. 'In Gujarat, for instance, a cricket tournament was organised to create an opportunity to canvass young men. The organisers were mostly Congress workers but the main sponsor was a BJP leader and the Sarpanch of the village where it was held. A Congress member made the arrangements and local leaders provided the prizes. Teams from different parts of the district came to participate in the tournament, which made it an excellent opportunity for both parties to reach out to young people from a wide area' (Jani FR: 15).

Youth Meetings

'The BJP also regularly organised youth meetings (*yuva sammelan*). We attended one such meeting in Gujarat, which hosted a group of 15 young people drawn from different castes. The journey was made in a huge auto-rickshaw festooned with coloured lights and had a BJP flag fluttering from it, so passersby could tell their party affiliations. The speeches emphasised the role that Narendra Modi had played in improving the medical and economic infrastructure of the state; no mention was made of L. K. Advani, the BJP's Prime Ministerial candidate, or of any of the other national-level BJP leaders. This meeting too ended with dinner, which went down very well with the young people' (ibid.).

Lunch and Dinner Gatherings

'Lunch and dinner gatherings were another popular kind of election event, which could typically be arranged to stay within the bounds of the legal directives of the MCC. These were often segregated not only by party loyalty by also by caste, for rules of commensality were still strictly maintained in large parts of the country. Accordingly, in Gujarat, we observed the Congress holding two separate feasts for its Dalit and upper caste (*kshatriya*s) supporters, as did the BJP. The venue, caterers and kitchen staff were exactly the same but the speeches made during the meal were specifically tailored to the audience with the usual promises and assertions of shared caste and religion. The large majority of those who attended either feast were drawn from among the poorest groups and mostly appeared to suffer through the speeches in return for the free meal' (ibid.).

On the Campaign Trail in Bihar

In Bihar, we were able to join the campaign trail of different candidates and see a series of smaller-scale gatherings. There, the main contest was between two state-based parties: Shahnawaz Hussain of the BJP–JD(U) (or Janata Dal [United]) and Shakuni Chaudhary of the Rashtriya Janata Dal (RJD) — and correspondingly between an agenda of development *versus* secularism. The JD(U), led by Nitish Kumar, emphasised its record on development (since gaining power in Bihar in 2006) and criticised the previous Lalu Prasad Yadav-led RJD government for having let the state to fall into ruin by its failure on this score. RJD candidates, on the other hand, criticised the JD(U) for their alliance with the national right-wing BJP party and their Hindu chauvinistic agenda, and emphasised their own secular credentials.

On a typical campaign day, we joined Mr Hussain's cavalcade of four Mahindra Scorpios in the outskirts of Bhagalpur town where he was speaking to a small group of people gathered around a tea stall. (The size of the convoy is restricted by ECI guidelines.) Of the four motor vehicles, one carried the flag and *kajkarta*s (workers) of JD(U), one had a small contingent of local police, one was Hussain's own car and the last carried other party workers. This cavalcade stopped at the local party office and Shahnawaz Hussain made his way inside. The office was a small, one-room thatched hut and was crowded with local party workers, who took the opportunity to complain about some other party workers' deceitful activities. Some of the local

(continued)

(*continued*)

village people who were present sensed an opportunity to voice their concerns, and complained about contractors who had not paid them their dues. But Shahnawaz Hussain firmly put them down, saying none of this was his responsibility, and went on to make a small speech to the gathering. As everywhere else, the central thrust of his campaign was the development work undertaken in his tenure. He introduced himself as the worker (*mazdoor*) who ought to be paid his wages (*mazdoori*) and given blessings (*aashirvaad*) and love (*sneh*). He further played with the metaphor, describing himself as the ideal servant of the people and emphasising that far from being absent, he had worked hard and spent his time among the people, rather than in faraway seats of power. 'I have spent more time amongst you than even a son who goes away to Delhi for a job' was the way he put it, drawing a parallel with Bihar's huge numbers of emigrant workers. He went on to enumerate the work done in that particular village with the village-level party workers prompting him with local details. Even though Hussain belonged to the BJP, he played down his party ideology and chose instead to celebrate Nitish Kumar's successes and the wind (*hawa*) that his electoral victory was likely to be. The BJP was only mentioned in the context of its likelihood of gaining central power as part of the NDA alliance, in which Hussain's supporters reckoned that he would be certain to win a cabinet seat and, by implication, enormous clout for his constituency. (This was a well-judged reminder because, as we saw with other candidates such as Subodh Rai from the CPM, people could respect a candidate's personal integrity but judge him, nevertheless, to be an ineffective MP because of his perceived inability to become part of a winning coalition in Delhi.) Hussain's next stop was the all-important Mamlakha village, where he had personally ensured the construction of a bridge across the river, before which the village had been completely cut off from rest of the district during the monsoon rains. This achievement was, therefore, the centrepiece of his campaign, and so, a grand meeting had been organised in this village for the inauguration of the party office, which was situated prominently by the side of the road. Soft drinks, tea and snacks were served while party workers made their speeches culminating in Hussain's own. Unlike some other BJP candidates, he did not participate in any religious ritual to mark the inauguration nor did he visit any local temples or other religious sites in the village, presumably keeping in mind the delicate situation of a Muslim candidate standing on a Hindu rightwing party's ticket. Instead, Hussain chose once more to speak of his development work and made reassurances of compensation to the farmers on whose land the bridge had been built. He also took the opportunity to draw unfavourable comparisons with a rival candidate who had given the contract for another bridge to his brother. That bridge had taken 11 years to build and had collapsed soon after, killing a small girl. The speed and probity of his own bridge were highlighted as a contrast, but rather than stating the obvious, he complimented his audience on being intelligent enough to draw their own conclusions about the better candidate, a ploy that was was rewarded with loud cheers and applause. Overall, the tenor of Hussain's campaign was assertive and confident, and he was able to judge his audiences in every situation, knowing when to reprimand squabbling workers, ignore uncomfortable complaints and flatter a large audience (Singh FR: 10–11).

Tailoring one's speech to every new venue was an essential part of a candidate's campaign strategy and success. For example, in Tamil Nadu 'the CPM candidate Nataraj spoke about caste in an area where there had recently been an issue about access to a temple, and about agriculture and irrigation in the next village, which was home to many landowners. In an SC hamlet he spoke all about Amma, and also made a point of thanking local (SC) men who had helped with the campaign, referring to them as "leaders". He also made detailed reference to the issue of corruption amongst DMK and Congress politicians and the nepotism of the DMK government' (Carswell and De Neve FR: 36).

Pit-stop tours by candidates across the constituency were typical everywhere and in some places they were heralded by entertainers. In Maharashtra, we saw a truck carrying a group of professional entertainers singing campaign songs to the tune of popular folk songs and a middle-aged dwarf man dancing to the tunes. To maximise participation from the audience that inevitably gathered around the entertainment, the comperes announced the name of the song along with the name of the folk song to whose tune it was going to be sung so that people could join in. It was evident that providing such entertainment was, in fact, the big hook to get people interested in the political messages. When this was missing, as we witnessed in Tamil Nadu, no one but the most loyal party workers showed up when the candidate made his pit stop in any place. In a well-functioning campaign, these various elements came together smoothly and in a coordinated way. Thus, in Meerut district in eastern UP, we saw the SP candidate start his day at 6 AM when he met with his party workers at the election office in Sardhana near the police station outside the town, and discussed the election strategy. Walking with his workers and campaign organisers down the main road, he talked them throughout the route which encompassed 16 villages he was to visit before the campaign came to a close. His supporters and workers had already been canvassing day and night for him in the most remote villages. Villagers, in turn, erected welcome stages and covered them with *shamiyana*s (cloth canopies), political posters, flags, and banners. The campaign party then went ahead to the villages in advance to announce the candidate's arrival. When Som reached the first village, Nagali, at 8 AM, the villagers were waiting with garlands and drummers outside the village to welcome him.

In a typical medium-sized political meeting in Khirkiya, Madhya Pradesh 'about 1,000 people had gathered in total, but given the blistering heat and the fact that it was an auspicious day for weddings, the low turnout was, in fact, not bad. The CM's speech was popular, according to the female party workers that we attended the meeting with: he focussed on the government's achievements: roads (Harda had received the greatest share of road money during the last few years); the canal, which they were trying to extend to Khirkiya; the wheat procurement bonus; and the ₹3 per kg price of wheat in the Public Distribution System (PDS). Much was made of the fact that the country had the most esteemed economist at the helm, under whose watch people were experiencing the worst *mehangayee* (inflation). He also talked about the disadvantages that he was facing with an opposing government at the centre — MP was being denied coal, as well as adequate wheat for its PDS. Did the centre think the poor in Madhya Pradesh were not real or poor enough? The local candidate, Jyoti Dhurve, was introduced as a dynamic female tribal leader, who had been head of the Jan Jati commission at the state level, but whose tribal credentials the Congress had tried to paint as fake. She was a *behen*, a younger sister, who needed their support. For most of the rally, we were standing next to two old men who did not seem to be moved by any of the claims being made from the stage. When the question of development of the canal system and Harda's water came up, they both shrugged and asked each other loudly: 'Have you ever seen the water that he is talking about? I know I have not seen a drop of it!' (Khirkiya remains unirrigated by the Tawa Canal). At the end as the slogans were being chanted, they initially kept their fists down, then one of them raised his half way, as the other one raised his eyebrows, uncertain whether to endorse a chauvinistic slogan by the BJP for whom they clearly had no sympathy. He finally lifted in with all the rest for the last shout — *Bharat Mata ki Jai!* ('Victory to Mother India!') Looking sheepishly at his friend he said, 'I have no problem lifting it in the name of Bharat Mata; that's fine with me!' Then they made a beeline for the exit' (Krishnamurthy FR: 14).

In UP, the Samajwadi candidate Sangeet Som addressed villagers in the language of kinship and family: 'Farmers have been suffering badly in Maya's regime. This government has neglected farmers to the limit. The price of sugarcane is at an all-time low, and farmers are having a bad time. Had it been the government of Mulayam Singh, you could have got a fair price for your sugarcane crop. Criminals are being protected openly by the State.' After this he narrated the incidence of a person who was threatened while talking over his mobile phone during Kadir's speech in Bhanmori — a Gujjar-dominated village.

There was talk that Kadir threatened the person to throw into the furnace. Som roared: 'Friends, we belong to *kisan parivar*s (farmer families) and I cannot tolerate this kind of threat to my brothers and elders. I want to suggest to you all that if you happen to meet him, tell Kadir "we will drag you out of your house and put you into the furnace".' Further, he said:

> Friends, I would rather be beheaded than let you down. I will save your honour and respect at any cost, even if that means I need to give my life and blood for you. I do not want to become a *neta* [leader]. I want to become your younger brother, elder brother, son or nephew or cousin, and want you to be so comfortable with me that you think of me as your relative and not your *neta*. It is a coincidence that I have a ticket from the SP. My deepest desire is to get your love and respect and your acceptance. I will return all this by caring for your respect, honour and *izzat*. I will change the definition of a *neta* or a leader, which is abhorred and hated and mocked in everyday language. I will change this image by working very closely with you and making a place in your heart — you will find me standing next to you at all times whenever you need me.

He then proceeded to defame the third contender too, casting aspersions on her character before his peroration:

> I am an educated, young and dynamic candidate who has lots of potential to work with you. I am a local candidate from Sardhana, which not very far from your village. So this is your chance to give an opportunity to a local candidate. In the history of Meerut and Muzaffarnagar PC [Parliamentary Constituency], all political parties have imposed outsiders on the voters (Kumar FR: 15).

Organising Large Rallies and Public Meetings

A key responsibility of the party workers was ensuring, by any means, that large crowds gathered at the public meetings they organised. As some party workers in Rajasthan explained to us, it was not enough just to be popular; they also had to make that popularity visible and palpable in order to attract yet more votes, especially from among those still undecided. They often arranged food and transport for people to attend and in Tamil Nadu we heard of DMK cadres offering factory workers ₹100 to attend a rally. Sometimes the candidate himself helped bring a crowd. For example, 'the SP candidate in UP ended his speech at one large village by asking everyone to join him with their tractors on the day of nomination in the city of Muzaffarnagar, in order to help him fulfill his target of fielding 20,000 tractors that day to show the strength of farmers in the district. In return, he promised to give 10 litres of diesel to each tractor'. But party workers also jealously guarded 'their' voters, sometimes causing great inconvenience to the voters themselves. 'Thus, for instance, AIADMK activists chose to take their constituents to a meeting in faraway Coimbatore, which was officially part of their constituency, rather than nearby Tiruppur which would have been far easier for attendees' (Kumar FR: 15; Carswell and De Neve FR: 35).

Party workers chose venues that provided high visibility such as crossroads or local fairgrounds. The approach routes to these locations were also carefully charted, taking into consideration bus routes and markets, though rarely the weather. The bigger rallies were invariably held under the midday sun which went some way in explaining the use of branded umbrellas and caps! Recent innovations such as big processions (*maha michil*s) sought to capitalise on these gatherings further and were typically organised at the crossroads of market towns where people could travel in from hinterlands located in different directions. The experience of being part of a procession that swelled with every new one joining it further heightened the mood of effervescence. And all along the route, tractors and buses that lay parked and festooned with colours of the political parties, sent out messages to all passersby.

The most visible gatherings were the mass rallies that were attended by thousands of people and addressed by the big party bosses who showed up to support the local candidate. But these sorts of mass rallies were rare and the appearance of national-level politicians rarer. Their visits were strategically fixed for trouble spots and for areas that were estimated to have large numbers of swing voters, where parties hoped that the presence of a big politician would turn the votes in their favour. But for all politicians, the ability to put their constituency on the campaign trail of a national leader was also something of a coup. Such a visit allowed the coveted photo opportunity in which the lesser of the two politicians could be seen in the same frame as the famous one. The impact of such an image was immeasurable and politicians went to enormous lengths to secure them. These events also tended to be the ones that were covered by the electronic media and were beamed to millions of households across the country. The management of these events was thus of crucial importance.

Rahul Gandhi's Rally

Attending one such rally in the state of Chhattisgarh, we joined the crowds of people who, like us, had begun their journey at dawn to travel to the midday meeting. On this occasion, Rahul Gandhi, the Secretary of the Congress Party, a great grandson of Jawaharlal Nehru, India's first Prime Minister, and heir apparent to the Prime Ministership was to be the star speaker. Along the route, for several miles, people travelled in any available transport from tractors, two-wheelers and bullock carts to get to the meeting, waving to the more fortunate who sped by on special buses provided by the party. The mood at the tea stalls along the road was festive and good-humoured, as stall owners made the most of this spike in demand for snacks and drinks. The roads leading to the fair ground where the meeting was to be held were lined with bunting and police vehicles and loudspeakers blared instructions for orderly queues, patience for the Chief Guest and details of missing persons. At the venue, the huge crowds were controlled through pathways made of bamboo fences that led to the vast marquee that shielded the audience from the sun and soaring temperatures. Vendors sold every kind of refreshment from ice creams to spicy nuts and eager volunteers thrust badges, caps and scarves in the Congress colours to new arrivals. The stage itself was set apart from the crowds, under its own huge awning. Giant, shiny cutouts of the smiling figures of Rahul Gandhi; Manmohan Singh, the incumbent Prime Minister; and Sonia Gandhi, the Congress President and Rahul's mother, flanked the stage. At the appointed hour, the vast grounds were full but Rahul Gandhi was nowhere to be seen, nor was his helicopter anywhere in sight. Rather, in a matter typical of political meetings of this kind anywhere in India, the local Congress leaders and those who worked for the party occupied the stage. The captive audience and coming elections provided them the rare opportunity to hone their speech-making skills. They extolled the virtues of their party, of its national leaders but also listed their own achievements at the constituency level over the past five years. In this case, they had been in opposition in the state government, so this meeting provided an ideal moment to criticise the opposition whole-heartedly. Their speeches were interwoven with entertainment which was provided by a couple of talented local singers who performed popular local songs and ghazals that the audience seemed to enjoy. The female singer was also clearly present to add some glamour to the event, incongruous as the silk clothes and heavy make-up seemed in the 40 degree Celsius heat. But gigs like this would undoubtedly lead to future commissions and the artists gave the performance everything they had, despite the din of the conversation under the marquee. The finale of their performance was the rendition of the rousing 'Jai Ho' song that the Congress had borrowed from a popular film and had made their national election anthem.

While the speeches and singing carried on, the increasingly restless and thirsty crowds were appeased with announcements detailing the exact location of Rahul Gandhi's helicopter and free bottles of water. After two hours of this, when the collective patience seemed poised to snap, the welcome drone of a helicopter was heard in the distance and the audience erupted in sheer relief as much as in excitement.

(continued)

(continued)

Those who had earlier been unfortunate enough not to find shade in the marquee were now rewarded with a clear view of the helicopter, and quickly relayed details of its colours, agility and speed to everyone else. Finally, after several hours of travelling and waiting, people were able to see Rahul Gandhi in the flesh. That his continuous travel during the election campaign had taken a toll on him was obvious: he looked exhausted, unshaven, crumpled, and his speech was brief and unremarkable. But later, while he was talking to people who were present at the meeting, these physical details were not commented on. It was as if a leader like Rahul was too 'big', too laden with charisma through birth and reputation, to be judged by his appearance on a single day. What was important was that he was physically present, far away from home in a small town in Chhattisgarh, addressing a local audience. What he actually said was interpreted differently, depending on the listener. For instance, a young man thought that the leader had urged local party workers to hold the older and more established workers to account in the ways in which funds allocated by the Central government were disbursed. While at no point had Rahul actually said this, his youth and his image as a critique of older Congress ways, was what was 'heard' by this young local man.

In contrast to Rahul Gandhi's rally was one featuring the veteran Lalu Prasad Yadav in Bihar, whose witticisms and ability to connect to his audience through the use of local languages was legendary.

Lalu Prasad's Rally

The meeting we attended was one in which Yadav was there principally to support his party's candidate Shakuni Chaudhary. The latter gave a lacklustre speech, unable to recover his ground from his poor development record during his tenure as a member of the state legislature. The attendance was modest, almost small, especially given Lalu's reputation, and it seemed that the opposition had the upper hand, not least because of their decent performance in the state government for the past three years. But it was evident that the meeting was really building up for Lalu's appearance though journalists joked that he would be furious once he saw the poor turnout. In keeping with the quintessential style of Lalu meetings, songs in praise of Lalu Yadav were sung and a Muslim lady recited some couplets that received a roaring round of applause.

Dum laboon pe tha dil ke zor se ghabrane se
Aur aagyi jaan mein jaan aapke aajane se
Is siyasat mein aap ko kya batayein
Kis kadar chot khaye hue hain aur
Kitni mohaabat hai lalu yadav se
Ke khub tapti dhoop mein bhi aaye hain

Tu lakh sitam dhale sitamgar, hum saab sehnewale hain
Aur ye janta bhi kasam kha ke nikli hain, ki aap logon ka boriya bistar sametwane
aaye hain
(Those who love Lalu Yadav have come despite the scorching sun because he will
be our saviour.)
As soon as Lalu's helicopter landed, almost magically, there was a groundswell of
people around the dais and the whole stadium was filled with people in a matter of
minutes. Perfectly aware of the mis-givings about his waning popularity, Lalu did
not miss the opportunity of calling out to one of the TV cameramen while on his
way to the stage, instructing him to take pictures of the huge gathering. Some people
sitting in front were equally prompt in shouting out their complaints of not having
any electricity and water but these were ignored as Lalu got down to the business
of his speech-performance. Lalu's speech primarily focussed on his commitment to
secularism and the importance of his party without which no secular government
could be formed in Delhi. Deflecting attention from Bihar's state of affairs, which
he dismissed as 'possible only because the money came from Delhi and not because
of Nitish Kumar' he chose instead to talk about the important of building a non-
communally divided nation, which he had always stood for. It was a calculated and
uncontroversial speech of about 20 minutes, which had no mention of the candidate
Shakuni Chaudhary for whom he was campaigning. Instead he held his fire against
the BJP as the communal forces his secularism challenged, and by implication, the
JD(U) who were in alliance with them. He criticised L. K. Advani as an unsuitable
Prime Ministerial candidate, pointing out his inability to realise any of his stated
objectives — primarily the temple at Ayodhya — and ridiculing his desire, even in
old age, to risk his life for a high-pressure job (*kahe ke banoge Advani ji, budhapa*
mein kahe ko aapna jaan dene ko taiyaar ho). The audience responded to his jokes
and sarcasm with enthusiasm and his colloquial style, the accent, tenor, sentence
structure, and speed of delivery, and use of the local dialect connected him with his
audience like no other. The audience was completely in sync with his speech and
statements such as 'Nitish Kumar said that Lalu should be bowled out at zero but
I have hit such a six that the ball has gone past the boundary' drew enormous applause.
His defiant confidence ('My doctors, i.e., those taking the public temperature, have
checked that I am winning everywhere') was infectious, if futile, and created a feeling
of wellbeing among his supporters that sustained them for the remaining campaign
period (Singh FR: 12).

We also attended a large rally addressed by Mayawati, the UP
Chief Minister, who, for a while, was a real contender for the post
of Prime Minister during the 2009 campaign period had her alliance
of parties won.

Narendra Modi in Gujarat, another politician who commanded
the loyalty of millions but had the allegations of having stoked the
anti-Muslim pogrom in 2002, took up the position of deliberately
setting himself up as a macho man.

Mayawati's Rally

At a rally on 2 May 2009, just four days before the election, crowds had gathered long before Mayawati's 11:30 AM arrival. She came several hours late. Buses full of her supporters filled all the lanes, roads and open spaces around the civil lines area of the city. The party buses went down the remote villages of Muzaffarnagar, Kairan and Saharanpur carrying people from distant rural pockets. In the Numaish Maidan of Muzaffarnagar city, almost 100,000 people were waiting amidst tight security in the burning sun to catch a glimpse of their Chief Minister. Amid a thick cloud of dust, Mayawati arrived in a helicopter to make a speech and comment on the merits of the BSP candidates. Women made up for more than a fifth of the crowd, and there was a large gathering of media persons — Indians and foreigners. So far, in other political rallies, the absence of women had been conspicuous even though a woman candidate was running for the Muzaffarnagar Lok Sabha seat. As soon as Mayawati reached the platform erupted into chaos and slogans — 'UP has become ours and now it is the turn of Delhi; and long live the unity of the *sarvajan* (all classes)!' and waiting political leaders began touching her feet one by one and offering garlands as she was seated on a huge chair. In her 50-minute speech, Mayawati began giving details of the different kinds of welfare and developmental work she had done in the state after becoming the Chief Minister. She also mentioned how the central government kept creating hurdles in the development of the state and the welfare programmes launched for the poor. She said that the only way to fight the central government was to send her to Delhi as the Prime Minister. Towards the end of her speech, Mayawati urged the crowds to proclaim their support and vote openly without any fear. She shouted a slogan, which was repeated and cheered by the crowd, *Chad goonde ki chathi per, mohar lagegi hathi per* ('Climb on the chest of the bully; it is the elephant that will get the stamp of approval').[5] Most of the people in the crowd responded in unison, repeating the slogan after her. Afterwards, as a woman put it, satiated with the performance, 'I had come to see Mayawati and now I have'. Others discussed the security arrangements, particularly how the two senior-most district civil servants — the Superintendent of Police and the District Magistrate — had run around like peons, given the importance of a VIP. People enjoyed talking about the aura of their leader. They also commented and talked about the speech, about how good and eloquent the speaker was. A large group of voters was busy discussing the quality of Mayawati's helicopter — whether it was a new or an old one, and whether bigger or smaller than the one they had seen before in another political rally (Kumar FR: 17–18).

Narendra Modi's Rally

Addressing the issue of terrorism, Modi said, 'When the dreaded terrorists entered our Akshardham, we did not have commandoes with us but our local police entered the temple and killed them instantly but when four children (*bachhe*) entered Mumbai, our Prime Minister's government could not do anything until they had exhausted their explosives.' He then asked 'What can be termed a great response to terrorism?' Immediately, BJP supporters shouted, 'Jai Shri Ram'. In a similar manner, whenever

---

[5] The elephant is the symbol of Mayawati's party, the BSP.

addressing opposition leaders attacked him, he would imitate that person and make people laugh by doing so. Mimicking Sonia Gandhi, he chose to talk about the sensitive issue of national security after the Mumbai attacks by terrorists that had occurred six months previously.

> Madam Sonia ji says terrorism is not an external issue and very much an internal one. But *bhaiyo* [brothers], her mother-in-law Indiraji always said that this is an external issue and other countries propagate terrorism in our country. When I recall hearing this, how can she forget it despite having had the great opportunity of staying in Indiraji's house.

This made people laugh even louder. Furthermore, he had the knack of playing with figures effectively. For instance, referring to the incumbent's achievement of high growth rates, he dismissed them by saying:

> When the Government of India is struggling to achieve a growth rate of 6 to 7 per cent, Gujarat has already achieved 10.5 per cent growth. When the Central government has put up a target for 4 per cent growth in agriculture sector, Gujarat has already achieved 14 per cent (Jani FR: 10–11).

The Importance of 'Being Seen'

At the meetings themselves (and as we shall see in greater detail in Chapter 3 on political language), a good oratorical style and catchy plays on words were essential ingredients for a memorable speech and politicians worked hard at honing these skills. But often what was actually said in a speech was almost of secondary importance. Given that the large majority of contestants lacked the talent for truly memorable performances, their speeches tended to follow a stock formula: they thanked the local organisers by name, welcomed the crowds, criticised the other contestants and their parties, made promises (though they rarely discussed policy), and then thanked the crowds and encouraged them to join in chanting their party's slogan. This raises the question that if so little was actually said, why did parties expend so much energy and resources on these meetings?

The same could be asked about the vast amount of paper on which handbills and pamphlets were duly printed, as it was rare to find anyone actually reading one, let alone discussing its contents. No wonder then that the pamphlets contained very little text and mostly displayed the name of the candidate and the colours and symbol of the party. However, these pieces of paper gained another life as wrappers and packaging material very quickly after they were discarded, thus continuing to give these essential bits of political advertising sustained visibility. What the unread pamphlets and empty speeches had in common was, therefore, their sheer materiality and visibility. Political parties needed to be seen as distributing the pieces of paper and holding the meetings, as they were ultimately the most effective way of communicating their presence and capacity for organisation to vast numbers of voters. It was as if their ability to do these things was proof of their eligibility to run a government for the people. The composite message that was communicated through the campaign gatherings, therefore, was a complex statement about organisational strength and the magnitude of support it already enjoyed, which was measured by the numbers of bodies physically present, the ability of the candidate to rouse a mass audience and the 'wow' factor of the event. We were informed of a tactic used by party workers to boost the perceived popularity of political meetings in Rajasthan, where they made people believe that thousands of persons were going to attend a particular party rally by sending supporters in buses with tinted windowpanes rather than clear ones. In truth, numerous half-filled buses with tinted windows were sent to the rally and despite the fact that the buses were partly empty, this clever scheme managed to portray the candidate as a very popular one, making him the talk of the town for miles across the constituency.

Candidates themselves were very careful with their visual self-presentation, paying close attention to the clothes they wore, the colours they chose, the expressions on their faces, the tone of their voices, their body language, and the props they used. This importance was brought home to us by the enormous emphasis that people attending these meetings placed on the visual impact in the post-mortem analysis of the events. Every aspect of the candidates' persona was analysed for coded meanings. In Bihar, for instance, after one perfectly ordinary meeting, people pointed out the 'pensive and nervous look' on the candidate's face, which was enough proof for them to pronounce that his chances looked shaky (*unki naiyya dol rahi hai*). The party's choice of candidates inevitably led to much discussion and debate as the merits and flaws of the candidates were dissected. In our site in Bihar, for instance, everyone seemed to agree that the BJP candidate was incapable of winning a single vote on his own.

However, his financial prowess, his hold over a gang of young boys for a show of strength, and his good looks, which were 'suitable for television and on stage' (*manch par chadhega, TV par aayega toh aacha dikhega*) were considered to be useful attributes. For these reasons, he was well known among the youth too, who frequently invited him to be 'Chief Guest' at their functions. People added that good looks were a particular preoccupation with image-conscious parties like the Congress and the BJP. In Madhya Pradesh, the constituency that we studied had been newly reserved for STs and so the BJP decided to field an Adivasi woman Jyoti Dhurve. 'Rumours had circulated that she was the incumbent MP's mistress and because she was a newcomer and no one had really seen her much, there was a great deal of curiosity about her. Accordingly, her party made sure she attended several community functions during the month full of religious holidays. On one occasion of a communal feast (*bhandara*), we observed her first spend a few minutes in prayer at a temple in the middle of a yard full of people before going round touching the feet of the elders and asking for everyone's support with folded hands. After she left, the impression she made was judged as largely favourable. People remarked that "She does not look like an adivasi, she has an educated face" and commented on her confidence. It was a well-conducted visit, for the pause of the prayer had given everyone an excellent opportunity to observe her unabashedly and by doing so she had also sent out the message that she could withstand such scrutiny. She was perhaps aware of the rumours about her and the curiosity a female candidate from an indigenous community was likely to generate, so she had decided to face it all head on. For male candidates, their vitality was often commented on. In the same state, we heard it said about Shivaraj Singh Chouhan, for instance, that he conveyed great energy even as he ran out from under his helicopter. As one farmer said, "You feel like he is willing to run a marathon for you when you see him do that"' (Krishnamurthy FR: 13).

Similarly, what politicians wore in public and especially on the campaign trail always held enormous significance. This is partly because in India, clothing does matter, and further, Gandhi's adoption of *khadi* as a statement of self-reliance and nationalism remains a lasting legacy in Indian public life. Accordingly, the sartorial styles of all politicians held meaning: Mamata Banerjee's signature simple handloom saris in West Bengal conveyed her incorruptibility and identification with the common person's problems, despite having been an MP for several years. Mayawati's shiny *salwar kamiz* suits in Uttar Pradesh made a statement about her having overcome her low caste and underprivileged Dalit background to become modern like the upper castes and won self-respect for her whole community. Male politicians, on the whole, adopted the ubiquitous white *kurta* and trousers out of inertia as much as anything else, although the choice of the more regional *dhoti* or *veshti* by Lalu Yadav or Karunanidhi respectively made more of a statement about their membership of a particular part of India. The visual impact of clothing in vast crowded public meetings is enormous and is often able to convey political messages of austerity, modernity and double standards as effectively and economically as written manifestos or speeches.

With each successfully held meeting, the campaign increased in momentum as word started to get around. More and more people tried to attend meetings held on later dates so as not to miss out on the chance of having 'been there' in person and seen to have participated in the campaign of a potential winner. For particular star politicians, it was, therefore, not uncommon for supporters of their rivals to attend as well, just to witness the spectacle and to have a *darsan* or glimpse of a famous leader.[6] This happened even in states like West Bengal where the surveillance and punishment of CPI(M) cadres for this transgression could be severe. As one young CPI(M) worker said, 'I don't know why I like Mamata Banerjee, but I do. There is something about her. I might not vote for her, but I had to at least go and see her [performance]'. And people echoed this sentiment about Narendra Modi, Jayalalitha, Lalu Yadav, and other politicians whom they found compellingly charismatic. The key to their brand of charisma was their ability to use a variety of communication techniques that could appeal to a wide variety of people and at all levels of what Sudipta Kaviraj calls 'the semiotic register' (2011b: 316). As Kaviraj's discussions (ibid.) of Gandhi's communication techniques have shown, his success lay in being able to communicate without words, to convey emotion even

---

[6] This is echoed in Walter Hauser and W. Singer's account (2001) where they report a voter at a rally addressed by Rajiv Gandhi in Bihar saying it is so many words, 'I have come to do *darsan*'.

from a great distance, to be heard even in a thronging multitude, and to use his words to equal effect with the colonial government as with illiterate peasants. He notes, 'Gandhi's use of rhetoric is exceptional precisely because he did not, unlike other middle class politicians, abandon the rhetorical resources of the semiotic register of Indian peasant society' (ibid.). Gandhi's particular brand of performative politics has, in fact, become an important element of the cultural archive of Indian politics. Everywhere in the country, it was evident that those politicians who paid attention to their clothing, gestures, language and silences with the purpose of communicating through each of them were the most widely admired. Thus, Mamata's energy, Jayalalithaa's stillness, the shininess of Mayawati's *salwar kamiz*, and Lalu Yadav's *paan*-stained mouth were read not merely as indicators of personal style and aesthetic, but were also encoded respectively with the meanings of fearlessness, power, modernity, and a connection with the man on the street. As Kaviraj (ibid.) notes for Gandhi, it is the deployment of this non-discursive range of symbols in order to make comprehensible the written and the discursive to an illiterate electorate that makes certain politicians win a mass following.

The Differing Conditions of Local Party Machines

Well-functioning local party machines campaigning in the organised and energetic ways described in this chapter contrasted conspicuously with less established parties or those that had become moribund. In much of the country, the Congress party offices told the story of a prominent national party whose organisation had been allowed to go to seed. The secretary of a District Congress Committee in Bihar remarked that because the Congress had not faced contested elections for 15 years (due to electoral alliances and the ability to form coalition governments relatively easily), younger voters had passed into adulthood without ever hearing about the party locally. This fact alone had lowered morale considerably for workers of the country's oldest and largest party. In Bihar, for instance, local Congress offices had an air of desolation. A handful of workers valiantly put up some bunting outside one in preparation for a hoped-for visit from the candidate. But he chose not to stop there. The campaign head office in the district capital also remained deserted until late in the morning and we heard that owing to a lack of organisational backup, much of the campaign was being coordinated from the home of the candidate Sadanand Singh, with his son as the chief campaign coordinator. When Singh went on the campaign trail, the lack of a strong Congress organisation became evident as his pit-stop meetings were not well organised. The audiences in most of them were children, young boys and random passersby who had been herded and prodded towards the venue by the convoy members after they stopped at the place. Most stops were in the houses of the village headman, or caste leaders, who were expected to deliver the votes, rather than in a public space in the village. Given that social visits to people's homes are still largely segregated by caste, such visits could never reach out to a broad-based audience. As a result, despite the shoe-string campaign, local Congress workers insisted that the fact that the Congress had decided to field its own candidate this time had given them a new lease of life (*marte ko pani diya hai*) and inspired them to work harder in the future (*hamare andar aab khoon daud raha hai*).

In Madhya Pradesh, we heard that the Congress had completely failed to mobilise its party workers, primarily as a result of disintegrating internal unity. Onlookers blamed it on the rot in the central organisation: 'When the main tree becomes weak, the branches will also naturally wither' is how one BJP worker put it. The BJP, in contrast, appeared extremely streamlined and well organised, with more of a campaigning strategy and many more workers on the ground. One of them, in charge of six wards of the city, reported that the party organisation contacted him regularly by phone to find out how things were progressing in each ward, and that all activities took place according to a schedule, and there was no question of him making individual decisions and plans. All this was a sign of being 'professional' he added, using the English term. In West Bengal, CPI(M) cadres described the same phenomenon in similar ways, talking of the Party as being the basis (*bhitti*) of everything.

This is the standard newer parties aspire to, but it is a challenge for them to achieve. The Trinamool Congress lacked the many years that the Communist parties had invested in training their leaders, and Trinamool leaders had to undergo crash courses where their speeches were planned and their delivery improved. To maintain quality and control, once the content was agreed on (usually a vitriolic diatribe against CPI[M]), the same speeches were repeated verbatim over and over during the campaign.

Implications of Changing Electoral Alliances for Campaign

As we have seen, there has been a rise in coalition politics in India in the past two decades, especially with the rise of smaller regional and caste-based parties and the decline of one- or two-party dominance (Ruparelia 2011). As a result, national governments have been formed by alliances formed by a cluster of regional parties led by a national one, e.g., the BJP-led National Democratic Alliance (NDA) government from 1999–2004 and the Congress-led UPA government from 2004–09. In some cases, these alliances were made after the results had been declared and different parties had seats to bargain with and the bigger parties knew how many more MPs they would need to form a government. But some of these alliances were also formed well before the elections such that two or more parties agreed to contest the elections by sharing seats among themselves, with candidates from different parties contesting for different seats and ultimately working together as part of the same team. This way, resources could be shared along with credibility for the future. For example, as we saw in the case in Bihar, the candidates belonging to the BJP–JD(U) combine could not only gain local credibility through the work that the JD(U) had done in Bihar but could also promise the voters that they would have influence in the national government in Delhi through the BJP who would lead the government. Thus, the BJP provided the promise of power at the national level and the JD(U) at the local. But these alliances were by no means permanent and every election brought with it new configurations and these, in turn, caused confusion and ambivalence on the ground. The voters would be confused who 'their' party was in alliance with at a particular election, and party workers never knew until the last minute before 'nomination' which party's candidate would be standing from their particular constituency. We were able to capture this vividly in our field site in Tamil Nadu, 'where the AIADMK, CPM, Communist Party of India (CPI) and Pattali Makkal Katchi (PMK) were in alliance with one other, while the DMK was in alliance with the Congress. For activists in our site in Allapuram, the results of the seat-sharing negotiations were a major disappointment: here, CPM and Congress put forward candidates on behalf of the AIADMK-led alliance and the DMK-led alliance respectively. So, in a village where we had never met a CPM supporter and had come across only very few Congress supporters, the seat sharing arrangements were a huge letdown for people on all sides of the political spectrum. AIADMK and DMK activists were disappointed that "their" party would not be standing. One DMK activist said "It doesn't matter who wins now!" while an AIADMK activist (an aspirant for the Coimbatore constituency) was reported to be considering leaving politics altogether because he felt so disillusioned. It was striking that the day after the seat-sharing arrangements were announced, AIADMK activists travelled to Tiruppur (which was outside their constituency) to meet and congratulate the AIADMK candidate there. In contrast, they had very little contact with their own candidate in Coimbatore.

Although activists on both sides said they would campaign for their alliance, they all agreed that this would happen with less enthusiasm. While they said they would work as hard for the alliance as they would have if their own party had been allocated the seat, they explained this in terms of "rules" and "duty". They would "obey the party leader, and work [for the alliance] because that is the rule". Another noted that he would work hard for the alliance to win: "Jayalalitha has strictly announced that they must not be careless (*assalt*) with the alliance parties. If votes go down because they are careless and they are not working hard for the alliance, the person responsible will lose their post". A local journalist observed that in the end the alliance parties would all support each other's candidates simply because they were dependent on each other in different constituencies: "If AIADMK doesn't work properly for CPM in Coimbatore, the CPM activists won't work properly here. That is *kuttani dharmam*, or alliance moral duty!"

But what is clear is that the party whose candidate stood in a particular constituency took responsibility for planning the campaign. Four weeks before the election, the local DMK activist, Vijay, had not even met with the local Congress man to discuss the campaign. Three weeks later, when we interviewed him again, we asked him why there had not been much campaigning yet. At this point, he sounded quite disheartened and admitted: "If we had a DMK candidate, it would have been much better; there would already be banners and flags up everywhere. But now Congress took all the money. Now I feel very disappointed with the Congress members and the candidate. Because I have a position within the DMK, I have to work, but ordinary members are very upset." While Vijay had hoped to be appointed as one of the booth agents for Allapuram, he had now lost all hope and said that a Congress member would almost certainly be appointed: "They pay ₹5,000 for that, and in MP elections even more, but even that I won't get this time." At different points we were told that the Congress candidate was going to visit the village, but as we got closer to the day of the election it became obvious to the activists that he was never going to turn up. This added to the sense of neglect felt not only by the DMK supporters but also by those of the Congress party.

Vijay's feelings were echoed by Mohan, an AIADMK activist, who similarly had to campaign for a candidate of a different party (in his case, the CPM). He first said that they were closely collaborating and used the following image: "In a banyan tree, there are big and small branches and they all grow in different directions. Like that, we have people who feel differently and who have different opinions, but in the end we all collaborate." However, towards the end of the interview, when we asked him how he felt about campaigning for an alliance candidate, he admitted: "If my own [party] candidate was standing, you wouldn't be able to talk to me right now. I would have organised everything in a major way, but now it doesn't feel as if the election is about to come. Even though I am responsible here, I am hardly working now, I am just sitting around without doing anything." A few days later he mobilised about 50 people from the village to go and see Jayalalithaa in Coimbatore, but we did not see a lot of activity within the village itself.

For voters, the discussions about seat-sharing and alliances are often remote and confusing. About three weeks before the election, when alliances, candidates and seat-sharing arrangements had all been announced, some voters were still unclear as to who was in which alliance. They knew they wanted to vote for "two-leaf" AIADMK, but didn't know who they were in alliance with. Here it became clear how important the symbols used by the parties were. The "two-leaf" symbol is strongly associated with M. G. Ramachandran, commonly known as MGR, and some activists raised concerns in the runup to the election about the fact that there would be no "two-leaf symbol" on the ballot paper. As a result, an important aspect of the campaign was to get across to voters that they should vote for the sickle and hammer. Wall paintings appeared in and around the village showing the sickle and hammer symbol and describing it as "Amma *cinnam*" or "Amma's symbol" in reference to Jayalalithaa. On some walls, the sickle and hammer symbol was painted in the red, white and black colours of the AIADMK, while in other paintings the symbol had all party names of the alliance written around it. Furthermore, the night before polling day, all the political parties distributed "voter slips" with the alliance symbol on them to remind their supporters which symbol to vote for' (Carswell and De Neve FR: 30–33).

Elections as Carnivals

Election campaigns in India, as we have seen, are extraordinary and temporally marked events. During a campaign, the entire nation appeared to shift into a new gear, leading actors from different segments of society to behave in ways that they did not normally do on an everyday basis. Officials were more efficient, voters were fearless and politicians humbled. Victor Turner in his analysis of ritual coined the term 'liminality' to describe such a phase. It was the period when a society marked a transition from one social stage into another. In order to mark the transition, Turner argued, members had to undergo a temporary phase, an anti-structure, when the normal rules of social life were suspended and a carnivalesque inversion was allowed to take place, after which order was restored. The participants of the ritual in Turner's analysis shared what he called a feeling of communitas, a shared sociability in which egalitarianism was reinforced, displacing everyday hierarchies. We might argue that, to a certain extent, elections in India are similar rituals. Evidence collected during this study showed that part of the enthusiasm of Indians for elections did indeed come from the curious levelling effect that election campaigns ushered in. But such reversals could also be inherently unstable and so brought with them the threat of danger, of radical possibilities, and of violence. The increased criminalisation of politics, as has been noted by all observers of Indian politics, has been a response to this threat.

One important reason for this constant threat of violence is that an election campaign, more than any other public event in India, brought about an unprecedented level of contact between the powerful and those on whom they depended for power. The public meetings, ubiquitous images of politicians everywhere and the appearance of party workers on doorsteps of people's homes led to constant discussions among voters about politicians and political parties, and our study revealed that across India, without variation, the assessment of those in power was negative. This world of politics of the rulers (*rajniti*) was seen as venal, corrupt and dishonest. A good example of the tensions of the world of *rajniti* was evident in an incident that we saw at close quarters in Bihar on the campaign trail of Shahnawaz Hussain, a BJP candidate. 'During a car journey to a meeting with the candidate's right-hand man Mr X and some party workers, talk inevitably turned to an assessment of the performance by the previous Bihar government led by Lalu Prasad Yadav. While Mr X conceded that Lalu's government had given the Yadavs and lower castes a sense of self-worth (*astitva*), he felt that not enough had been invested in education, development and employment opportunities. So we asked if the newfound self-worth had, in fact, not been good for democracy. And was democracy not a good thing? He answered, "Yes of course we must have democracy, it is a good thing" (*prajatantra hona chahiye, acchi baat hai*), but then with a tinge of sarcasm added that sometimes though there was "rather too much democracy" (*kuch zayada hi prajatantra hai*). When we asked him to explain what he meant, he added with a sardonic laugh, "Sometimes people have too much freedom, anyone can do as they please, say what they want and behave how they want" (*Kuch zayada hi freedom mil jati hai*). He was of course referring to how the electoral process had brought about "a silent revolution" by which lower castes such as the Yadavs had been able to capture power and redefine the rules of public conduct. On an everyday level, social practices of caste had been greatly reduced (for instance, it was hard to find the reprehensible "two-cup" arrangements for upper and lower-caste customers at tea stalls) and rules of social conduct generally had to be revised. Further, the greater devolution of governance to locally-elected Panchayat bodies had allowed a huge number of new actors and politicians to enter the arena of *rajniti*. If there was any doubt about what Mr X had meant, they were dispelled later in the day when we were returning home in the evening and a jeep carrying two men with a small flag with the scissors symbol — of an independent candidate, N. K. Yadav — zipped passed and overtook our car. Mr X recognised one of the men in the car and sternly instructed his driver to overtake the other car. As the two vehicles came closer, the driver of our car hung back slightly as the road was very narrow. Mr X got very agitated and commanded the driver to get ahead of the other car. The driver reluctantly did as he was instructed, and just at that point, the man in the other car caught sight of Mr X and gave him a sheepish smile. Mr X, on the other hand, merely said peremptorily through the open window "Come and see me at home this evening!" (*aap aakar milye mujhe ghar par*). As the car sped ahead, he commented 'This is democracy for you' (*Yeh hai aapka prajatantra*). He explained that the person in the car used to be a manual labourer in his house but thanks to Panchayat elections was now a sarpanch and his assistant has become *mukhiya* (headman) of their village. Clearly the sight of his erstwhile retainers campaigning for a rival Yadav candidate was too much for the Rajput Mr X. Their command of a car (the ultimate sign of prosperity and upward mobility) and that too one that could overtake his was altogether unbearable at many levels. This one incident encapsulated the changing hierarchies of social caste, the erosion of class-based patronage politics and the greater opportunities that democratic ideas and electoral politics had brought about. To fight elections was a game but for the game to impinge so personally was intolerable. "As I said, democracy is good, but sometimes there is too much democracy!" (*Haan theek hai, accha hai, voh hi hum bole na, bahut zayada democracy hai*) was all he could bring himself to say to convey the complex cocktail of emotions' (Singh FR: 8–9).[7]

Ordinary voters were keen to emphasise the distance between that world and their own (*lokniti*). But while the two worlds could be kept apart otherwise, during elections, the privileged world of *rajniti* was forced to intersect with the world of *lokniti* due to the pressures of the politics of vote-banks, caste politics and clientism, all of which were an inextricable part of electoral politics. This contact was often explosive as politicians attempted to win over voters at any cost. The threat of being bullied, bought and beaten was ever present. But the need to woo voters also caused a strange levelling effect. In their dusty campaign journeys the laundered clothes of elite politicians were sullied, their well-groomed and arrogant heads had to be bent low to enter the humble dwellings of voters, and their hands had to be perpetually folded in their plea for votes. People were, of course,

---

[7] For a comprehensive discussion on whether caste still matters in India, see Corbridge et al. (2013: 239–57).

aware of the hypocrisy of such gestures, but nevertheless delighted in the sheer visual effect of the reversal. And finally, on the day of voting itself, the ultimate reversal took place, as voters became kings (*ek din ka sultan*) and politicians were reduced to nervous wrecks as they waited for the results.

Voters, Politeness and the Triumph of the Democratic Ethos

But elections also brought out the tensions within the world of *lokniti* itself. The possibilities of such tensions coming to the surface were everywhere and the fissures ran predictably between communities defined by caste, class and religion as also, of course, by party allegiances. As a Yadav shopkeeper while speaking of the Jat–Yadav rivalry put it, 'During the elections the tension between the Jats and the Yadavs is comparable to Hindu–Muslim tensions'. Another person while speaking of the relationship between these two communities stated that 'during elections the poison boils and comes to the surface. They cannot even sit on the same stage' (*zehar ubal ke upar aajata hain. Woh ek manch par bhi nahi baith sakte*) (Falcao FR: 5). In some cases we found that the elections provided the excuse of converting long-standing family disputes into political rivalry. But rather than the barely concealed violence of the *rajniti* world illustrated by the example here, we found a wholly different ethos in popular politics, namely, a remarkable display of restraint and politeness on the part of everyone concerned.[8] People were polite to campaigners who appeared on their doorstep even when they did not support their candidate; workers from different parties rubbed along with each other when they needed to share space; supporters of different parties attended each other's political meetings; and officials were polite to hesitant voters. It was as if there was a collective recognition that the stakes were too high, the divisions too deep for anything but the most circumspect behaviour in order to maintain basic decorum. In western UP, for instance, in a village full of diverse political alliances, BJP supporters were seen to be attending SP meetings even though it was

---

[8] Again, Hauser and Singer (2001: 299) confirm this in their work on Bihar where they observe that politeness is part of the 'ritualized function of the elections'.

unlikely that they would change their minds about who they would vote for. The same was true in Tamil Nadu, where the AIADMK was in alliance with the CPI(M) in 2009 and the DMK was in alliance with the Congress. This was fairly extraordinary given the otherwise high levels of adrenaline and excitement during the weeks of elections and the vituperative rhetoric that was freely used by politicians in their speeches. A number of factors might help explain this ethos of civility among the voters themselves in such a climate of fierce competition. First, there are several institutional restraints that are placed on conduct in public life. The importance of the MCC as imposed by the ECI has been discussed at the beginning of this chapter. This forced the players who had the most at stake in the electoral game, namely politicians and political parties, to conduct their campaigns according to rules that are laid out. The threat of fines and worse still, disqualification, which took place routinely were severe restraints. Second, the capillary nature of the Election Commission's organisation and its 2 million-strong workforce means that observers acting on its behalf are present everywhere. As these officials were drawn from local populations of schoolteachers and clerks, it was often difficult to identify their presence, and this caused further nervous vigilance on part of political actors. That they reported directly to the ECI, which was in turn backed by constitutional authority, gave their authority the teeth that most other regulatory bodies lack. Further, 24-hour media channels ensured that no incident, especially those that invited the attention of the ECI, went unreported, not least because controversies always sell, and politicians were keen to avoid any adverse publicity. During the 2009 elections, an inflammatory speech made by Varun Gandhi in the northern state of Uttar Pradesh during his campaign on behalf of the BJP, was the most notorious example of this kind of indiscretion. Unsurprisingly, we found that people all over the country had heard of the incident and discussed it avidly. His defiance in the face of ECI warnings made matters worse for local party workers who found that this issue attracted a disproportionate amount of attention and questions from the electorate.

Among voters, the importance of politeness stemmed perhaps from an instinctive desire for survival as much as it did from norms of civility. Elections come and go but in the end people need to live together. While political loyalties divided people during elections, they needed to nevertheless live with these divisions as indeed with others. Thus, there was recognition of political differences but also a respect for the differences that existed between them. Further, when it came to each other's political meetings held in the village, maintaining a polite atmosphere was, people explained, largely due to a desire to put forward their village's reputation as a civil place to the visitors who had organised the meetings. The norms of village sociality overrode political divisions, if only for an evening, in order to put forward a hospitable face to the outside world. This did not mean for one moment, that political loyalties were weak or meaningless. If anything, it was people's unshakeable allegiances that allowed them to be accommodating of the norms of politeness. Besides, alongside political loyalties, other allegiances based on religion or kinship also continued to exist. This fact was made starkly visible in a village in eastern Uttar Pradesh where one could see each household flying the colours of the party they supported. 'It was either the blue of the BSP or the red and green of the SP and so on. To a certain extent, these party divisions coincided with caste membership and so it was possible to guess the caste membership of the household by looking at the colour of the flags they were flying. But right next to these political flags were also a second set of flags, which also every household had on their rooftops. These belonged to the Nirankari sect of Guru Jaigurudev who had a wide and diverse following. The flags of these sects, unlike those of the political parties, were seen across different castes and neighbourhoods in the villages' (Narayan FR: 9).

In the example from Tamil Nadu, there was another factor at work. Every election brought with it a new configuration of alliances between national- and local-level parties. This therefore led to parties who had been in opposite camps in one election to ally with each other in the next. While party leaders made these calculations with abstract electoral arithmetic in mind, at the ground level, it meant that real people were either pitted against each other or thrown together in alliance. As a result, friendships could be tested, neighbours alienated from each other and families divided. Thus, people treated these alliances with a certain formality, not allowing them to intrude into personal relationships. 'On at least one occasion, an individual known to be an active supporter of an opposing party was involved in 'welcoming' the candidate by lighting firecrackers. In the particular case we observed, that man in question made light of it, saying someone had asked him, and he had done it to be polite' (Carswell and De Neve FR: 36). In the end it was easier for most to be polite even to their political adversaries for the sake of social cordiality. Of course, in the end, the most important factor in facilitating civility was that people knew that ultimately their vote was secret. It was therefore possible to agree with everyone, disagree with no one and yet be able to register one's opinion. The secrecy of the ballot was therefore perhaps the most important factor in maintaining decorum in the campaign period. In the final chapter of this book, we will return to this issue of decorum or the 'virtue of civility' to examine its role in maintaining India's democracy. But we next turn to the particular uses of language during an Indian election.

III
Political Language

This chapter examines different aspects of the use of language across India during elections in a wide variety of settings. We explored this issue while staying mindful of Sudipta Kaviraj's assertion (2010) that ordinary language is often more advanced than scholarly language in capturing popular perceptions. This is not because it has greater rigour, he argues, but because it has the agility required for capturing what people confront in a particular historical moment. The social world is plastic and politics is an activity that appreciates this plasticity. 'This is the evolving streetwise language of political description which simply follows new developments in political experience with constantly refashioned vocabularies — usually in colloquial vernacular' (ibid.: 5). As noted in the Introduction, Indians talked about politics all the time during elections and their everyday language did indeed have the requisite creativity and plasticity to describe the politics unfolding around them. They modified official English words to describe local events and used local idioms to explain philosophical notions of citizenship and participation. Entirely new words were coined to describe unprecedented events, everyday sayings were given new inflections of meaning, euphemisms were used to hide political tensions, and so their discourse had a general liveliness and accuracy that the official language of social science and political commentary would find impossible to capture. In this chapter, we present some examples of 'streetwise language' in order to respect this richness of language (ibid.) and to examine whether the manner in which people talk about politics says something about how they think about politics.

During an election, it has to be noted, it is mainly men who conduct public discussions of politics. This is because the venues where these discussions occur are traditionally masculine places where men gather to talk, exchange information and gossip and generally to shoot the breeze. While this was generally true in everyday life, during an election, these spaces also hosted regularly attended gatherings often focussed around a charismatic and loquacious opinion-maker. Thus, in Rajasthan for instance, a particular street corner was taken over by a Chotu Ram's soapbox every evening for several weeks in a row, where he talked about how Dalits had been forgotten throughout the government's term but were then used as a 'vote-bank' at the time of elections. Dalits and non-Dalits alike either heard him out or ignored him, but in any case, his message inevitably spread beyond his soapbox and subsequently featured in later discussions among other people. Elsewhere we found members of a faction in 'opposition' to the ruling party routinely occupying the rickety bench outside a particular grocery store where they spent endless hours discussing the day's happenings and new developments and finding new critiques of the incumbents. Being 'seen' at these gatherings was a mark of expressing sympathy for the opinions being aired, and for this reason, neutral but curious men made sure to circulate among different clusters and meetings during the campaign period. Some tea-stalls would have put 24-hour news channels to shame, with the quality of their in-depth analysis and predictions of electoral outcomes. These discussions then filtered back into people's homes as men brought back news of the day and of what they had seen and heard, repeating statements made by others word for word and sometimes passing off the particularly witty and intelligent comments as their own in order to impress their families. Younger members would also contribute the jokes and slogans that they had picked up during the day and these would be further shared by neighbours and visitors who, in turn, would file them away mentally to repeat to new audiences. Women, who were often missing from public discussions of politics, were nevertheless interested and often asked questions, sometimes awkward ones, and this, in turn, required the men to clarify various points, revise their positions or defend them against criticism. In this process, ideas about parties, candidates and the elections would travel back and forth between different kinds of spaces, circulating among a wide network of participants, gathering embellishments and annotations with each iteration and thereby creating a whole discourse about the elections.

One feature to note about the language of politics, and in language more generally in India, is, ironically, the use of English. While it is true that India's middle class forms the largest population of English-knowing people in the world, they are still only 12 per cent of the national population (Census of India 2001). In fact, in most of the areas where the CEE project was conducted, people were not fluent in English but nevertheless considered English to be the language of aspiration, opportunity and modernity, like the rest of India. For them, English remained a language that was remote and yet constantly present in the public sphere — shop signs, advertisements and news bulletins regularly used it as a *lingua franca*. However, it remained incomprehensible to the vast majority because their schooling had not equipped them with the same fluency in reading and writing that a small proportion gains through 'English-medium schools'. It was, instead, a language that was heard and partially adopted through frequent usage of some words. These words tended to be the ones that have been used for a sufficiently long period of time in India (e.g., 'Congress', 'cricket', 'film', 'army') and have entered local lexicons and been thoroughly domesticated and are now used as though they had always belonged to Indian languages. This is obviously truer for words that do not have equivalent words in Indian languages, like the ones cited here. But even where there is an alternative, the English word is used instead. Perhaps the best example of this is the word 'politics' itself. While the word *rajniti* is the literal translation of the word 'politics' in various Indian languages, it is used in a very specific sense in popular usage. *Rajniti* is used to describe what remote, privileged and powerful people in immaculate white *kurta*s do. In contrast to *rajniti*, the word that is used to describe the vast domain of popular politics is simply: 'politics'. This word borrowed from English has now been thoroughly assimilated into the Indian lexicon and is used by even those who speak very little or no English. In contrast to *rajniti*, 'politics' is an umbrella term to describe a range of popular activities such as agitation, mobilisation and struggle including student politics, ecological movements, land rights agitations, and the women's movement; i.e., it is used to describe what people can see themselves doing. So even though the word 'politics' comes from English, it is used to describe a domain in which people identify themselves as participating. The term *rajniti*, on the other hand, is derived from the classical language of Sanskrit and lacks the colloquiality associated with popular politics. (I shall return to the distinction between the two words at the end of this chapter.) Another English word inducted into the popular lexicon is 'vote'. When people describe what they will do on polling day, they are likely to say '*Hum* vote *zaroor dalengey*' (I will vote for sure) or when party workers assess the support they have they say 'vote *ki banavat hamare paksh main hai*' (the vote/final result is looking in our favour) or 'vote *bikhar raha hai*' (the votes are getting scattered, i.e., we are losing our votes). We heard the word *matdan*, which the ECI formally uses to refer to the process of voting, being used for more philosophical discussions of voting, thus assimilating it into a wider Hindu understanding of the notion of *dan* or giving without any expectation of return.[1] In Bihar, however, where there had been a move towards boycotting of the polls in our research site, we did hear a pun on the word which when broken up generated the meaning 'do not give' (*mat* = 'do not'; *dan* = 'give'). For processes and practices describing electoral procedures, polling officials also seemed to prefer the English words like 'mock poll', 'strong room', 'polling agent', 'machine', 'presiding' (for 'presiding officer'), even though it must be noted that the ECI provided them with a list of the same terms in various Indian languages. Other examples of the English word being used instead of the vernacular alternative were: 'police', 'canvass', 'machine' (for the EVM) and 'aspirant'. These were similar to the word 'secular', which was used as a composite adjective to describe a person, process, party, and ideas instead of the more cumbersome literary Hindi equivalent *sampradik sadhbhav*. There were several other English words that people used liberally while speaking in other languages, sometimes modifying their usage to suit the purpose, such as 'direct/indirect' to refer to access to powerful people; 'readymade *neta*' (politician); 'underground' to refer to clandestine happenings or issues that were not openly stated. Those candidates who were given a ticket by bypassing the party organisation and hierarchy and were brought in from outside because of their wealth, caste or religion were called 'parachute candidates'. Such quirkiness in the use of English words in political discussions was symptomatic of a wider tendency in the use of English among non-English speakers in India. In Bihar, for instance, among the English words that percolated into the vernacular and made surprising and sudden appearances were 'Indian *vasi*' (Indian nationals), 'constitutional morality' (responsibility to vote as citizens of the country), 'dominion' (federal structure), 'ladies *log*' and 'gents *log*' (*log* is a word for 'people'), 'judicial' (right), *behav* (behaviour), and 'professional' (lacking moral values, responsibility or ethics).

---

[1] There is a longer discussion of the notion of *dan* later in this chapter.

But ultimately, such a list was finite and 'the number of such English-only terms was quite limited. A second category of terms consisted of those for which either an English or a local language version was used, and for which the choice of language was likely to depend on the level of literacy/education of the speaker, the person one was speaking to, and the context of the conversation. Typical examples of such terms from English/Tamil were: "vote" or *vakku*; "election" or *theerthal*; "election commission" or "*theerthal* commission"; "politics" or *arasiyal*; "alliance" or *kuttani*; "party" or *katchi*; "two-leaf" or *irettalai* (to refer to the two-leaf symbol of the AIADMK); "campaign" or *pracharam*; and "candidate" or *veetpaalar*. For these words, the English and Tamil were used interchangeably. While a wide range of people, even those with less education, knew the English words for these concepts, were aware of their meaning and could understand them when they were used in their presence, tended to use the Tamil equivalent word when they had to pick a form to use themselves. Moreover, when combined with other words, such as *vakku chavadi* or "election booth", *kuttani dharmam* or "alliance loyalty/duty" and *uzhal illaame katchi* or "corruption-free party", it was always the Tamil that was used in conversations' (Carswell and De Neve FR: 23). This slightly different adoption of English words in Tamil Nadu indicated a further nuance in the way in which English has been adopted in India, namely that many words are familiar to the ear and people generally understand the meaning, but are unlikely to use them because they lack a precise knowledge of them. Similarly, in north India we found that terms such as 'vote bank' that were regularly used in media discussions were never found in popular usage. Instead the word used was *samikaran* (equation) such that Nitish Kumar's support base in Bihar would be described as a 'luv–kush' or 'kurmi–koeri' *samikaran*.

There was a further layer to such bilingualism for there were a number of popularly-used terms relating to politics for which the vernacular was used without exception, even though the speaker might have known the English equivalent or at least have heard it. Here are some typical examples. 'When villagers in Tamil Nadu talked about voting as a "right", they always mentioned *urimai*, a Tamil word that also means "hereditary rights", used, for example, in the context of certain castes having specific "rights" in temple festivals or of an uncle having the "right" to marry his sister's daughter. It was the same *urimai* that was used to refer to the democratic right to vote in contemporary India. Another word frequently used in conversations about democracy

and voting was *kadamai* (duty), again always mentioned in Tamil'
(Carswell and De Neve FR: 24). Similarly, elsewhere in India, words
such as *odhikar/adhikar* (right) and *kartobbo/kartavya* (duty) were
used instead of their English counterparts. The Hindi/Bengali word
for citizen — *nagarik/nagorik* — was used widely and so was the
Tamil word *kudimagan*.[2] In the same vein, we never heard 'democracy' being used. Instead, people used words such as *jananayakam*
or *makkal atchi* (Tamil) or *jonogono tantra* (Bengali), which meant
the same thing: 'people's rule'.

This in itself was interesting because it was clear that these English
words that were used by non-English speakers were used in similar
ways by English speakers. However, some English words like 'duty' or
'rights' or 'citizen', which were not part of common usage, were used
only with a certain degree of self-consciousness, and so did not travel
to other language vocabularies. On the other hand, informants who
talked to us about *kadamai* or *nagorik* often belonged to the lowest
socio-economic categories — piece-rate tailors, daily wage labourers or farmers. They considered these concepts to be important and
worthy of discussion and used their native languages to describe
them.

Names

The play with language and acronyms was also evident in the way
people talked about political parties. Given the large number of political parties and their names, acronyms are a must. The ECI has a total
of 363 parties on record, which are usually known by their initials. For
example, the Bharatiya Janata Party, whose name consists of Hindi
words, is listed as 'BJP'. In Hindi writings, it is usually referred to as
Bhajpa, which takes the first syllables of the three constituent words
of the party's name to make up the short form. However, English
acronyms of party names are also occasionally used as vernacular
terms in Indian languages. One example of this took place in Bihar
when people used the word *mai* to describe Lalu Yadav's traditional
supporters. The term was derived from the acronym 'MY', i.e.,
Muslims and Yadav.

---

[2] The Tamil word *kudimagan* meant both 'citizen' and 'drunkard', which
led to no end of amusement.

Alongside their acronyms, political parties are also always associated with a party symbol. In an electorate of with a high proportion of illiterate voters, this practice is essential and it was one of many prescient decisions taken by the ECI at its inception in its effort to make the electoral process transparent and user-friendly to the Indian electorate (see Jaffrelot 2006). These symbols have traditionally been thoroughly quotidian images such as a lantern, a flower, a bicycle, an elephant, and so on. On EVMs, therefore, party names are listed alongside their symbol and during campaigns, candidates remind voters to push the button next to their party symbol. These symbols have become synonymous with the political party they stand for and in campaigning and conversation the two are used interchangeably. In Kerala, therefore, we heard loud-hailers telling people to press the button next to the 'clock' the day before the election as a last-minute reminder to vote for the NCP, the Nationalist Congress Party. Similarly, Jasuben, a woman from the Thakarda community in Gujarat explained how local leaders gave their advice about who to vote for: 'If the Bhabha (caste leader) says *phul* (flower, i.e., lotus) then I vote for the BJP, if he says *panjo* (hand) then I vote for the Congress'. Naming parties by using the words for their respective symbols, therefore, worked at two levels. The party symbol came to stand for the party itself and became so closely associated with the party that they grew to be virtually indistinguishable over time. Thus, it is impossible to mistake the hammer and sickle as associated with any party but the Communists and similarly, the hand with any other than the Congress. However, people also used the words for these symbols euphemistically to avoid naming political parties openly as this allowed them to maintain certain vagueness when discussing politics. As with Jasuben's village elder above, they could dispense advice about whom to vote for without stating it explicitly. This veiling was essential because in many parts of India, election campaigns were also extremely tense times and to be overheard discussing political parties could expose one's political loyalties and make one vulnerable to others. This vagueness caused party workers immense frustration because they were keen for people to come out in the open and support them unequivocally. As one put it: 'Nowadays if the lotus blooms in one household, the elephant is also present as is the hand as is the lantern' (*aaj aisa hai, ek ghar mein agar kamal khil raha hai toh, haathi bhi hai, haath bhi hai aur laltern bhi hai*). In another instance of ambiguity, when a frustrated RJD worker was asked if N. K. Yadav, an independent Yadav candidate whose election symbol was a pair of scissors, was eating into the support for the RJD candidate, Shakuni Chaudhary, thus allowing his chief rival — BJP's Shahnawaz Hussain — to forge ahead, the question was posed euphemistically: 'Is the lotus blooming or the lantern burning bright?' (*Kamal khil raha hai ya laltern jal raha hai*). The answer was equally enigmatic and played with what scissors could literally do: 'The scissors [the symbol of the Independent candidate] are cutting into the support' (*Kainchi vote kaat rahi hai*) (Singh FR: 8). This kind of play on words was common. In Madhya Pradesh we came across another instance where a group of women managed to avoid a direct confrontation with aggressive workers from a party they did not support. On their walk to the polling station, these women passed the local BJP worker who reminded them to press the '*phul wala* button' (the button next to the lotus, the BJP party symbol) on the EVM. 'Yes, yes!' one of them replied immediately, 'don't worry we are all *phul wale bais*' (lotus-women) but then, a few steps later, once she was out of his earshot, she sang quietly, '*Phul phul*, April fool!' and everyone burst out laughing (Krishnamurthy FR: 10). Here, the euphemism was combined with a bilingual pun. The joke was on the workers and the cleverness of the voters became even more evident.

The Language of Caste

It is widely agreed by observers of Indian society that one of the most significant changes in the social and political landscapes in past decades has been the simultaneous decline of caste-based practices across India along with a growing assertion of caste-based politics. There is a clear decline of the caste-based framework of social organisation, the *jajmani* system, and the social/ritual hierarchy and various everyday practices that divided and ranked castes according to strict rules of separation are being gradually weakened in many parts of the country (Jodhka 2012). The notorious 'double-cup' system, for instance — a once widely observed practice at tea stalls across the country whereby one set of cups was reserved for upper castes and a different set for the rest, in replication of the rules of pollution that people maintained in their homes for visitors — has now more or less disappeared. Even a generation ago, it was unthinkable for an upper caste person to receive water from someone from a lower caste. While these practices continue within the domestic sphere, they have been considerably weakened in the public. This has, to a large extent, been influenced by the growing challenges that lower castes have posed to the hegemony of the upper castes through direct agitations and through what Jaffrelot (2003) calls India's 'silent revolution' — challenges that have been facilitated by the growing influence of lower castes in elected bodies and popular politics and greater recourse to constitutional rights that guarantee equality to all citizens irrespective of caste or any other social distinction (Jaffrelot 2003; Mosse 1994, especially pp. 93–94).

Therefore, it did not come as a surprise that this changing landscape of caste, i.e., the weakening of caste practices in public alongside a growing assertion of lower caste political parties, was reflected in the language that people used to talk about caste. First, constitutional categories have been appropriated for local use in inventive ways. The most widespread example of this is the category of Other Backward Classes (OBCs) and its various spin-offs. While 'backward' was rarely used to describe the lower castes, its antonym 'forward' was regularly used to describe the upper castes. To describe lower castes, however, people rarely used the official term 'OBC' and instead used their individual caste names such as *koeri*, *kurmi*, *yadav*, *baniya*. It was as if the stigma of the term 'backward' was no longer acceptable in public discussions, and while much electoral politics was organised around harnessing the OBC vote, the growing electoral and consequent social prominence of the same castes did not allow for them to labelled in terms that made their status explicit. Yet the use of the term 'forward', which was not an official category, was an economical way of referring to those upper castes that were excluded by the OBC category. Unlike 'backward', the word 'forward' was by definition non-derogatory, at least among non-English speaking peoples, and therefore could be used without controversy. The use of the term 'Dalit' was similarly complex and context-driven. Researchers reported that across the country, the use of the word 'Dalit' in everyday language was somewhat rare. While it remains an important term for activism and mobilisation, ordinary people, including ground-level party workers, are much more likely to use individual caste names like *dhobi*, *chamar*, *nai*, etc. This is not dissimilar to the usage of the word *harijan*, which has largely fallen out of popular use, with the exception of the term *harijan tolla*, which refers to village neighbourhoods where Dalits lived. The same is also true of the term 'Scheduled Tribes'.

However, as scholars have noted, the entrenched power of upper castes is far from being a thing of the past. In our field site in Gujarat, 'even though the village had a large number of Dalits and OBCs, the politically dominant caste in the village was still largely the upper-caste *kshatriya*s. Some things have changed here too, especially the "double-cup" system, which is now a thing of the past. Also, in political practice, the *kshatriya*s have to keep the rest of the village in the loop before making any decisions. However, the upper castes continue to harbour a sense of entitlement to power and privilege. This is strikingly reflected in the term *sahukar*s, which is used to refer to the *kshatriya*s. One of the *kshatriya*s in the Gujarat site described this inherent sense of privilege thus: "To rule the people is in our blood and that's why we are now in politics in big numbers. Whether that is the Panchayat or even the Vidhan Sabha'" (Jani FR: 10).

Metaphors

As mentioned already, the use of euphemism and analogy was common in popular language, even among people of very little education. In particular, there were two metaphors that were widely used to compare the process of elections; one was to compare it to weddings and the other to compare the process of casting one's vote to giving *dan*. I would like to discuss these in some detail here in an attempt to tease out the significance of these comparisons.

As we noted in the Introduction, in 2009, the dates of the five-week-long election period also coincided with the 'auspicious' wedding season, and perhaps for this reason and others, people drew constant parallels between a wedding and an election. Both the ECI and the political parties were genuinely worried that people would be so caught up in wedding preparations and celebrations that they might not turn up to vote at all. One of the catchy slogans coined to mitigate this worry was: 'Vote first, the wedding can follow' (*pehle matdan, phir kanyadan*). This slogan was catchy also because it played on the word *dan* (to give) which was used both in the context of a wedding or 'giving away a daughter' (*kanyadan*) as well as to refer to the process of voting itself (*matdan*). As we shall see later, this play on words deriving from the complex meaning of *dan* was used by people in their reflections on why they vote. They explained that to give without an expectation of tangible return was the spirit of *dan* and that this was the sentiment behind casting their vote. This slogan, therefore, had resonance with popular usage and was particularly catchy. It is also possible that the wedding season provided fodder for the extensive use of marriage-related metaphors for describing the electoral process. We observed that officials anticipated the elections with the same mixture of dread and excitement as they did weddings and exams (*yeh pariksha bhi hai aur shaadi bhi*) and so, it was not surprising that officials repeatedly drew parallels between the various stages of a wedding and the process of conducting the election. They referred to the paperwork and paraphernalia (*chunav samagri*) of the polling process as wedding prestations (*dan dahej*) and the EVMs full of registered votes at the end of polling day was likened to the return of the groom's party with the bride. Candidates and party workers also evoked parallels with a wedding in various ways. In Bihar, one of the independent candidates came to his nomination rally dressed in red and riding on a mare (*ghodi*) like a bridegroom, with lots of party workers dancing in front of the horse, just as any groom's party (*baaraat*) would. In other nomination rallies too, the candidate came garlanded with party workers dancing to the beats of *dhol* and local music, as if accompanying a groom to his wedding. That people widely consumed and understood parallels between weddings and elections was evident in an incident during the campaign of one of the candidates, Shakuni Chaudhary. As he was getting ready to leave and party workers crowded around him and jostled to get ahead, one of the workers remarked — 'Let the groom go first, the groom's party should always follow him!' (*arey dulhe ko toh aage jane do, hum toh barati na hue, peeche peeche aayenge*). Later, when a candidate went out to canvass votes (*prachar*), his action was likened to going out to get his bride (Singh FR: 19). While addressing voters, we heard workers of political parties say to them that deciding whom to vote for was the same as choosing a groom for one's daughter, and would then go on to list the qualities that made their candidate the ideal groom. In Rajasthan, a campaigner explaining how to decide which Congress candidate to vote for put it thus: 'When you give a daughter in marriage don't you check the family's credentials as well as those of the groom's? The son of a millionaire could turn out to be dullard!' (*Jab rishta dekhte ho toh phir dono parivar aur ladke ko dekhte hain. Parivar crorepati ho sakta hain par agar ladka bavla lallu ho toh phir?*) (Falcao FR: 13) He thereby appealed to the voters to take both the candidate and the party into consideration when deciding whom to vote for.

In their riposte, voters when pressed to explain how they would decide whom to vote for used the same analogy to explain that they would give their votes to the candidate of their caste in the same way that they would marry their daughters within their caste (*Ka ho bhaiya, beti te vote jaat ke bahar debe jaat hain ka*). In other cases, where relations between the party and supporters were more strained, people would say things like: 'It's not like I am negotiating my daughter's wedding, why should I worry about my decision so much?' (*beti thodi na de rahe hain jo itna sochen*). This particular retort, made by a Dalit voter in Bihar, was intended not so much to dismiss the importance of the voting decision as to indicate his frustration that his community had been completely neglected by campaigners during this election. What he meant, therefore, was that he felt undervalued and underrepresented in a way that he would not feel at his daughter's wedding.

Dan

There was also a whole discourse around the play on the word *matdan* itself, which means 'to vote' in many Indian languages. This literally translates to 'giving your opinion' but the use of the word *dan* as suffix, assimilates this secular act with other cognate acts such as *annadan* (the gift of food), *goudan* (the gift of a cow), *bhudan* (gift of land), *shramdan* (gift of labour) and *kanyadan* (the gift of a virgin daughter) — all of which are gift exchanges of a sort. As Jonathan Parry explained in his nuanced and scholarly study among the priests of Benares, '[t]rue *dan* is a voluntary and disinterested donation made without ostentation or expectation of *any* kind of *this*-worldly return' (1989: 120). The giver also typically occupies a lower status than the recipient in acts of *dan*. These gift-giving practices are widely practised across India and so, while it should come as no surprise that people drew the parallels, the fact that the people who drew them were among the poorest was what made it significant. An elderly marginal farmer-labourer compared voting to the *dan* of food or giving away of a daughter in marriage, which were all acts through which *punya* or merit accrues to an individual. Sixty-year-old Saroj Kashyap explained why such giving was virtuous.

> We take so much from the government and the government is doing a lot of things for the people. They supply electricity and give different kinds of ration cards and the poor get wheat and rice at a very cheap

rate. Many old people are also getting old age pension. My mother-in-law is one of them. So we should also do something towards forming a government, and the least we can do is vote. It is our *matdan* by which we contribute towards the formation of the government. If we do not vote, how will the new government be formed? All the money that the candidates and the government spend on the elections will be a waste. And finally, all this expenditure will fall on the people after the elections. And if the elections have to be held again, the people will have to bear the expenses.

As this comment demonstrates, there was a clear recognition of the spirit of exchange in the implication of *dan*. Just as pilgrims in Benares hoped to gain merit in exchange for their *dan* to the priests, voters felt that their vote was what they gave in return for a stable government. As Saroj implies here, people viewed casting one's vote as a small donation that brought them not only the material benefits of pensions and grain but also saved public funds by avoiding repeat elections. Therefore, they considered it their duty or *dharma* to vote. However, as we have seen, there was also a great deal of scepticism regarding the performance of governments and politicians and that, perhaps, led another person to comment wryly: '*Matdan* is like *dehdan* [donating your body for a good purpose, i.e., the ultimate sacrifice] but this gift has true meaning only when the person understands your feelings behind it'; thereby indicating that politicians were not the worthiest recipients of *matdan*. This man's statement brings out an important anxiety among all givers of *dan*, namely that the recipient must be worthy of it. Again, as Parry points out: 'Good *dan* (*sudan*) is given to a "worthy vessel" (*supatra*) "without desire" (*nishkam*)' (ibid.: 128) and if the giver chooses an unworthy recipient, he becomes responsible for the latter's sins. In electoral terms, we might gloss this as 'people get the government they deserve' but by drawing parallels between *matdan* and *dan* given in other contexts we are able to recognise that voters suffer the anxiety of choosing correctly. The priests in Benares had their own anxieties because while giving and receiving *dan* was among the six duties of a Brahman '*the* most problematic aspect of a *dana* [was] that it is an unreciprocated gift' (ibid.: 76). According to them, 'there is no such thing as good *dan* . . . It is all vile (*nikrist*); whoever takes it burns his hand' (ibid.: 67). Therefore, they had to make sure that the gift was passed on (much like a hot potato, as Parry remarks) to avoid the burden of sin accrued by a large gap between receipts and disbursements. Whether or not politicians felt the burden that the priests of Benares did, we cannot be sure, but it is possible that they have little idea about the meaning that people invested in their votes. For very poor people who could not otherwise afford the expense of donating a cow or food or labour, the ability to perform *dan* of *any* sort had a special poignancy. As a middle-aged woman trying to feed a large family on a tiny budget said, 'We don't have money, but during elections, we get a chance to give. That is why it is our duty (*dharma*) to fulfil this because it is an opportunity for us to earn some *punya* and perform an act of good *karma*.' Seizing on elections to serve the function of gaining merit was an especially sound decision because *dan* by those who had little to give away was considered especially virtuous. As Parry goes on to qualify, 'the merit acquired . . . is proportionate to his or her means — the widow's mite being in theory the equal of the jewel-encrusted treasures of the prince. It is also proportionate to the worth of the recipient, which is defined largely in terms of his reluctance to accept gifts' (Parry 1989: 120).

Neologisms and Jokes

One very evocative term that we came across, used to capture the day of polling itself, when time itself seemed to stop and all was held in suspense, was the imaginative formulation, *katl ki raat* — i.e., the night of the hanging. To describe the mixture of anticipation and uncertainty that accompanies such a moment, a man explained that it was the sort of night when you wanted your wives and daughters to return home and be safe for one never knew what was going happen (*bahu, betiyaan ghar paar aajani chahiyen, kuch pata nahin kya ho*). Jokes coined by ordinary people also circulated widely. One such joke, parodying the UPA government went: 'How does the UPA vehicle move? Manmohan Singh is at the wheel, the Communists control the brakes and Sonia controls them all with a remote control' (UPA *ki gaadi kaise chalti hain?* Manmohan Singh steering *pe baitha hain,* Communist break *par per rakhte hain aur* Sonia remote *se sabko* control *karti hain*). The capricious nature of electoral fortunes was referred to repeatedly as a wave (*leher*) or wind (*hawa*) and when they turned dramatically in someone's favour, they were referred to as a typhoon (*aandhi*). Such change was palpable and voters sensed it in a number of ways, not unlike the way one feels a storm brewing in one's bones. In such a climate, if asked on what basis they would decide whom to vote for, many voters replied: 'The way the wind is blowing' (*jahan leher hai vahin ho lete hain*).

Political Rhetoric

Perhaps the most innovative use of language in the Indian political landscape is the case of Dravidian political rhetoric, as shown by Bate's masterful study (2009) of the topic. The Dravidian movement in Tamil Nadu, as an integral part of its assertion of a Dravidian identity as opposed to a dominant Brahmanical Tamil one, replaced the 'high' *sen* Tamil with a Dravidian lexicon drawn from Sangam poetry and neologisms. As a result, all Tamil words that were derived from Sanskrit were removed and replaced by a 'pure' Dravidian Tamil, which bore little resemblance to the demotic Tamil spoken by Brahmins and non-Brahmins alike. As a result, political leaders of the Dravidian movement routinely delivered speeches that lasted hours in a language that was little understood by the audience, but which they duly sat through. Here, rather than serving as a communicative function, political language was used to assert a political ideology that its supporters subscribed to. The use of language as performance was also evident elsewhere in India during the 2009 elections, as we shall see in this section.

A powerful weapon in the armoury of populist politicians like Mamata Banerjee, Lalu Yadav and Narendra Modi, who could sway thousands at political rallies, was the language and rhetorical style they used in their speeches. These politicians were able to connect with the masses that came to hear them through devices that connected what they said with what people knew.

Narendra Modi, the chief minister of Gujarat and star campaigner of the BJP that was in the opposition at the national level, was particularly adept in communicating with vast audiences. Asking the audience questions and waiting for their answers was one of his favoured methods. To start with, he took care to choose the language he spoke in. Whenever he addressed local people he always spoke in Gujarati, but he was also aware that his mass rallies were often covered by television and so made it a point to speak in Hindi when he turned to the cameras to provide a soundbite. Given the vastness of his audience he also deployed rhetorical tricks that simultaneously connected him with each one of them and also united them as an audience. For instance, in a typical speech at Bayad *taluka* of Sabarkantha constituency, he asked the audience: 'Do you think that the party in power should give an account of their work at the time of election?' To this the audience roared: 'Yes!' He reiterated: 'Do you think the party in power should give an account of their finances?' 'Yes!' they said again. Having elicited the response he wanted, Modi then pronounced: 'But the Congress is not ready to do so'. This was a fairly economical device to sow suspicion against the incumbent government among the public without having to provide any concrete evidence. The audience, having vocalised their assent to the fairly bland opening questions, were then made complicit with the much more serious charge levelled immediately afterwards. The use of this kind of device was to establish an immediate and visceral connection between an audience of thousands and a lone speaker. By responding to the questions posed to them, members in the audience were made to feel involved at the rally rather than being treated as passive listeners to be talked at by the politicians. By answering in unison, the voice of thousands also merged to mouth a single word, thereby creating an effervescent atmosphere that everyone could individually experience.

The use of such devices by politicians takes considerable skill. They have to take the gamble of posing a question to their audience hoping that they will indeed answer. For them not to do so would pose irreparable damage to their own reputations. Furthermore, the question posed should elicit an unambiguous and monosyllabic answer to create the desired effect of agreement, unison and frisson. The complicity created at such meetings also facilitated a wider dissemination of the messages themselves. We found that within hours of having attended Modi's rally, those who attended, including party workers, were using his very words while explaining to those who hadn't attended why they needed to vote for the BJP. His famous slogan — 'I am not corrupt nor will I allow corruption to flourish' (*Hun khato nathi ane khava deto nathi*) — was repeated endlessly from those in his inner circle to district-level workers, from farmers to village-level *karyakar*s. His formulations were catchy and memorable for people to repeat them verbatim.

Mamata Banerjee of the Trinamool Congress in West Bengal used another rhetorical device to great effect. The politician is also an amateur poet and is known for the rhymes she constantly invents. At public rallies she exhorted her audience thus:

> *Tata salem er kole*
> CPM *dole*
> *aar luchir moto fole*
>
> (The CPI[M] leaders are in cahoots with Tata and became fat on their money).

Other slogans that she made up many years ago and has used in several campaigns since in her bid to oust the Communists from power are now well known and well rehearsed. Thus, rather than repeating them herself, she often says the first line and waits for her audience to recite the next one:

> Mamata Banerjee (MB): *hamla rukhey* vote *din* [stop the nonsense and vote]
> Audience: *trinomul ke* vote *din* (cast your vote for Trinamool)
> MB: *bhikkhe noy chaichhi rin* [I am not begging nor asking for a loan]
> Audience: CPM *ke bhalo kore kobor din* [bury the CPM once and for all]
> MB: *shokal shokal* vote *din* [vote first thing in the morning]
> Audience: *nijer* vote *nije din* [cast your vote yourself] (Chakrabarty FR: 14)

During the 2009 campaign, in the wake of the Nandigram agitation against the forceful takeover of agricultural land by the Communist government in order to build a factory to manufacture the Tata Nano car, Banerjee's party's slogan was *Ma, Mati, Manush* (Mothers [referring to mothers who lost their sons to Communist atrocities], Land and People). This rhetorical device achieved many objectives all at once. First, it established her long career in politics and the familiarity with which people treated her and her words. There was a consistency of message too, which, in Mamata's case, has been to remove the Communists from power in West Bengal. But it is also interesting that the lines spoken by the audience hold the key messages that she intends to transmit: vote for Trinamool, bury the CPM and take ownership of your vote. By making her audiences actually say these lines themselves, she manages to hammer her point home.

In Bengal, there has been a long and well-documented literary tradition that celebrates such rhyming couplets. Children learn them in their early years; adults repeat them as nostalgia and to teach future generations. By appropriating this form, Banerjee indicated her literary prowess while also packing them with political meanings that are then endlessly repeated and propagated through the population. The rhythm and rhyme acted as effective mnemonic devices and the question-and-answer game between the speaker and the audience demonstrated fun, fidelity and frisson. But the language at Trinamool political meetings also reflected the rather less literary figures that were part of the party. A slogan such as *marbo ekhane lash porbe shosane* (one kick will land them in the cemetery) conveyed their intentions regarding the Communist candidates. Nor were these sentiments conveyed with any subtlety. In fact, as the campaign gathered momentum, the vitriol flowed freely from speakers from all sides of the political spectrum (Chakrabarty FR: 12–15).

The politicians' felicity with language impressed a wide range of people and was noted and appreciated by the intended audiences. As one man said at a tea stall discussion about Narendra Modi's style: 'I like Modi's language very much. Each statement is like the dialogue of a popular film!' This ability to connect with his audience combined with his sharp memory (remembering to thank his local party colleagues by name) and his effective use of numbers in a speech — 'When the Government of India is struggling to achieve a growth rate of 6 to 7 per cent, Gujarat has already achieved 10.5 per cent growth. When the Central government has put up a target for 4 per cent growth in agriculture sector, Gujarat has already achieved 14 per cent' — won him enormous credibility with his audience. The people enjoyed the manner in which he delivered his speeches and this liking translated easily into support. As a result, his controversial opinions about Muslims also gained credibility. For instance, he proclaimed that

> Muslims in my state are the wealthiest ones in the country and compared to other states. More Muslims in Gujarat have savings accounts in banks as well as comparatively stronger presence in government jobs. So it will be now better if the Government in Delhi stops the politics of minority appeasement in the name of Gujarat (Jani FR: 11).

Regardless of the veracity of these claims, or indeed the point that he was making, the message that people took away from it was a different one; one that perhaps people would have liked to believe themselves. What they took away after this particular speech was: 'Modi *sahib* told the truth that all these Muslims are earning very much'. A prejudiced view when bolstered by a leader's rhetoric made it somewhat less controversial.

As the examples of Mamata Banerjee and Narendra Modi show, the language of political campaigning played a crucial role in building the reputation of a politician. Similarly, Sonia Gandhi's acquired fluency in Hindi, Atal Behari Vajpayee's poetry and Lalu Yadav's witticisms have all contributed to their stature in the public imagination. During the 2009 elections, politicians like Banerjee and Modi were able not only to capture the attention of audiences at their mass rallies but also to ensure that their messages remained in people's minds by using rhetorical devices to transmit their ideas quickly and effectively across a wide area. One of the executive members of the village dairy was talking to us about corruption and he suddenly said, *ame khaie nahi ne khava daie pan nahi* ('I am not corrupt nor do I allow corruption to flourish'), repeating what Modi had said in his address.

This issue of the transmission of messages is a generally interesting one in all parts of India and indeed in any setting where speaking and listening are involved. At a meeting in Chhattisgarh, while Rahul Gandhi spoke about farmer's loans and the National Rural Employment Guarantee Act (NREGA), a young Congress worker insisted directly afterwards that what Rahul Gandhi had said was that young people are the future of the country and that they should challenge their local level's older (and corrupt) workers. It was evident that Rahul Gandhi's embodiment of the youth, and by implication, his support for them, was interpreted as more significant than the words that he had actually spoken.

Politics and the Demonic

The different aspects of the uses of language considered so far in this chapter come together most powerfully in the most ubiquitous discourse of all — discussions about politics and politicians. While Indians discuss and argue about politics all the time, the frequency of these conversations rises during elections, as indeed their intensity. The sudden ubiquity of politicians among the people during their campaigns led, in particular, to conversation about their nature and the character of the world that they inhabited. During an election campaign, such ideas were aired more frequently than at other times because the contrast between politicians' mannered humility when desperately seeking votes and their guaranteed neglect of the very people who had voted them to power afterwards was made more stark. In this section, we would like to present the variety of formulations we heard across India, in order to convey how creative people were with their language in conveying their ideas. As we shall see, popular assessments of politicians led to wider assessments of the nature of politics itself, and it is worth paying attention to how people described this issue.

The perceptions of politicians themselves were uniformly negative all over India. 'Our politicians are submerged in irregularities and corruption. Every other day we read about a scandal through the newspaper' and other statements like these were ubiquitous. During a campaign the following statement was representative of what people universally noted:

> When an election comes they all come and say we will do this, we will do that, we will favour you, and for that our party should come to power. But once when they come to power, nothing really happens or changes in our lives. It's all a farce. They only know how to show us a dream, but it always remains a dream. They never fill any of the promises.

An old woman said: 'What is there to trust? When they win and they do something good for us, then we will believe them. Now they are just talking nicely to get our votes, but once I vote they won't come back to help me' (Carswell and De Neve FR: 28). This hypocrisy on the part of politicians was what grated most and was described thus by a young man: *Netaon ke khane aur dikhane ke daant alag hote hain* (Politicians have one set of teeth to show to the world but another that they use for eating). In this rather vivid metaphor, the two-faced nature of politicians was highlighted, as was the monstrosity of their beings. The language used to describe this demonic nature was varied; one woman called them 'stained white dhotis!' and others called them a 'thorn' in the side of the body politic. But the same person who used the metaphor of the thorn also qualified the statement by pointing out that a thorn could only be removed by another thorn, which was why it was not enough to just criticise politicians. One also had to join politics oneself.

When we pursued this with questions of what people thought politicians actually did when they got voted into power, the answer was fairly unequivocal:

> The various tricks of making money is what they call politics. All politicians do is look for ways of making money (*fayada*) — either they get a handsome amount from their party masters or take advantage by illegally forfeiting or by producing fake documents, or they take bribes directly from people, for which there are no checks and balances. Even their political godfathers give them green signal.

If this seemed too harsh an assessment of the entire political class, a Congressman himself who had served as the President of a Panchayat rather unashamedly confirmed it. We spoke to him to gain an alternative point of view and had expected a defence of the probity of politicians. Instead, without mincing words, he unabashedly admitted,

> [w]e are in politics to gain something. Earlier my father was the Sarpanch and later I was the Sarpanch for two terms. Now our seat has been reserved for the Scheduled Tribes so we have a Sarpanch from an ST, but de facto I run the entire show, not only because I am the vice-Sarpanch but also because I have experience of doing the job. We will do anything for profit. Why would I be in politics if I could not gain something from it? [*Fayade ke bina Rajniti me rehne ka kya matlab!*] (Falcao FR: 4).

It was interesting that this man could be so candid about the naked instrumentalism of his career and politics. That he belonged to the Congress, a political party that had over 150 years of standing in India and had been at the forefront of the independence struggle made his statement even more galling. There was no pretence in his words; he offered no platitudes about working for the people to act as their representative or trying to make their lives any better. He made it clear that joining politics and winning elections was simply a way of making money and asserted forcefully that he wouldn't bother doing it if he could not make any material gains through it. Further, he also implied that holding the post of the Sarpanch had come to be seen something of a family tradition whereby he 'inherited' it from his father. Clearly the delimitation exercise that changed constituency boundaries and reserved seats for members of the STs precisely in order to unseat such entrenched interests had not changed this sense of entitlement at all. The Congressman had continued to remain in charge by deftly occupying the post of Deputy to the newly elected novice member of the ST. When we expressed our astonishment at this level of cynicism, the responses from politicians across political parties, were consistently patronising. As a BJP leader in Rajasthan put it: 'One doesn't join politics for a noble and honourable life!' (*Sadhu aur udarta ke liye thodi na rajniti mein judte hain*). The reason for this, he went on to explain, was because, 'principles do not work in politics; you have to draw your own lines and destroy the lines drawn by others' (*Rajniti mein sidhant nahi chalti hain, is mein* line *bhi kheechni padti hain aur doosron ke line bhi katni padti hain*). This kind of cold-blooded cynicism about the nature of politics appeared to cut across all parts of India. Those who entered politics, despite having described politicians as thorns in the side of the body politic, explained their own decisions to join by politics by saying that a thorn could only be removed by another thorn. 'A young man who served as DMK treasurer in Tamil Nadu said without reservation, "Those who are genuine cannot face the election." The certainty in this formulation thus prompts us to query the reasons behind such an assessment of politics and those who enter it. What it is about politics that doesn't allow "genuine people" to function or indeed ideals to flourish?' (Carswell and De Neve FR: 26)

On this issue too, people used a wide variety of metaphors to explain what they meant. In Chhattisgarh for instance, one person said that politics was like a swamp (*daldal*) because it sucked you in the moment you stepped into it. 'People may be good to start with' said one man, 'but once they enter politics everything changes. Their language, their lifestyle, their clothes, body language, friends, every-thing changes. All they want to do is line their pockets' (*Sabhi neta apan jebla bhareke koshish karthe*) (George FR: 14). This metaphor of the swamp, as a foetid seduction was used to describe not only the murky waters of politics but also the helplessness of those who entered it, being sucked in despite their original intentions. As a middle-aged man said in a conversation comparing today's politicians with the past, 'We can't believe in politicians anymore. They seem to be innocent before they get to their post. But then they get to their post, and they become like a politician! All politicians are thieves and robbers' (*yella arasiyal vathigal thirudhargal*) (Carswell and De Neve FR: 26).

In Maharashtra we heard about the local multi-purpose credit society in which many well-regarded individuals had got 'spoilt' after becoming office-bearers. While people found the corrupting influence of politics inexplicable, they nevertheless tried to offer explanations.

For instance, in the same site, they explained that the leader of the Gadakh faction in the village, who was an artisan belonging to an OBC caste, was a close associate of a former MP from the district, even though the ex-MP was really the Gadakh's local rival. They claimed that the former MP had asked this OBC faction leader to take a loan unofficially on his behalf from a local credit society, and had then used the money himself and refused to pay it back. This obviously created trouble for the faction leader and so the ex-MP had reportedly agreed to bail him out in return for a switch of political loyalties. This convoluted and unconvincing account exemplified the sense of confusion that people felt about what went on between people in power. Money always seemed to be a factor, both to be stolen from public funds and as a way of bargaining between rivals. While people did not state it in obvious terms, it was implied that the former MP belonged to a higher caste and hoped to discredit the OBC caste leader publicly by pilfering funds in his name. New entrants into politics such as this OBC leader always needed to prove themselves as capable of handling power in the face of competition from entrenched interests and were often coerced into bending to the will of more established politicians, even if it meant giving up their party loyalties. Thus, personal political ambition was seen to override ideology associated with different political parties. A political career emerged as an end in itself rather than as a means to a loftier end. Furthermore, as is evident from this example from Maharashtra, the corrupting influence of politics could exist at any level, whether the management of a small credit society or a vast parliamentary constituency.

There were other ways in which people tried to explain the inexplicably corrupting nature of politics. The following story illustrates the specific reasons for why a woman in a small town refused to enter politics. She was a housewife whose husband worked as an agricultural assistant in the state government's agriculture department and also had substantial landholdings. The woman ran their readymade clothing store and had established an active women's self-help and savings group. She had contested the previous Panchayat elections against the present Deputy Sarpanch of the village. Though she lost the election, the NCP offered her the party ticket for the elections to the Panchayat Samiti, the second tier of the three-tier system of the rural local self-government in Maharashtra. She explained that she did not have the necessary financial resources to contest the election but the *taluka*-level leaders agreed to fund her campaign and help her in whatever way possible. However, she refused again, which some people explained, was a result of her perception of politics. She said that as an elected Panchayat Samiti member she would have had to go to party meetings and other such programmes and that it would not be proper to go unaccompanied by a male member of her family. Being a government servant, her husband could not accompany her, and hence, her eldest son would have to go with her instead. Furthermore, there were political and party meetings where women did not go, sending some male member of their family as their representatives instead. This would inevitably have to be her son. Since those present at such meetings reportedly consumed alcohol after they are over, there was every possibility of her son becoming a habitual drinker. She cited this as the main reason for her refusal to enter politics. She also explained that greater political involvement might lead her to neglect her children.

The anxieties of joining political life for women could be caused by small but not inconsequential worries of neglecting the family and the need for a male chaperone. A young Dalit widow in another state of India said,

> I don't know what all happens in politics. But I am sure that politics is not my game. It is for those who could mint money. Today money, muscle and mafia are the mainstay of politics. I have my three children to look after . . . what could I gain out of it? (George FR: 14)

But as the story here showed, a woman was capable of finding solutions to these problems. The *real* worry, as people said, was that her son would get corrupted in the process of facilitating his mother's political career. The consumption of alcohol was the material threat, but it also stood for a wider depravity that the mother feared her son would be corrupted by. It was stories such as this one that circulated widely and constantly that reinforced the perception of politics as something that should be kept as far away as possible from one's life. It is for all these reasons that one person said, using the English word, '*mujhe rajniti se* allergy *hai*' (I am allergic to *rajniti*) (Falcao FR: 11).

The cause for the irritation was the reality that was present for all to see. Despite legislation to encourage new actors into the democratic process, entrenched interests continued to hold sway. *Ek murkh se ninyanve bhudhimaan pete bharenge* (one fool feeds 99 clever ones) — meaning that the person who was corrupt was often a puppet in the hands of many more who controlled the strings. Some labelled this *Haan Sirji, Na Sirji rajniti* (Yes Sir, No Sir politics). And despite this, older upper-caste politicians resented the presence of the newer lower-caste actors in what they considered their arena. As one upper-caste Rajput man put it, 'They no longer go hungry for food, but they are now hungry for power' (*Bhookhe nahi hain phir bhi bhookhe hain*). But what disappointed many who belonged to the same lower castes as the new entrants into politics was that even a small taste of power was enough to extinguish the fire in the belly for social justice, which was replaced with desire for material benefits. 'There is a whole queue of Bahujans waiting for the BSP to win for this reason' (*Line mein hain*), one Dalit bitterly said of his compatriots.

No wonder then that a group of young women in Tamil Nadu described politics as a sewer (*sakkadai*) and politicians as cheats (*mosadi*). To most, *rajniti* was a blight on the country (*Desh ka kodh rog rajniti hain*) that contaminated everything. A woman in Rajasthan used a telling analogy to describe the change for the worse in politics and society saying: 'Earlier traders used to adulterate flour with salt, but now they don't bother with the flour at all and just sell salt in the name of flour' (*Pehle aata mein namak milaya jata tha, ab aate ke jagah namak hi bechte hain*). So noxious was its effect that it was seen to adulterate everything it came into contact with. Again, using an innovative analogy, people called politics *kanja ka tapka* referring to a type of drink made with carrots and buttermilk which when added to milk curdles it and renders it useless. The implication was that politics was a kind of adulteration of social life that made it futile. But others, perhaps in order to preserve some integrity in the rest of their lives, refused to accord politics such omniscient importance. These people insisted that ultimately there were only three things that human beings fought over: wealth, women and land (*jar, joru* and *jameen*) so the fight over votes was ultimately irrelevant. But while it was possible to believe this at other times, elections made the fight over votes all too apparent. 'This is the Politics of Liquor and Chicken' (*Daaru Murge Ki Rajniti*) said someone damningly. Others pointed out that the incentives also came couched in a threatening message that said, 'If you are with us, we will serve you cream, if you work against us, we will cream you' (*Agar aap hamare saath hain toh hum aapko doodh nahi kheer khilayenge, aur agar aap hamare khilaf hain toh hum tumhe cheer denge*). Whether the messages conveyed the carrot or stick, they manifested themselves in excess, reducing the gullible electorate to stupor or violence. A 25-year-old woman said,

> I hate elections since that is the time we have lots of quarrels at home. My husband is completely drunk for the entire period. Although he doesn't beat us he doesn't care for the family either and is submerged in some other world. I have seen many husbands beating their wives and children in our village. I just feel helpless when all this happens.

Elections thus seemed to distil the very essence of corruption and greed that people had come to associate with politics. But rather than being able to ignore it and put it to one side, the world of ordinary people inevitably came into contact with that of the politicians and was thereby corrupted. A lawyer summed up such electoral politics leading to a democracy as 'not a government of, by and for the people, but a way of ruining people's lives using a system that used people' (*janta ke raj mein, janta ke dwara, janta ki aisi ki taisi*).

Why, then, we may ask, yet again, do people bother to vote? Why do not more people think like the 65-year-old man who remarked: 'Politics is the most abominable thing in the country and elections are only means to extend that. Why should I waste my time on deciding which snake is the most venomous one?' Instead, despite their eloquent formulations and severe indictments about the nature of politics and politicians, people continued to participate in elections in high numbers. Was it because they thought like the person who said, 'When election nears, I think it is our chance to take revenge and show our power' or was it because of something more? We need to look at what happens on Election Day to understand this further.

As the evidence in this chapter demonstrates, the language of politics as it is used in India, serves as a useful entry point to probe further the ideas that people hold about politics. The ways in which terms are coined, learnt and circulated indicates the popularity of the ideas that take hold of the popular imagination and those that don't. With the discussion of concepts such as *dan* we saw how people take familiar and deeply understood concepts from different aspects of social and spiritual life and use them to reflect political values. Their dissection of the notion of *dan* inherent in the word *matdan* as a way of casting one's vote without hope of any material gains in return was an illustration of this. The imaginative parallels that officials and voters alike drew between weddings and election indicated how seriously people took elections — likening the giving and harvesting votes as contracting a marriage in the family — but also hinting at the festive character of the event itself. By taking people's own formulations as a serious object of enquiry and reproducing them in the original (rather than as reported speech) as we have done in this chapter, I am in agreement with Schaffer's take on political language among the Wolof speakers of Senegal. In his book *Democracy in Translation*, Schaffer observes,

> everyday political language need not always be viewed as something to be reconstructed. Social scientists can, alternatively, take political language — ambiguities, valuational overtones, and all — as an object of enquiry, and use this enquiry to gain insight into shared understandings about the political world (1998: xi).

This chapter has attempted to provide that kind of insight.

IV

The Polling Station

It was evident that for voters their experience of the process of casting their vote itself was a very important one in determining their enthusiasm for voting. The journey to the polling station, the way in which queues were managed, how polling officials treated the voters, the accessibility of the voting process, and the simplicity of the procedure were all important factors in encouraging people to engage with the electoral process.[1] It was on this day, more than any other, when people felt special and empowered as the most important actors on the political stage of the country, when they engaged with the state to *give* something rather than to receive. Voters everywhere seemed to be aware of the gravity of this right and their role and responsibility in discharging this duty properly. But for many of India's illiterate and poor voters, the journey to the polling station could also be intimidating because of its formality of procedure, the encounter with officials and the exposure it brought. The need to look presentable, to conduct themselves with dignity in front of the officials and other voters and not to make mistakes while voting were all worries that preyed on the minds of people. For middle-class voters, Election Day was perhaps the only time they ever entered a government school building and came into contact with members of the lower classes in their own neighbourhood with whom they would otherwise seldom mingle. From the point of view of the millions of officials who conducted the elections across the country, this day was one of reckoning, the culmination of many weeks of planning, training and hard work. It was their performance on this day that would be the ultimate test of

---

[1] It is interesting to contrast this with emerging reports of how people are humiliated and insulted as they stand in queue at local centres all over the country to get their Unique Identification Number (UID), something that is purported to give them greater dignity in the future.

their own abilities as well as the country's record for holding free and fair elections, which was so essential to its global reputation as a democracy. Officials felt this burden of responsibility acutely, and approached it with a mixture of excitement and adrenaline as before a big sporting event. For candidates, political parties and their workers, Election Day was a one full of nervousness and frustration. After months of relentless campaign-related work, Election Day brought with it a reprieve, when they had to restrict themselves to doing only a few circumscribed tasks such as encouraging voters to visit the polling station and manning the desks outside the booths but keeping a low profile in order to avoid attracting any unfavourable attention from keen-eyed and vigilant election observers in their area. Those with transport, therefore, often spent the day visiting various polling stations exchanging news and guesstimates on their mobile phones with other workers. And so, on Election Day the polling station itself became an important site where the voter, political parties and the state of India came together in conducting the business of democracy. Such a confluence of actors was rare in normal life and unsurprisingly created a culture and mood of its own. It is for this reason that we identified exploring the 'culture of the polling station' as one of our principal research questions to collect fine-grained data on Election Day.

The Run-up to Election Day

In Chapter 2 we examined the role that the political parties played in the weeks preceding Election Day. In this section, we will look at the part played during this period by the officials of the ECI who are ultimately responsible for delivering free and fair elections.[2] In an average national election, 11 million officials are on election duty and each of them has a specific role to play. The 543 constituencies with their 8 million polling stations are divided up according to a

---

[2] Article 324 of the Constitution of India vests in the ECI the powers of superintendence, direction and control of the elections to both Houses of Parliament. Detailed provisions are made under the Representation of the People Act, 1951 and the rules made thereunder. Under the same Act, the ECI nominates officers of the Government as Observers who report directly to it.

timetable of different phases of the elections to allow for movement of security personnel and monsoon winds. In 2009, the elections were held in five phases with some parts of some states covered by different phases (see Map 1.1). The national grid is divided across the states and in each of the 30 or so states of India and a Chief Electoral Officer is appointed (usually drawn from the Indian Administrative Service or the state administrative services) who for the duration of the election period is answerable directly and only to the ECI based in New Delhi. (S)he is thus relieved from other duties and obligations to the state-level administrative structure and also crucially, by implication, from the interference of local political bosses and officers. At this level, election officials work in tandem with the administrative and police machinery, many of who are drafted in specifically for election duty. Local-level officials assigned to election duty are drawn from a wide range of white-collar professions. Schoolteachers dominate this group, but it also includes clerks, bank officials, government employees in administrative posts, and so on. Duties are differentiated according to rank; for instance, bank officials perform the duty of patrolling magistrates or work in counting centres whereas a primary school teacher is likely to be a polling official. Within the world of officials, these distinctions are finely calibrated and the success of the polling process depends on getting these allocations right, as we shall see later. But, regardless of what their specific job is, election officials greet elections with a mixture of dread and excitement. 'It feels simultaneously like an exam and a wedding!' (*Yeh pariksha bhi hai or shaadi bhi!*) said one official in Madhya Pradesh.

Election duty can be an onerous affair for these men and women. The officials get paid very little for this extra duty and the state does not arrange any board or lodging facilities for them during the two or three days of polling-related work. To maintain neutrality in the conduct of elections, the process of 'randomisation' ensures that election officials are not appointed in the area they come from and that they do not know their allotted polling booth until they report for duty at the district headquarters the day before polling. Therefore, election duty inevitably involves travel to an unfamiliar area. While in the district capital, the polling officials have to make their own arrangements and their meagre allowance often gives them very little choice. The polling duty becomes particularly arduous for those appointed in far-flung areas that involve a long day's journey to get there. Once at the polling booth, officials have to rely on the goodwill of the locals for food and shelter. In a number of our research sites, the officials spent the night before polling day in the booth itself, often a building with intermittent or no running water or electricity. Given that elections are frequently held in the heat of the summer months, this is a physical challenge, especially as the approach of Election Day is source of stress and tension. No wonder then that officials refer to election duty as 'serving the nation' (*desh seva*) and elections as the 'great festival' (*chunavi mahaparv*) not without some irony. Given these circumstances, we may ask how the ECI manages to mobilise its huge task force, drawn from among public servants, to perform with an unmatched efficiency in the conduct of elections? This is an important question to pose if one recalls that the ECI was instituted soon after Independence when '[b]ureaucratic functioning was deeply afflicted by the two cultures in Indian politics. The modernist decision-maker at the level of ministries shared no common language with the village clerk whose ideas of social reasonableness were radically different' (Kaviraj 2003: 232). One answer lies in the constitutional authority of the ECI that gives it a wide range of powers during the electoral period in order to maintain the probity of the electoral process. It has the ability to transfer any partisan members of the administration who cannot be trusted with fair conduct or to design the election to be held in several phases, covering different districts of the same state at a time. This allows it to focus its entire energies and resources on monitoring the elections closely and intensively as they unfold. Regarding the performance of the election officials themselves, the Commission's biggest sanction is that they are all employees of the Government of India and are therefore subject to an annual review while still in service. Any mistakes made by them on polling duty lead to a black mark on their all important Annual Confidential Report (ACR), thereby adversely affecting promotion opportunities.

To prepare them for their duties, the officials normally attend three rounds of training. In Bihar we were able to sit in during the second round of training at the Chomu tehsil office and the following account describes what went on there; this is typical of a training session anywhere in the country. First, a presentation was made addressing all aspects of what to expect on Election Day and the preparations required to ensure the smooth running of the elections. Accordingly, the division of labour between the various officials in a polling booth was explained along with a description of the work allocated to each of the three polling officials (PO) and the presiding officer (PRO). Also described was the exact procedure that was to be followed every single time a voter entered the booth — their entry, verification of identity (which documents could be accepted besides the EPIC as permissible identity proof), the procedure for recording essential information on the information sheets with the appropriate symbols, how to mark the left index finger with indelible ink, and finally the importance of ensuring their utmost privacy while the voter cast their vote at the EVM. Officials were familiarised with the EVM using dummy machines and shown how to connect it, how to seal it with the different strips of paper and tags, how to conduct a mock poll to satisfy the concerns of the party agents, how to issue ballots, and finally how to turn off and seal the EVM. Foreseeable problematic situations such as doubt about the authenticity of voter's age, women refusing to unveil their faces for identification, or alternatives if the voter's left index finger was missing were also discussed and procedures to handle the situations were specified. The provision of 'No vote', i.e., an option available to voters to refuse to cast their vote once the ballot was issued in their name, and the procedure to be followed in such a case was also explained to the POs.

These training sessions were, for the officials, a little bit like being back in school. And they behaved accordingly! Given that several to-be PROs were schoolteachers, it seemed as though they were borrowing liberally from the repertoire of their students in their cocky questions, heckling but nervousness before the tests. The training provided was comprehensive but invariably rushed given the extensive nature of the rules and qualifications encoded in the election manuals. During the sessions, talking to the officials revealed that not many had a complete grasp of the all the complexities of the process and during the test, the officials freely asked each other for answers, even turning to visiting ethnographers for their input. Even those conducting the sessions were not always sure what the answers to some of the questions were. But in the end, it seemed to turn out well for the experience of officials who had served in previous elections helped them to do the right thing and to perform much better than their peers in the assessment viva. As a final resort, they were reassured that they could consult the rule-book if the need arose.

History

It has to be remembered that the experience of voters in 2009, who were able to successfully cast their votes in a streamlined and efficient operation such as the one we observed, was the result of many years of an evolving electoral practice. The use of EVMs at all polling stations instead of ballot papers, for instance, was the result of a long list of experiments that the ECI has been conducting with the technology of democracy. Since the first elections were held in 1951–52, the ECI had constantly struggled to design and deliver an electoral system that would ensure a free and fair election. For a newly independent nation, even the process of drawing up electoral lists brought unexpected problems. The first Election Commissioner Sukumar Sen had to stand his ground against Nehru's impatience to hold the first elections by insisting on redrawing the electoral lists when it was found that most women's names had been listed as the 'wife of' or 'daughter of' a man. The basic foundations of a new democracy could not be laid, he argued, on such a patriarchal challenge to the notion of a universal citizenship. Further, in this process were of course the very high levels of illiteracy in India (more than 80 per cent) at the time of independence that made even something as simple as the design of ballot papers a challenge. Four decades later, in 1990, more than half the population was still unable to read or write. Moreover, the large number of candidates and political parties meant that on an average, the number of candidates competing per constituency has remained above 10. The challenge was therefore to find a way to present the voters with their choices in a comprehensible form, while maintaining the secrecy of the ballot and delivering a solution that would work at a mass scale. The system unsurprisingly went through a process of trial and error several times.

One of the first innovations was the introduction of the system of electoral symbols to depict political parties, first on ballot boxes and then on ballot papers. This built on the colonial practice of colour-coded ballot boxes for each candidate. However, officials would also 'help' voters write the name of the candidate of their choice during the colonial period, which severely compromised secrecy. The system of electoral symbols solved the problem especially once they began to be placed next to the candidate's name on the ballot paper for ease of identification for those voters who could not read. The ECI has remained the ultimate arbiter in the assigning of symbols to political parties, although the latter have always been able to express their preference. Political parties in India have used these symbols to great effect, almost developing them as brands over the decades. The most well-known ones are the use of the *charkha* (spinning wheel) by the Congress for its popular association with Gandhi, variations of the hammer and sickle by the Communist parties and farming symbols by the newer pro-peasant parties. In addition to the symbols themselves, the colours in which they were designed have over time come to be associated with those parties — red with the Communists, orange with Hindu chauvinists, green with Islamic parties, combinations of colours such as red and black with the AIADMK, or saffron, green and white with various Congress parties, and so on.

As we have seen, party symbols are used liberally in all campaign materials; party supporters are encouraged to sport clothing, umbrellas, caps, and scarves marked by the party symbol and in the colours of the party thereby creating maximum visibility and subliminal awareness among voters during a campaign. Great play is also made on the names of parties and the symbols. For instance, Mamata Banerjee critiqued the mighty but alienated Congress through the adoption of the name 'Trinamool' ('grassroots') Congress for her new party and a logo depicting the same, famously designed by Mamata herself on the back of an envelope. Through this one detail, she managed to make a statement about herself and her new party — her artistic abilities and spontaneity in contrast to the high culture of her political foes in the Communist parties, the flowers in her logo that contrasted with the gritty hammer and sickle, and the grassroots nature of her party that hoped to be in touch with ground reality that the well-established Congress had lost touch with. Similarly, the emergent leader Akhilesh Yadav of the Samajwadi Party made the most of his party's symbol, which is a bicycle. In the two years before an all-important election, he cycled thousands of miles across Uttar Pradesh, India's largest state. By doing so he could convey a message about his down-to-earth nature, his accessibility, his desire to identify with the common person despite his expensive overseas education, and his youth and vigour with which he hoped to replace his ageing and unwell father as the head of the Samajwadi Party.

By the time the 1962 General Elections were held, the voting procedure had more or less come to resemble the system as it is currently conducted. It went through many changes, all of them aiming to make the procedure as confidential and easy to conduct for a large volume of voters as possible. With each iteration the paperwork involved has been steadily reduced while greater measures to protect the voter from the control of external authorities, inside or outside the polling station, have been introduced. The history of the changes are replete with examples of considerable attention to detail — the choice of a public building surrounded by an open space for queues to house the polling station, the decision to offer separate queues for women for their comfort and the design of the stamp with lines in a clockwise direction to detect irregular markings on ballot papers are all examples.[3] The two most radical and recent changes have been the introduction of the EPIC and the EVMs as essential elements of all state- and national-level elections and while both innovations were met with understandable wariness by voters, parties and officials alike, their uptake so far has been encouraging. Like many before these, the new practices have been introduced with specific goals in mind but they have stabilised over time depending on how enthusiastically they have been adopted by voters. For instance, when the EVMs were first introduced, many expressed fears about the possibility of tampering with the technology but illiterate voters in particular found them liberating because having to press a button was far less awkward than having to handle papers and stamps. By 2009, when the entire national elections were conducted using these, few questions were raised by anybody. But by far, one of the most ingenious procedures to be introduced in the Indian electoral process has been the marking of the left index finger with a vertical line across the skin and nail in black indelible ink. While this was introduced during the tenure of the second Election Commissioner to prevent voter fraud, it has taken on a life of its own over five decades. As we see through our data, it has become a coveted badge of pride across India that also creates peer pressure to go and vote. It is worth noting the fact that such a practice when it has been tried elsewhere in the world has failed. Bosnia tried the use of silver nitrate ink that was visible only under a special light but it turned out to be too complicated and unreliable, requiring special bulbs and other paraphernalia to detect it which went missing when they were needed. Elsewhere, people took exception to having their bodies marked, seeing it as an invasion of privacy by the state. However, in India, these factors have not come

---

[3] See Jaffrelot (2006) for a detailed account.

into play. The technology is simple — a little stick to dip in a bottle of ink is all that is required and the results are there for all to see until the ink fades off the skin after several weeks and the mark on the nail grows out with it. It works in India because bodies are routinely marked as a sign of participation in a ritual in various religions and cultures across the country — be it a thread tied round a wrist, henna on a bride's palms or the forehead marked by repeated bowing to the ground five times a day by a devout Muslim. In the same vein, to have one's fingers marked by black ink provided visible evidence of one's participation in elections.

The Day Before

The day before Election Day brought with it a mixture of relaxation for some and heightened activity for others. For election officials, it was possibly the busiest day of their year, the day of *samagri vitaran* (distribution of materials). These gatherings were huge as thousands of polling officials reported for duty, found their teams, located their assigned desks, collected the bag of materials required to conduct the polls, found their armed escort, and boarded the buses that transported them to their respective polling booths. The local administration organised these gatherings in large sports fields or other similar spaces and the atmosphere in the grounds was a cross between a village fair, school annual day and boot camp. At one end, under a huge marquee, officials were greeted with lists pasted on walls and notice boards with details about their assigned teams, polling stations and bus numbers. Desks where materials and forms were disbursed were set up at another end and an endless stream of announcements over the tannoy directed the gathered officials about where to go and which buses to board when. A first aid centre, water coolers, chairs, and the shade of marquees was also provided to the waiting officials. The *chunav samagri* (election materials) includes about 60 assorted items in anticipation of a variety of needs during the polling process. For the paperwork of the elections, there were multiple forms, stationery, tags, seals, and wax; and the all-important EVMs that had been extracted from the 'strongrooms' where they were stored between elections. The auxiliary needs of the officers spending the night at the polling booth were also catered to with medicines and mosquito repellents also being supplied. All these were packed into a white cloth bag that each team of polling officials was issued with, except for the precious bottle of indelible ink that was stowed away in the PRO's pocket. Mingling among them, it was hard to overlook the distinctive mood among these groups of men thrown together for the first time who would be spending the next 36 hours together discharging a most important duty. As the buses roared off the grounds in clouds of smoke and dust, one could not help but feel some pity and admiration for their passengers. We recalled the remark that one officer had made to us, referring to the coarse white cloth of the bag with all the election materials 'Look! They are sending us to our duty complete with our shrouds!' (*Dekhiye! Kafan ka kapada dekar bheje hai!*) (Singh FR: 23).

In the village the mood was altogether different as all campaigning stopped 48 hours prior to polling, bringing an unexpected silence after weeks of cacophony of the campaigns. Families remained tense as last-minute inducements by political parties left their menfolk in an alcoholic stupor and the arrangements for organising time the next day were discussed. Party workers used this time to hand out 'voter slips, i.e., small pieces of paper on which the party's (or alliance's) symbol and the candidate's name were printed on the left hand side and the voter's name, roll number and other details on the right hand side. While voters did not need such a slip to enter the polling booth to vote, in some places where parties had the manpower, they were widely distributed allegedly to speed up the voting process within the booth — with a slip, the voter could be swiftly identified, ticked off the list and allowed to vote. However, the distribution of voter slips also allowed parties to do last-minute canvassing work in the village and send out a final reminder to their supporters to vote the next day. For illiterate voters or those who were uncertain about the alliances that their party had entered into for the election, the voter slips provided an important reminder of the symbol that they needed to vote for as this was often the symbol of the alliance partner rather than their own party. In places like Allapuram, Tamil Nadu where most people were either AIADMK or DMK supporters, this was particularly helpful because the candidates for their seat often belonged not to their own parties but to the CPM and Congress, alliance partners of the AIADMK and DMK respectively. Reminding voters of the alliance symbols was doubly important in 2009 because these alliances were exactly the opposite of those at the previous election!' (Carswell and De Neve FR: 43)

The arrival of the election team in the village heralded the start of a liminal 24 hours in the village. Here is a typical scenario that we witnessed in our research site in Meerut district in western UP. On the afternoon of the 6 May the two polling parties arrived in a bus from Victoria Park, Meerut. The polling party consisted of a presiding officer, and polling officers 1, 2 and 3. In addition, a security team — one sub-inspector, three constables and two home guards — accompanied the polling parties along with a bus driver. The *patwari* or village revenue officer offered his services as a local guide to the team. He accompanied the party to show them the school building and briefed them about the village. The bus was parked next to the school at the southern entrance to the village. As soon the party arrived, the news spread like wildfire across the village, children being the chief messengers, and before long the husband of the *pradhan* (village president) came running to see them. The familiar school building was suddenly transformed into a site of great curiosity as a result of the strange bus parked next to it. The children surrounded the bus and groups of young men stood around discussing the polling party and the logistics required to house them for the night. They were interrupted by the *pradhanpati* (husband of the village president) who bustled in, ordering two Gujjar boys to bring string cots from the nearby houses for the guests to be seated, and returning to his home briefly to re-emerge with refreshments for the party along with some more young men. Rare treats of chilled carbonated drinks were produced, as were biscuits on the best china, in the makeshift sitting room set up in the schoolyard. The polling officers accepted these gratefully but then confined themselves for the rest of their stay to the school building, starting on the work required to convert two classrooms into booths 293 and 294.

A large proportion of the 8 million polling stations set up during an Indian general election are school buildings and across our 12 research sites, this was the case in most. These buildings are often the only *pukka* structures that the government owns and are therefore marshalled for a variety of uses throughout the year: for dispensing polio drops, voter IDs, holding Panchayat meetings, census-data gathering, etc. In fact, in a village at least, people are in no doubt where to go for any government-sponsored activity and head to their local school building. While on an ordinary evening the school grounds would be used by local children for cricket games, on the day before polling, access to the building was closed as the polling agents began their preparations for the next day and the night ahead. Being outsiders, making arrangements for the night and for meals was particularly tricky as accepting too much hospitality could be seen to be compromising. They were therefore careful to maintain a business-like manner and kept conversation with locals to a minimum though sometimes, the pupils of the school and local Panchayat members were drafted in to help. This involved cleaning, rearranging furniture, designating separate entry and exits to the booth, putting up posters, removing all campaign materials from the vicinity of the building, and making provisions of drinking water for the voters. Further, the area outside the building also had to be demarcated as a special polling zone in which all talk of 'politics' had to be avoided. 'A 100-metre line was drawn on the road to indicate the area within which no one was allowed to discuss politics or display party symbols on the day of election, as well as a 200-metre line further down the road, to indicate the wider area within which full law and order had to be maintained. No raised voices were tolerated within that area and if anyone created problems within this zone, they could be removed by the police. The officials were also required to complete some of the paperwork on this day — documents such as affidavits for individuals accompanying visually challenged persons, affidavits to be used in case the legitimacy of a voter's age was questioned, and so on' (Carswell and De Neve FR: 41–42).

In booths that were designated as 'sensitive' there was added worry about local tensions and outbreaks of violence in the charged atmosphere before polling day and all polling stations were provided with security personnel, mobile police teams and extra election officials on standby, in case the Zonal Magistrate felt the need to call in backup. A conversation with the police and a polling officer revealed how nervous they were before the day of elections. In our site in western UP, they were worried about the social composition of the village and sources of possible tension. The polling officers stationed in the booth, working as they did at the coalface of the polls, seemed distinctly anxious about the voters on whose goodwill they were reliant in order to conduct a peaceful and efficient election. In Bihar, at a booth where there had been a small fight between Hindus and Muslims on the day of polling a few years ago, there was an extra contingent of security forces, two of which manned the gate in the forecourt and two others the terrace that had been fortified with sand-filled gunny bags. In 2009, the ECI also deployed roving cameramen with video cameras to record any unusual happenings. In Rajasthan, two polling booths within our constituency under study were identified as 'very sensitive' (*atti-samvedansheel*) which seemed surprising given the apparently peaceful state of affairs. On enquiring as to why it was so, we were told that there were two cases in which a polling booth with no history of electoral violence is classified as 'very sensitive' in the EC's 'mapping exercise' in preparation for any election. One scenario was when the registered voters in a particular polling booth all belonged to the same caste. In such a case the chance of fake votes being cast was considered high, as there would be no opposition to challenge it. The second one was when the local population consisted mostly of people from one community but was not a completely homogenous group of voters. In such instances, the minority group was considered to be vulnerable to pressure from the majority to vote like them.

'At about 5 o'clock in the evening the Sector Magistrate (SM) arrived in a jeep on his rounds of all polling stations under his jurisdiction. He stayed long enough to make sure that the officers had everything they needed, paid them their honoraria (presiding officer — ₹1,100; polling officers 1 and 2 — ₹800; and polling officer 3 — ₹450), reminded them to complete the paperwork the same evening rather than leave it for the next day when so much else had to be done, went over these instructions twice, and disappeared in a cloud of exhaust fumes to the next polling station to do the same. The officers resumed their tasks and within a few hours the polling station was ready for the next day' (Kumar FR: 9–10).

Meanwhile party workers continued last minute preparations late into the night. In some places they didn't sleep at all and spent the night distributing liquor to constituents. While this had become common practice in many places, the police were reluctant to crack down on it owing to fear of reprisals from the party that came to power. Among the workers, on the other hand, an unusual combination of competitiveness and bonhomie across parties was created as they tried to find out the rivals' strategy while simultaneously trying to dodge the police. In places like Gujarat we found that all-night performances of *bhavai* (a local theatrical form in Gujarat) had been organised as entertainment, followed by the worship of the local village deity at dawn. 'In Tamil Nadu, despite heavy rainfall, a booth agent for DMK went from house to house to distribute voter slips for his party till 2 AM.' When asked whether he found this work exhausting, he said, 'we only do this once in five years but we have to do this because people expect us at their doorstep irrespective of how late we manage to show up.' He confirmed that by working through the night he had managed to cover all the areas, even the surrounding farms. 'I haven't even taken a bath yet as I have to be back at the polling booth by 6 in the morning! . . . But I will go to sleep after the booth closes and only wake up on results day!' (which was several days away) (Carswell and De Neve FR: 44–45).

Election Day

The day began early at 5 AM. Before the doors to the polling station could be opened to the public at 7 AM, a mock poll was conducted in the presence of the party agents who then 'witnessed' and signed a 'clean' machine, after which the EVMs were sealed. These party agents were those whose names had been vetted by the Sub Divisional Magistrate (SDM) on a list of names allotted to specific polling stations. The sealing process itself was an elaborate one. The first sealing strip was signed first by the party agent and then by the Presiding Officer. After the consent of the polling agents, a tag with the details of the EVM and Polling Booth was attached to the machine, which was then sealed again with wax and marked with a stamp. Finally, the flap of the EVM was shut, the address tag detailing its exact location on the day of polling was attached, and the machine automatically recorded the time that this process was conducted. After this was done, the wait for the voters began. Outside the polling station armed guards took up their posts. Posters detailing various aspects of the voting process were also put up. 'In Tamil Nadu we saw three posters that had been put up within the school grounds. Two posters were pasted on the veranda of the school building, one above the other. The top one showed the design of the EVM and the one underneath explained in Tamil how to cast a vote. The third poster was pasted on an opposite wall detailing the use of the EVM in English. In addition, another poster on the compound wall to the left of the gate provided information about the presence of observers, the importance of free and fair elections, and the availability of Form 17(A), which voters could fill out in case they did not want to vote' (Carswell and De Neve FR: 45). Each of these was an attempt towards greater transparency and information about the election process.

In the meanwhile, the voters too went through their own rituals of preparation. Election Day is always a public holiday in India. 'On the morning of 23 April in eastern UP, a 35-year-old Chamar youth named Amarnath who lived in the low-caste neighbourhood of Shahabpur rose early in the morning, took a bath, and holding a flag of the BSP, went to the memorial of Sangram Singh (a local freedom fighter) in the middle of the village's mango orchard and offered prayers. The evening before, he had 'accepted a bag' from the BSP, which indicated his willingness to serve as a polling booth agent of the BSP by carrying the bag of papers of the agent. He planted the flag on the *samadhi* and then went to an ironsmith's shop around 200 metres from the polling booth which was closed for the holiday, and sat down at the shopfront with his friends to chat. His friends Sohan, Kallu, Babban, Ramu, and Bhole were all between the ages of 20 and 25 years, all confident new activists of the BSP who had joined the party during its drive to include younger, literate and marginalised youth. This was in stark contrast to other political parties whose workers tended to be much older. As a local *pradhanpati* remarked caustically, "The BSP has started a factory for producing leaders and all young dalit boys are now becoming leaders. And it is not just dalits, many youths of other castes are also becoming important leaders of BSP." As local activists they had gained prominence and even the fear of the police by becoming important power brokers at the crucial local institutions of the block office, courts and schools. For these young men, Election Day provided an important performative platform to display their leadership skills and sobriety on an important public occasion. As a result, Amarnath and his friends were among the first to cast their votes at the polling station, after which they settled down with copies of the voters' list and a dummy EVM to help voters with last-minute questions before they entered the polling station' (Narayan FR: 15).

Voters knew that the polling station couldn't be far when they saw flags and bunting lining the way there. About 100 yards from the station, they came to desks at which workers from various political parties sat. Those who did not yet have their voting slips could collect them here. People could, in principle, go to any party's stall and not necessarily to the party they would be voting for, but there were people who wished to indicate their loyalty and the desks gave them an opportunity to do so publicly. In some areas we saw parties disbursing leaflets that resembled the EVM with the respective party's symbol and candidate's name indicated at the same point where they were on the actual EVM inside the polling station. This was to indicate to the voters where exactly on the EVM to press the button to vote for the party of their choice.

The dynamics around these desks were always worth watching, as they frequently encoded a multiplicity of meanings. Consider the following scene in Tamil Nadu. 'Around 6.30 AM on Polling Day, outside the polling station, just beyond the 100-metre zone, two DMK–Congress activists dressed in white *dhoti*s set up a desk and some chairs under the tree next to the small Ganesh temple. They sat down behind the desk with the voters' list in front of them and explained to us why they were there. Around the same time a second desk was set up under the temple tree, just behind the DMK–Congress desk. This was the desk of their arch-rivals, the AIADMK, manned by their own activists, to which AIADMK voters would come to collect their voter slips in case they didn't know their number. The KMP (a smaller party) had also set up a few chairs under a tree at the other side of the school, partly because there was no place under the temple tree and partly because they wanted to access voters coming from Thottampalayam and the farms, where they knew they had more supporters. By 7.30 AM there were two men in white *dhoti*s sitting at the DMK–Congress desk and about eight men around the AIADMK desk. Other party workers — all men — were squatting on the floor around and in between the desks. Many of them were party workers drawn from among the SCs dressed in their everyday clothes and none of them in *dhoti*s. Gradually, the first voters started to turn up: first, a lady by herself and then another, followed by two ladies walking together. Some people walked directly to the school to vote, while others approached one of the desks first to collect their voter slips or to ask for clarifications or just for a chat with people they knew. By 9 AM about 10–12 people sat around the AIADMK desk, with a regular flow of voters approaching. The DMK desk, on the other hand, seemed rather quiet with hardly anyone coming forward to collect their voter slips, but that was because most of the DMK slips had been handed out the evening before. The AIADMK desk, with lots of men in white *dhoti*s and lots of motorcycles parked around, looked rather intimidating and some women seemed somewhat hesitant to approach it. By 10 AM it got busier with more people moving between the desks and the polling booth. Some men and women came alone, others in small groups; activists went back and forth on their bicycles to drive older voters to the booth, and children played everywhere. By 1 PM activists reckoned that about half the votes had been cast. Suddenly, without any warning, A. S. Mani, the sitting MLA of the DMK party, arrived along with two other party leaders in three large four-wheel drives. They had a large group of men accompanying them and they all gathered around the DMK–Congress desk. Suddenly the air crackled with tension. For the first time during the day, the balance changed and the AIADMK table with its many activists and supporters suddenly looked small by comparison. The AIADMK people watched the DMK gathering intently, watching them swap news of turnouts and support from the other areas that Mani's entourage had just visited. They stayed for a few minutes before moving on but after their visit the DMK group somehow no longer seemed small or the AIADMK group overwhelming, and the atmosphere soon relaxed again' (Carswell and De Neve FR: 44–47).

The political parties thus played out their own election drama in the scene at their desks outside the polling station. It was a very public performance in which all aspects of their presentation — the furniture they used, the provision of shade and water, the freebies they gave away, the strength of people manning them, the crowd around their tables, and the visits of party heavyweights — were noted by passing voters and other parties. The use of a borrowed bench from the school building to the chairs hired from the local tent house could indicate the prosperity of the party. Even when work was slow, workers had to sit ever vigilant at these desks to show their loyalty and capacity for hard work. They stayed in anticipation of unexpected visits from candidates and future leaders, hoping to be noticed and given more responsibility in the future. Workers clustered around 'their' desks not only to visibly demonstrate their allegiance, but also to network, attract passing voters, hand out voters' slips, and to help them ascertain if they had the correct ID. Young men on motorcycles stopped by these desks briefly with news of turnouts, campaigns, swings, and incidents of violence elsewhere in the constituency. Political parties therefore utilised this forum to demonstrate their influence and organisation to the voters one last time before they entered the polling booth. But they also used this just as much to send out messages to their rivals. In Maharashtra, for instance, the Shiv Sena's organisational machinery seemed to be in a serious state of disarray on the day of polling. The only senior and experienced activist sitting on a ramshackle bench at a lone desk was a middle-aged farmer who had been with the party for almost 15 years. But when asked, he claimed that that the picture of disarray was deliberate because had the Sena's machinery appeared stronger, the dominant faction would have sensed the danger and swung into action thereby pressurising swing voters. So their nonchalance was a deliberate ploy to disarm the opposition. In Madhya Pradesh too, we witnessed a similar dynamic between

political parties, here between the Congress and BJP. 'The BJP table —
which began the day under a tent but was later taken down by the
order of the Collectorate, and then went up again —was manned by
an old retired schoolteacher, Masterji, and a young boy. The Congress
table was presided over by the young Municipal Councillor of this
ward referred to by everyone as Panditji. A couple of children helped
him at the desk, while another middle-aged Congress character, a
well-known contractor around the town, pulled up a chair nearby
and followed events. Many voters stopped by at these tables to confirm that this was the right booth and that they had the right slip to
show the officers. A few had to be told that they had not brought
the right documentation and would have to return later. On a couple
of occasions, when the party workers were sure that this was one of
their supporters, a young man would be assigned to run them home
on their motorcycles and bring them back. But some were less lucky,
such as a very old couple who had walked a long way but forgotten
their voting cards. They ended up hobbling back home and returned a
couple of hours later. The trader- and service-class voters came in by
motorcycle, typically with wives riding at the back. A couple of young
men came in on their own first, checked out the process, and only
then went back to collect their wives. As and when people stopped to
check their names on the voters' list or get voter slips made, Panditji
and Masterji would urge them to vote for their parties, asking them
to press the no. 1 or no. 2 buttons depending on whether it was the
Congress or BJP desk. Throughout the day various people who knew
the party workers stopped to chat. One young BJP worker who had
come from another station to this one for a short while insisted that
he could tell from their faces which party they would vote for, but
refused to explain what indicators he looked for. He could just tell.
But the old experienced Masterji said that was nonsense and that you
could never really be sure. The notion of an anonymous vote was, we
found, generally taken very seriously. Around noon, three old men on
their way back from casting their votes stopped between Panditji's and
Masterji's desks and began a conversation with both of them. They
were three retired schoolteachers and old friends — of whom one had
moved to a village after retirement, but still came to vote in Harda
— and were spending the day with their friends. They were former
colleagues of the BJP man and the teachers of the young Congress
worker and teased both of them now, scolding them for failing to live
up to promises. As their banter came to an end, one of them said to us,

"You have to keep at both sides. After all, only by flipping both sides can a *chapati* be properly cooked!'" (Krishnamurthy FR: 10)

Some political parties, depending on their resources, made an effort to urge people to go and vote on the day. These efforts ranged from party workers such as Dhankunwar in Chhattisgarh who went knocking on doors in her village urging people to go and vote, offering to babysit or bring in the cattle to free up women's time. In wealthier scenarios, parties offered to provide transport to people who were either too infirm to make the journey to the polling station or needed persuasion. The unusually continuous supply of electricity and water, the holiday, the hot weather, and family gatherings were significant disincentives! Therefore, depending on the party's wherewithal, cycle rickshaws, jeeps and tractors, adorned by the colours and symbols of the sponsoring party, plied the roads all day to transport people, dropping them off outside the 100-metre radius of the polling station. Almost everywhere, this boosted turnout figures considerably. Given that this would strictly count as campaigning, election observers would be within their jurisdiction to ban it, but on the whole they looked the other way as ultimately it bolstered the electoral process and vehicles seem to carry supporters of all kinds irrespective of their party affiliation. Significantly, we saw very few instances where even the old and infirm were also given lifts *back* to their homes, thereby highlighting the naked instrumentalism of party politics. The case of Dakkad ji in Rajasthan was a poignant illustration of this insensitivity among others too. 'Dakkad ji, whose voter ID card indicated she was 80 years old, had been brought to cast her vote by some party workers. Once at the school building, she was faced with a long walk across the yard and a flight of steps (or a very steep ramp) to reach the polling booth. After much effort a breathless Dakkad ji managed to reach the polling room, cast her vote and come out. While she rested outside some women asked her in whose favour she had cast her vote. Dakkad ji very matter of factly said that she did not understand how the EVM worked so she just pressed the first button on it. In the meanwhile, as some people were making attempts to find Dakkad ji a vehicle to take her home, they were greeted with the welcome sight of a jeep approaching the polling station. It was a press jeep from which about half a dozen journalists descended. They surrounded Dakkad ji asking her questions about her age, why she voted, etc. For the ideal photo to accompany their story, they wanted her to pose in front of the polling station and so old and hunchbacked Dakkad ji made the arduous trek back to the building but this time, extremely excited at the prospect of her photo being published in the newspaper. But as soon as they had got their scoop, the journalists zoomed off as quickly as they had arrived, leaving Dakkad ji to trudge her way back home' (Falcao FR: 24). Elsewhere we found people having gone to enormous lengths to be able to present to cast their vote. In one extreme case a man in Kolkata had arranged for an ambulance to bring his mother to the polling station from her bed in a hospital. All over India, migrant workers routinely travelled to their rural homes where they were registered as voters, sometimes in perilous circumstances, travelling standing for hours on overnight trains and risking the wrath of their employers just so that they could cast their votes on Election Day.

Despite all the drama going on outside the polling precincts, the atmosphere in the courtyards of the school building was solemn. People tended to form orderly queues, waited patiently even when they were long, spoke in low voices, and kept conversation to a minimum. Even those people we had spoken to before smiled at us in recognition but seemed disinclined to chat. The sobriety of the occasion was particularly noticeable given that most other social gatherings in India are noisy affairs. 'But here at most people discussed the sudden change in weather or something similarly innocuous. One woman explained this disinclination to make conversation by saying, "It would create competitiveness . . . we don't want to create a bitter relationship with people from other parties. We just stick to making jokes!" Further, it was as if the act of travelling together to vote, of queuing together and sharing the experience created a different sense of bonhomie. Mr Shanmugam, a Gounder activist and booth agent for the DMK pointed out: "Look, people of all parties are standing together, activists of the DMK next to those of the KMP. Political relationships are different from personal relationships. We don't have that bias in us. We differ in political opinions, but not otherwise". And the sight of people from different social strata together standing shoulder to shoulder in two queues, one for men and one for women, was indeed remarkable and discussed by many. In Tamil Nadu we witnessed the wealthier Gounders to the middle-ranking Nadars and Barbers to Adi Dravida Christians and SC Matharis all milling about together' (Carswell and De Neve FR: 48). In the state of UP, one Chamar woman pointed how significant this social mixing was given how rare it was the rest of the time. In rural India, at Panchayat meetings or religious gatherings it was still customary to sit with one's caste group and in urban centres too, people were usually divided by class regarding where and with whom they mingled. The low-caste Chamar woman therefore said: 'I realised the value of casting my vote through the experience of standing in the same line and the same room alongside people of other castes'. She added that this was an unprecedented privilege for her because in her natal village that was Jat-dominated, her caste members had been forcibly kept away from voting and had never been able to make it as far as the polling station, and so her own first time experience of visiting the polling station felt momentous. In another part of the country, an upper-caste Rajput woman commented that in *her* natal village that was Rajput-dominated, it would have been impossible to imagine that one could be standing right next to a Chamar woman in the *same* queue. Thus the queue itself represented a microcosm of the political equality that elections created. In a society deeply divided by caste, the polling queue created an unusual communitas.

When voters finally entered the polling booth, they were greeted by a row of four desks at which sat the polling team. First of all, under the watchful eye of the Presiding Officer, the first polling officer checked the name and other details on the EPIC, matched it with the voters' list and then loudly announced the name of the voter so that the polling agents of different political parties who sat outside the room could tally it with their voters' list. After this, the voter moved to the second polling officer and presented the ID card so the voter's identity could be verified and recorded on the voting register (17a) with the details of the nature of the ID proof used. The voter was required to sign or put a thumb impression against his/her name and was then given the official chit. It was the task of the third polling officer to apply the mark with indelible ink on the index finger of the voter before he/she could walk over to where the EVM had been placed, shielded by a piece of cardboard to preserve secrecy. Only one voter was allowed to cast their vote at a time and in case of any questions, the presiding officer was available to explain the working of the EVM. The atmosphere inside the polling booth was calm and unhurried. Voters were not rushed and yet the entire process of checking their ID to pressing the EVM button was dealt with quickly and efficiently. Occasionally we saw polling officers discreetly announcing their own party loyalties — a saffron pen used by the BJP-sympathising officer was an example. But on the whole, the process was largely neutral. After casting their vote, the voters exited the polling booth through a different gate than the one through which they had entered to allow for a smooth flow of traffic.

Voters looked immensely relieved as they emerged from the station, clutching their precious voter ID cards with newly inked fingers. And the experience of voting was seen to be transformative in some fundamental way. One of them said jokingly: 'After this mark, we are all similar, and have become equal after voting. Each vote has the same value, no matter whose it is. That makes us all equal today.' For first-time voters this was an important rite de passage and they looked relieved to have made the transition to adulthood successfully. Emerging from the polling experience, one voter remarked, 'That was like being in the *garba grha* (sanctum sanctorum). The EVM is like a god who is sitting inside and no one except the devout can enter. Even the priest (i.e., presiding officer) has to sit outside of this area'. In fact, this particular aspect of the voting process, that of the secrecy of the ballot, was an aspect that many people talked about and valued above all else. For instance, one woman in Madhya Pradesh, the least literate among a group of four, who had been particularly nervous about the EVM and whether she would be able to work it out without assistance, strode out of the exit of the polling station with the greatest confidence and a triumphant smile. When asked which button she had pressed to see if it had been the 'right' one, she shot back immediately, 'Why does anybody need to know that? I know what I did!' It was as if once she had been through the experience, it further emboldened her to not compromise on the secrecy of her ballot.

For those who were unable to vote, the day took on a wholly different flavour. In the majority of cases that we saw, it was because they had the wrong form of ID or had been unable to get their EPIC cards made in time. In Delhi we met a woman who could not vote because her name as spelled in her voter identity card was found to be different from that in the voter's list. So she went to the desk of the Congress party to notify them and the workers there in turn called the election in-charge of the area and went to the concerned booth to argue for the authenticity of the voter ID and after a long discussion she was finally able to vote. One young man who struggled in vain to find his name on any voter list at various polling booths found the whole process not just disappointing but also humiliating and embarrassing. 'I have been made to seem such a loser' (*mera to pappu ban gaya*). In Chhattisgarh, about a third of those who voted were allowed to do so on the basis of other means of identification such as a ration card, BPL card, NREGA card, etc. Elsewhere though we saw people turned away even when they produced their ration cards. One such poignant example was the case of Kankuba, who was widely known in the area as she provided little pots of drinking water to the thirsty near the bus station in return for a few pennies that some gave her in return. Her name was on the voters' list but she did not have an EPIC and so brought her ration card along instead. But she was asked for a photo-identity, as the ECI had identified a list of photo-identity documents such as a driving licence, property documents, PAN cards, government identity cards, Job cards, etc. as acceptable evidence. 'Sahib', she said, 'I have never had a photograph taken of me in all my life. Please read this ration card, it shows my name on it. Please let me cast my vote as I don't have money to make any other sort of *dan* [donation] so at least let me do the *matdan* [donate a vote]'. When the officer still refused, she left in a huff brushing back tears, saying, 'If you don't care about an old lady coming from such a far distance I also don't want to care about you'. Like Kankuba, women all over the country faced a similar problem for very few ever had their names in the property documents, and there was no question about them having a driving licence or PAN card as most of them were daily wagers, and women often didn't even have the identity cards called Job cards of the NREGA. The only document they had was the ration card, which did not however carry a photograph. Part of the confusion arose from the fact that many voters (and even booth officers we talked to before the elections) were under the impression that they would be able to use their ration card as a form of ID — as they allegedly had been able to do in the past — only to find out that it was unacceptable this time around. This in turn led to comments about the ECI having become stricter, even though there were rumours that ration cards were being accepted elsewhere at the discretion of the presiding officers. In the end, the 10 per cent figure that shows up in the NES survey of people who could not vote because of the lack of proper identity, were people like Kankuba and others who fell foul of this confusion. Elsewhere we found a 65-year-old man, who had been similarly turned away, waiting in the veranda of the school for three hours in the hope that the polling officers would change their minds and leaving shattered when this did not happen. But even when people had the right papers, unexpected complications arose, as with a young man in Rajasthan. He had brought with him three types of identity cards because previously he had not been allowed to vote because of inappropriate IDs. To ensure there was no trouble this time he made several trips to the block office to correct mistakes in his voter ID card, till finally, just a day before elections, he was assured that there would be no problem in casting his vote. On Election Day, however, when he went into the polling booth he was turned away, because the photo on the voters' ID list did not match the one on his ID card. Much confusion ensued till finally the SDM was telephoned and clarification on the case was sought. He was finally allowed to vote and when we spoke to him he said with a great sense of relief: 'I am glad I could vote, one has to vote out the government in order to prevent them from becoming a monopoly'.

As we have seen in this section, the polling station is a site where one can observe in real terms the overwhelming enthusiasm that exists in the Indian electorate about being able to vote. In the instances in which people were unable to vote for a variety of reasons, what was striking was that in most cases they had tried everything in order to be able to, and sometimes at considerable inconvenience to themselves. It would therefore be expected that if these efforts did not bear fruit we could expect them to express their irritation and annoyance with the system. However, we often found them in tears experiencing a profound sense of failure and humiliation that indicated that they invested far more meaning in the exercise than as a mere bureaucratic formality. In the same fashion, those who were able to vote did not just seem relieved to have got it over and done with, but expressed a sense of exhilaration at having accomplished something deeply meaningful.

For the polling officers, the atmosphere remained filled with tension throughout the day, as everyone concerned concentrated on following the ECI guidelines strictly, keen to avoid any errors or cause for complaint. The polling officers generally refused offers of food, for consuming the salt of a host's food was considered to create a tie of obligation in many Indian cultures and the officials were keen to avoid such debts to local party workers. They satisfied themselves with endless cups of tea and cold drinks instead. The presence of 'micro observers' at the station as well as the unexpected visits by roving observers fuelled this tension further. As researchers we experienced this tension all too personally. Almost everywhere, local presiding officers were often reluctant to allow us to enter the polling booth, take photographs or speak to the officials. This was despite written permission from the headquarters of the ECI in Delhi that allowed us to do just this and we too did not have photographic evidence attached and attested on these letters. Fear of being caught out in what they saw as transgressing the strict ECI rules was overwhelming. One could see why election officials had described conducting elections to taking an exam.

Towards the end of the day, the numbers of voters tended to surge. In several places we saw people literally running to the polling station, jumping fences and taking short cuts to make it there before the doors closed. As the evening drew close, everyone looked visibly exhausted and happy to finish the polling, and as one officer remarked as he locked the door to the polling room: *Hathi nikal gaya hai, aab toh sirf poonch rah gayi hai* (The elephant is nearly through, just his tail remains). As the remaining paper work got done, and the EVMs sealed, the atmosphere finally lightened. The officials looked relieved and even slightly sad that the extraordinary camaraderie created among them through sharing the election duty had now come to an end. 'Here we flow together like a river, but when we leave this booth, we will all revert to becoming separate tributaries' (*yahan par toh hum sab pani ke jaise hain, bahar ja kar saab apne apne rang mein dhal jayenge*), said one officer. The paperwork usually took until 6 PM when the patrolling party transported the EVMs back to the strongrooms where they would be stored until counting day.

'Vote Puja'

In the city of Kolkata in West Bengal, people often call elections 'Vote Puja' (vote worship). While this is a tongue-in-cheek label for the seemingly endless effort put in by politicians to garner votes, the witticism also captures something of the atmosphere of the day. Much like any other public holiday, Election Day brings with it a similar holiday spirit. Besides the effort of voting, the rest of the day provides a sudden mid-week reprieve, an opportunity to catch up with friends, cook a special meal and take an afternoon siesta. In rural India too, we saw that people who could afford to, did not in fact return to the fields after casting their votes, and used the opportunity instead to spend the rest of the day enjoying family reunions and a shared glow of a community activity well performed. For most women, the trip to the polling station was also 'an outing', a legitimate reason to travel beyond the confines of their dwellings with their friends. For young brides who were married outside their villages, Election Day provided an excuse to visit their natal villages and see old friends and relatives. Accordingly, to do these precious outings justice, women took care with their looks and clothes. Some wore new outfits and make-up, particularly young married women. The older women, too, were in their new or 'best' clothes. In most places women tended to vote in the second half of the day as they tried to complete most of their household chores and caring for their children before leaving the house. Rambati, a Gujjar woman in her mid-40s in western UP summarised it all:

> It was a hectic day for me since I had to finish all the household work in addition to bathing, wearing make-up and making sure that I had a new sari. It took me the entire morning to wind up the household chores including taking care of the cattle.

While men tended to come alone or with their wives, women also travelled to the polling booth in groups of four and six or sometimes even more. With their arrival, the sombre polling station would be transformed as their colourful clothes, black *burkha*s (veils), embroidered *chadar*s and flowers in their hair added instant colour to the otherwise drab courtyards. Little children sometimes accompanied their parents to the polling station and were keen to be taken just as seriously as the adults. One five-year-old girl in Gujarat came with her mother, dressed in her best *chaniya choli*, holding a passport-size photograph of herself, and demanded that her finger be inked just like her mother's. Election Day therefore took on many layers of meaning, echoing other festivities and special days on the calendar.

It was therefore particularly productive to pose the question — 'why do you vote?' — to people as they emerged from the polling station. The experience inside the sanctum sanctorum and the excitement and relief of having accomplished the task made even normally shy or disinterested people loquacious as they used flamboyant metaphors and eloquent language to describe the importance of what they had done. For instance, Dayavati Ahir — an anganwadi worker in Khanpur — felt that her vote was a contribution that she as a citizen of India had to make in order to maintain her citizenship and in return for what the Indian *sarkar* (government) and *desh* (country) was doing for her. She said:

> I have got a job and am being paid by the *sarkar*. I have a ration card and ID that gives me identity as an Indian citizen and the *sarkar* is

doing so much for the poor and putting lots of money into development of villages. So it is our duty to vote. It will help to elect a leader who will participate in the government and help villagers in many ways by bringing good government schemes for village development. If we do not vote, how will the government be formed? So it is our moral duty to vote and it is up to us whom we vote for. This is our right.

When we asked a middle-aged lady emerging from a polling station in Kerala to explain how her single vote could possibly make a difference to the results in a vast constituency of millions of voters, she shot back: 'Even an atom is small, does that mean it does not have any power? My single vote is like an atom; it may be small but it packs a lot of power'. In eastern UP, Sugiya, a 62-year-old Dalit woman, put her reason in different philosophical terms. She said that the politicians were doing what was their *dharma* (moral duty), i.e., ruling the people, so it was important that ordinary people did what was theirs, i.e., casting their vote. 'In Tamil Nadu, we had another set of responses that reinforced the spirit noticed elsewhere. "It is a sign that I belong to this nation; if I don't vote then I don't have an identity . . . It is our right, it is our duty." When asked to explain why it was a 'duty' a young man said: "it is our duty to elect our leaders. I feel empowered to choose them." Clarifying this sense of empowerment, another lady added that rather than this being something imposed from the top, they felt an ownership about this duty: "If there is something in my house, then we say it's mine, well it's the same with the country . . ."' (Carswell and De Neve FR: 47) In the next chapter, we shall examine the implications of these responses in greater detail.

Conclusion

As we have seen in this chapter, voting day was a day like no other in people's calendars. It marked a fairly unique moment in their lives when they were able to experience what it is to be 'king for a day' (*ek din ka sultan*) in a fairly real way. And this sense of popular sovereignty was created mainly because of their experience of the voting process itself. Being able to vote on equal terms with every other citizen of the country regardless of gender, caste, class or any other marker of social status provided a rare opportunity to see the principles of equality enshrined in the Indian constitution actually put to practice. As David Gilmartin observes, 'the tension between the people as a sociological construct at the time of elections and as an ineffable utopian ideal nevertheless remained critical to the structuring of sovereignty. Only by standing apart from both state and society, could the people serve as sovereign. And yet, only by making their voice heard through elections, could the people rule' (2007: 56). Given the otherwise widespread social inequality of everyday life in which people faced discrimination on one ground or the other, to be treated at par with everyone else on this one day had immeasurable value. The polling station became a site of social levelling, when in the presence of the state and society people could stand apart from both. Regardless of the clothes they wore, the quality of their education, their skin colour or their age or gender, they mingled and queued to form a sovereign collectivity. It is difficult to think of any other context in Indian public life in which there is such a visible and palpable assertion of popular sovereignity.

Further, the officials who conducted the elections also strove for a standard of efficiency otherwise largely unknown in Indian life, which made the whole process of voting fairer. The assiduous maintenance of voters' lists, the voter awareness drives and the rolling out of the EPIC scheme gave any voter who had the right identification the guaranteed opportunity to vote. But most importantly, the fact that they seemed to turn away anyone who did not have the correct identification, regardless of how important they were or how 'well-connected', gave the ordinary person, the *aam admi,* an all too rare confidence in an institution that was genuinely universally available to all. The fact that the secrecy of the ballot was maintained even after the introduction of EVMs boosted voter confidence even more. Given that incidents of 'booth capturing' and voter intimidation used to occur within living memory in some parts of India, the genuinely free and fair nature of the 2009 elections was valued by most.

The importance of voting day was of course much greater because of its stark contrast with all other aspects of electoral politics. Unlike the noisiness of the weeks of campaigning that preceded it, this day was unusually quiet and sombre. Campaigning was also dominated by the antics of politicians and their supporters who tried every trick in the rule-book (and those that they could hide despite the rule-book) to persuade voters, intimidate opponents and blow their own trumpets to garner votes. Their one and only goal was to win the election at any cost — as a result the naked instrumentality of the tactics that they used to feed their greed for power lay exposed. In contrast, voters very rarely stood to gain anything material from casting their votes. Of course people voted to support particular candidates or parties but there was also a widespread understanding that regardless of who won the elections the lot of the common person was unlikely to improve much from one election to the next. Voting for the average voter was therefore always an exercise of hope rather than one in guaranteed dividends. Instead, their showing up to vote was a statement of a combination of motivations. There was instrumentality of course — to elect a leader who would represent their interests and address their needs — but also much more. These latter, less manifest reasons are what political scientists and others would call the 'expressive aspects' of voting namely, the feeling of having done something good and virtuous by voting.

For such a sense of participation to flourish, it was vital to have others present and it was therefore no wonder that people on the whole enjoyed being seen to vote and made others noticed their participation. The anthropologist Victor Turner (1974) coined the word 'communitas' to describe the feeling shared by the participants of a ritual and defined it thus: 'Communitas is the mode of social relatedness during liminal moments is, a "community of feeling" that is tied neither to blood or locality' — which is strikingly similar to what Indian voters say about the atmosphere at the polling station. The bonds of communitas, Turner argued are 'anti-structural in that they are undifferentiated, equalitarian, direct, non-rational . . . Social structure is all that holds people apart, defines their differences, and constrains their actions' (ibid.). As we have seen in this chapter, the queue at a polling station facilitated 'direct unmediated communication' between individuals free of social structure and generated a rare egalitarianism among the participants, overturning the hierarchies of the normal social order. In this Indian voters were not much different from their Swiss counterparts among whom, rather astonishingly, turnout rates at elections dropped when a postal ballot was introduced as an experiment. While the authorities believed that the convenience of voting from the comfort from one's home might encourage people to vote, in reality the opposite was true. In the *gemeinschaft* world of Swiss cantons, people enjoyed the feeling of community that the collective exercise of an election brought and the shared experience of voting together at the same place heightened that feeling (Dubner and Levitt 2005). I would argue that in India, this shared sense of communitas was extended beyond voting day itself by the black ink mark, which continued to testify to its bearer's participation for several weeks after the event. As one voter said only partly in jest: 'After this mark we are all one, and have become the same after voting. One vote has one value. That makes us all equal today'.

This chapter has shown that voting day was one such moment in the ritual of elections. We saw how people valued the unusual nature of this moment, in its expression of the elusive ideals of equality and fairness. A shared feeling of communitas marks them as discussed in the section on the atmosphere of a polling station, and this quality provides a critique of social structure and strains towards universalism and openness. The weeks of campaigning that culminate in Election Day are marked by communitas that suspends the rules of normal social order and brings instead a rare flowering of egalitarianism. This experience in turn heightens people's awareness of their most fundamental and universal attributes as a citizen of India. It therefore has the potential to be ultimately transformative and revolutionary.

V
Why Do People Vote?

Having considered various aspects of the electoral process so far — the campaign, the ways in which ordinary people talk about politics and politicians, voting day, the experience of voting, the role that officials play in conducting the elections, and the shared feeling of communitas that elections in all their carnivalesque nature bring — we can turn our attention to the reasons that voters cite for why they vote. 'Why do people vote?' was one of the key research questions that this project explored and the results of what people said when asked this question are presented in this chapter. By evaluating the answers we aim to get a better grasp of the meaning that a vote holds for people and thereby hope to strengthen our understanding of one of the least understood, yet key, aspects of a more substantive view of politics and elections.

But let me begin with an ethnographic vignette from eastern UP that provides a flavour of the sort of conversations that were sparked when someone was asked 'why do you vote?'

Vignette

In the burning sun of the afternoon of 16 May 2009, when votes were being counted for the general elections, we caught Ali at his tube well outside the village. Ali was waiting for the errant power supply to come back so that he could re-start irrigating his sugarcane crop. While we sat on a cot in a thatched hut next to the tube well, his cousin brother Hasim also joined us. We started the conversation asking if Ali voted in this election since we had not seen him at the polling booth on the polling day — 7 May 2009.

'I was out of the village on the election day', Ali replied quickly. Before we could ask next question, Hasim interrupted, saying, 'Well, he would not have voted even if he had been in the village at the time of voting'. Hasim's tone was sarcastic and he also sounded angry. We could see that Ali was not very comfortable with this interruption, and was trying to avoid looking at Hasim, who went on: 'You see, he is a very selfish person and does not want to contribute anything to the country and government', looking pointedly at Ali.

'That is not how it is', said Ali, finally breaking his silence. 'I really did want to cast my vote. But I had an urgent business in Mawana. This is the first time I did not vote; otherwise I cast my vote in each election whether it is a village panchayat election or a Vidhan Sabha election'. Ali was defensive but his cousin was unrelenting and remained critical. In a long, heated conversation in which we had to calm Hasim and Ali down several times we discovered much about how these two barely literate young men in a village in eastern UP felt about politics, democracy and elections.

We found both Ali and Hasim agreeing on the point that casting vote was their fundamental right and the only right they had that could not be questioned by anyone. As Ali emphasised: 'I can vote for anyone. I am free to vote, and I should not waste it. I can cast my vote at my will. No one can force me to cast vote in his/her favour'. Through his voting right, he felt he was a free citizen of India and contributed some-thing to the country/*desh*. The right to cast a vote gave him recognition and the sense of being a citizen of India. And the people of Khanpur added, having gathered round to participate in this intense conversation between the cousins, they felt pride and honour when they exercised this right with freedom.

On the polling day, we had seen Hasim and his family come to cast their votes. This was quite remarkable, as it was the time to sow sugar cane and they would have taken valuable time off to come to the polling station. We met others who had travelled from the nearby towns where they worked to come and cast their votes. Interestingly, many of them were Chamars who were so angry with Yogesh Verma and the performance of the BSP that they made it a point to return to the village just to cast their vote for the Congress candidate. Everywhere there was a remarkable commitment among the voters, who had all made sacrifices of time and money. Hasim and his family clearly believed that voting was as important as sowing the crop and so had started their sowing especially early to make time to vote (Kumar FR: 6–7).

As we shall see such conversations were not uncommon and the complex triangulation of motivations that we witnessed in the above incident was evident among people across India. In this chapter, I will tease out these different motivations to examine them in greater detail in order to provide reasons for *why India votes*.

While we now have excellent data showing correlations between the socio-economic groups, residence patterns, education levels, gender, and voter turnout, we continue to remain unsure of why some people vote more than others and what they think they are doing when they vote. As noted before, Indian citizens have plenty of reasons to be dissatisfied with the performance of governments and they do not hold politicians in great esteem either. Why then do they bother to vote? And why do poor people vote more than middle-class ones? And why does 80 per cent of the population continue to prefer a democratic albeit inefficient system to an efficient authoritarian one? (Lokniti 2008; NES 2009). Given that the aim of this project was to go beyond the formalist aspects of elections and to investigate the meanings and motivations that would explain high voter turnouts in India, it seemed important to ask people for their explanations directly. We decided to explore this question by posing it directly to people in as many words. As noted in the Introduction, elections are a good time to ask people about politics as the buzz of an election campaign appears to make everyone more loquacious than they otherwise are, including ordinary voters. In Gujarat for instance, people offered a wide range of different reasons for voting — 'to make a king' (*raja banaye bar*), 'everyone votes so I do too' (*sabjan bot deethe tau hamuman deethan*), 'to elect my leader' (*apan neetala chunhe bar*), 'to get my favours' (*hamar kaamla baayebar*), 'to turn the right candidate victorious' (*sahi ummedwarla jitayebar*), 'to express my opinion' (*apan matla jatayebar*), 'I have a right to vote' (*bot deyeke adhikar hai*), 'to make a government' (*sarkar banayebar*), and 'to vote for our country' (Jani FR: 7). As we shall see, in this chapter, these reasons for voting were not confined to Gujarat but offered across the country.

To start with, let us look at the reasons that we expect people to give for voting. These are reasons that political scientists are already familiar with and are the ones that are attributed to voters generally, but here we wish to consider popular formulations in the original to see if they add further nuance to our understanding.

Resignation

For many, especially women, they voted out of a sense of inertia, out of a feeling of not having any choice in the matter. When asked, a group of women in Madhya Pradesh who earned a few rupees every day by mixing grain in a trader's shop replied, 'We always vote . . . Oh, we just do. People come, round us up in rickshaws and trucks and tell us that we must vote. So, we vote'. When asked if it meant anything to them they said, 'No, not really. I mean, what do we get? Who gives the poor anything anyway? Nothing, we get nothing. But we vote anyway'. While these women did not make much of the act of voting, as we can see, behind their inertia there was also a sense of resignation (*majboori*) that was echoed by others elsewhere in the country. 'What else can we do, there is no other way' (*Aur koi chara nahin hain, kya karen*) is how many put it. But others also felt a sense of compulsion more prosaically. In Gujarat, an old woman was under the impression that voting was now compulsory (an idea that had indeed been floated by the chief minister of the state) and another one who insisted that 'someone had come from the government and told us that they will stop our *anaj-pani* [livelihood] if we didn't vote'.

It was worth noting that these sorts of responses came from women, and could easily give the impression that women were less politically aware than men. In some cases, we saw illustrations of these. 'In the same constituency on Election Day we met an old woman who rushed in and made it through the doors of the polling station minutes before it closed. When asked why she had bothered with the effort she said rather candidly, "I didn't want to vote but my husband scolded me and told me if I didn't go and vote then the government would punish me; so I came running out of fright". We decided to follow this up and visited her home the following day to quiz the husband. He laughed loudly, "Yes I indeed got angry with her and told her that government will punish you. Had I not told her this she would have not come to vote". Then added rather patronisingly, "We have to use these tactics with our women otherwise they waste their vote. They don't understand that this vote is worth crores of rupees". Inevitably, statements such as these from men have tended to convey the impression that women in India vote because they are told to do so, and this might be one of the reasons why women nearly equal men in voter turnout figures nationally. In fact, we found that in some places women were so used to being told who to vote for that they did not hesitate to ask for the advice even of the visiting researcher: "why don't you tell us who we should vote for" (*aap hi bata dijiye kisse vote karein*)' (Jani FR: 8). This did not come altogether as a surprise for we were aware that large numbers of women, especially in more patriarchal settings, remained cut off from public life and discussion and relied on men for news of the outside world.

Yet, as ethnographers, we also knew that *all* women were unlikely to be so susceptible to men's diktats, and so we continued to probe this issue further and we shall return to it later.

Instrumentality

Predictably, a second set of responses to the question 'why they vote' were along the lines of what the rational-choice theorists have taught us namely, that many people use their vote instrumentally, to get something. As a young man in western UP put it bluntly,

> I will vote for the leader who will save me from the *pilkhan* [police] and who will get my work done in a government office. I was thrown out from the post of an operator in the village powerhouse. Nobody helped me. I met Dr Yashwant Singh Rana, a BSP minister, who helped me to get a job. So I am in his debt and I have to repay it. In addition to this, BSP is still in power and will remain for a couple of years [in the state government]. I do not want to spoil my relationships with Yashwant who helped me when no one else did. He can also help me in the future. In fact he is the one who can save me from the arbitrariness of the police, and I will vote for him openly (Kumar FR: 8).

This man's explanation clearly illustrated how voting for someone was a way of paying back a debt of gratitude. For many in rural India, their lives were inextricably linked to the institutions of the state as they need to access loans, permits and allowances, and each and every household is connected in one way or the other way to local government offices. Their illiteracy and 'knowledge deficit' forced them into positions where they required the patronage of those who could give them access to the world of application forms and information and who were therefore essential for survival. Promising them their vote therefore became a strategy to build links with political leaders and get acquainted with the local officials who frequented the offices of political leaders for immediate and future needs.

In order to do so, however, it was also important not just to vote for that person but also to be *seen* to be voting for a particular politician openly, which meant that one declared publicly who they were going to vote for rather than keeping their vote secret. By doing so, one could, as this young man did, not only pay back the debt to the politician in full public view but also as a result exert subtle pressure of a noblesse oblige on the politician and his agents to continue to help him in the future. His less subtle urban counterparts, in Delhi, labelled this reciprocity a 'deal' between voter and politician.

In some cases the nature of the exchange could be immediate rather than a deferred promise. So in return for voting for a candidate, voters could extract immediate material benefits during the campaign period itself — a constant supply of electricity and a relaxation of patrols on unauthorised encroachment of land and the dreaded 'ceiling' drive on properties of illegally utilised properties were some of these. This betrayed the cynicism with which voters held politicians, not trusting them to honour their promises in the future and preferring to close the transaction in the here and now. Inevitably, money too entered into the exchange. *Jo dega vo payega* (Whoever gives [money] gets the vote) said one person bluntly, and another added that elections were a sort of 'business opportunity' for the voters to capitalise on the vulnerability of the vote-seekers. *Yeh election ki raunak hai*, he said meaningfully, indicating that elections wrought their own magic. But this seemingly clear-cut transactional exercise of 'vote-buying' as much as vote-*selling* was blurred by further elaboration. Equally nonchalantly the same men continued to say that ultimately, they took money from all the parties who offered it and after doing so cast their vote not to the highest bidder but by taking into consideration what they enigmatically termed 'other considerations'. It is no wonder then that political parties increasingly consider buying votes as the least reliable way of winning elections. In his conclusions based on a comparative discussion of vote-buying in several democracies, Frederic Schaffer notes, 'vote buying is far from a surefire strategy — even when accompanied by a panoply of instrumental, coercive, and normative strategies to boost the rate of compliance among voters. Where balloting is at least intermittently secret, many people defect' (2007: 186). What these discussion and statements show us is the following: people vote out of a sense of obligation and as a way to show their appreciation for any material help that they receive from political parties. The reason why they vote therefore has something to do with whom they vote for. But by qualifying that they do not always vote for the same party that gives them the largest material benefits, they suggest that there might be more to their rationale for voting.

In Tamil Nadu we heard of similar instances of incentives being offered. 'We were told by many different informants (from all parties) that the January 2009 state by-election in Tirumangalam (Madurai) where Alagiri (son of Karunanidhi) was the DMK party organiser was fraudulent: 'This [bribery for votes] started in Tirumangalam election — [people were given food and] under the banana leaf there were two coupons [which you can fill in and get something that will be paid for by Alagiri] and ₹2,000'. Details of the amounts paid varied, with figures of up to ₹7,000 being quoted. While some told us that bribing for votes was only possible in local elections and by-elections but was impossible in national elections as it would be simply too costly, there is evidence that such fraudulent practices did occur in the 2009 elections. We came across cases of migrant workers in Tiruppur returning home to Madurai *because* they were expecting to be paid ₹1,000–2,000 by the DMK. Prabhu, a tailor from Madurai, went home to vote and ended up getting ₹500 for his vote — and he did vote for DMK. But what was interesting was that on the whole the majority opinion was that bribing voters just wouldn't make sense, partly because an MP candidate simply could not afford to pay people over a large constituency, and partly because they would lose real voters. Mohan, a party worker, explained: "Now we've got genuine voters, but if I start giving money, they will always expect money and it will become difficult to manage. So, we wouldn't want to create such a situation"' (Carswell and De Neve FR: 25). While such pragmatism on the part of party workers could be expected, the response from voters themselves to such blatant attempts at buying their votes is even more startling. As one poor woman said to us,

[i]f you were as poor as us and never got to eat meat or buy a sari, then you too would accept them if someone was handing them out. But what on earth does that have to do with whom we vote for? We will vote for who we want; my vote is too precious to be bought for a litre of kerosene!

What this woman was trying to explain was that monetary incentives by political parties did not function like other gift-exchanges in which a sense of obligation was created by accepting a gift. Instead, because there was such an overwhelming consensus about politicians being corrupt and stealing public funds — 'they take half of our tax for their personal use' — their handouts during election campaigns were seen as a small payback of that loot which required no reciprocity and certainly not with something as disproportionately valuable as a vote.

Loyalty

In several parts of India, people also had predictably straightforward reasons for voting: it was to see their choice of leader or party in power. The details of which parties were considered suitable varied across the country but the common motivation for voting was *who* they were voting for, i.e., a particular party or candidate. People in the state of Gujarat, for instance, stated this plainly: 'We have come to vote because we want to see Narendra Modi [the state Chief Minister] as the winner. And our family supports BJP so we have come here to vote for the *Kamal* [i.e., lotus — the election symbol of the BJP]'. Further questioning revealed that they had no idea about the name of the particular parliamentary candidate they had voted for. As one woman put it, 'I just saw the symbol and pressed the button' and then added brightly, 'I think it was Narendra Modi's name written on the machine'. These women were very clear that they wanted Narendra Modi to run Gujarat and even though they were voting in a national election in which Modi himself was not even a candidate, they intended to vote for his party in order to keep his opponents out. A local BJP worker added the gloss, 'We should vote to make the lotus bloom in Gujarat and to stop the dark forces from impeding the development process in Gujarat'. As is evident, especially from the gloss, the loyalty to a particular politician or party (Narendra Modi and the BJP in this case) could be because of their particular charisma but also because they stood for ideas that could easily be challenged by others. Some people therefore used their vote to keep out such challenges at all levels of government. This commitment to a particular kind of politics was evident in the reasons that 30-year-old Gorelal Ratnakar, a landless agricultural labourer in the state of Chhattisgarh, gave: 'to vote for the party that will keep the communal and casteist forces away from power'. He went on to explain:

> I vote for the candidates who are devoid of communal and casteist feel-
> ings since these two aspects divide our society. Caste has been a factor
> of dividing human beings right from the beginning of history. I wish
> to see a government free of the caste and communal bias. Communal
> and casteist parties don't do any real work but just make a lot of noise
> and engage in anti-people activities. I vote for the creation of a secular
> government where every citizen will get equal right to live and self-
> respect (*izzat*).

This young man's involvement in Dalit activism had given him an added eloquence and so he was able to explain his support for a certain kind of politics of equality rather than one particular political party, whereas others explained their loyalty more simply for certain candidates and the parties that they belonged to.

Protest Vote

Commentators on voting behaviour have pointed out that in India, voters tend to alter who they vote for depending on which tier of democratic elections they are voting in, and the difference in how people vote in state and central elections has been an important one. Utilising national elections to send a message to the state legislature or vice versa is in fact a well-established feature of Indian elections (Yadav and Palshikar 2009). This trend was in evidence in 2009 too as in our site in western UP, where we found many people were very critical, disappointed and angry about the performance of the incumbent MLA of the Hastinapur constituency whom the villagers had voted for in the 2007 state assembly elections. The incumbent MLA from the BSP had not visited the village once in the two years since then which was in stark contrast to the weeks preceding the election when in his search for votes he had spent considerable time in the village hanging out with everyone and eating in the homes of poor farmers and labourers. But since then, he had not made even a brief visit or shown his appreciation for their hospitality and their financial contributions to his victory in any way. As a result of this, the voters in Khanpur were looking forward to the Lok Sabha elections in which they saw an opportunity to teach the party of the errant MLA a lesson. In Chhattisgarh, a similar warning message was directed at the Congress. A 75-year-old man made this clear in explaining why he would vote and who he would vote for and it is worth considering his quote in full to understand his frustration:

> In Chhattisgarh we know the BJP will win and I will vote for BJP this time round. But before this, in every election we have always voted for the Congress. But the Congress has now ruled for longer than they deserved to. We didn't benefit from the Congress rule in all these years. I was landless when they came to power and I am still landless. Congress lost because of whims and fancies [*manmanapan*] and

gautiagiri [a state where one individual has a hold on land and other resources and the rest of the village particularly from the lower-caste background only works for them as bonded labourers]. Sycophancy [*chamchagiri*] is another reason for the deterioration of Congress. The British looted, but the Congress *raj* has plundered us. They failed to remove untouchability. Untouchability is still vibrant in our village. We aren't allowed to dine with others, and in case we are invited to some auspicious ceremonies they ask us to either bring our own plates or wash them after eating. Even when they serve a cup of tea we have to wash the cups ourselves. Satnamis also do the same with us on many occasions as we are considered much below them in terms of caste hierarchy. In all the village functions we are asked to stay at a distance. In earlier days we were the palanquin (*palki*) carriers. We had carried a number of *palki*s of Gautias and Malguzhars. For this we used to get some small remuneration annually. These days we don't have that work anymore yet the people at the top still associate us with that kind of lowly work and want us to remain without any land and resources. Most of them are from Congress. They can't fulfil our hopes and aspirations of a better future for future generations. That is why I will vote. I will vote for a change so that my hopes and dreams can be realised for my grandchildren at least. Still I believe that the government could do better for us. I supported the Congress for many decades, but now I will vote for the BJP to see if they could bring in a change in our status (George FR: 11).

In this tirade, the man's anger and bitter disappointment with the Congress for having failed to live up to its reputation as a party for the poor was evident and worse still, its complicity in perpetuating old social hierarchies was evident. By describing the Congress Party's tenure in the state as Congress *raj*, he wished to indicate its over-long stay in power and his own intention to use his vote as a weapon to send them to the opposition benches for a while. His decision to vote for the BJP therefore had nothing to do with his hopes for that party as being the better bet for social change, but merely as a foil to teach the Congress a much needed lesson. Clearly he was not in a minority as the Congress lost seats in Chhattisgarh.

We found a similar anti-Congress sentiment at play in our site in Maharashtra where we found that lots of caste Hindus voted for rival parties mainly to ensure that the Congress did not get elected. They cited various reasons for voting against Ramdas Athavale of the Congress among which was his alleged misuse of the Prevention of Atrocities Act in the Pandharpur area and the possibility that this would happen again elsewhere. Yet at the same time, there was no particular enthusiasm for his main opponent Bhausaheb Wakchoure of the Shiv Sena party. Rather, voting for him was regarded as choosing from the lesser of the two evils and a way of keeping the Dalits from gaining influence through a Congress MP, who they were sure would get the lower-caste vote (Datar FR: 4). By choosing to support a non-Congress candidate, the upper-caste Hindus hoped to reign in both the power of the Congress but also those of the lower-caste voters whose support it enjoyed. In Bihar, a conversation with some Muslim 'bunkers' revealed that they intended to vote against the Hindu nationalist party if only to make a dent in their support base. As they put it 'Whether we vote or not, someone will eventually form the government. But if we haven't voted at all, i.e., for the opposition, it could be assumed that we voted for the BJP' (*Chalo hum bhi vote nahin diye toh koi na koi toh sarkar ban hi jayegi na. Aur agar hum bhi vote nahin diye toh iske matlab hai ki hum log ka saab ka maat hai uske saath hogaya*) (Singh FR: 17). In this example, the vote against the BJP was not as much to limit its chances of winning but to ensure that the party did not get the impression that most of the votes had been in their favour. For this reason these voters felt that it was important for the opposition parties to also register a significant number of votes, even in their defeat.

Thus, as the examples here show, people preferred to use their vote to send out a message against a party, however dominant, rather than not vote at all. In the first two examples, the defeat of the Congress candidate had less to do with enthusiasm for the BJP or Shiv Sena than the electorate sending a message to the Congress; in the last one, the vote was an assertion of a negative vote against the BJP by Muslim men. But there were other reasons behind this type of 'negative voting'. In fact, in the same research site in Maharashtra, we came across an elderly farmer who lived in a Congress-dominated area and said that he always voted for the underdog, namely, the strongest non-Congress candidate. The reason for this was simple. If the candidate won, he would have contributed to his victory and if he lost, he could have the consolation of having won some votes at least. This way, as the farmer's young companion, a shopkeeper explained, the Congress would always be kept on its toes and other parties would always feel encouraged to contest. In contrast, in the Delhi constituency where we conducted our study, voters seemed to do exactly the opposite by wanting to maximise the utility of their vote by voting for the winning candidate. The undecided voters therefore waited to see which way the wind was blowing by talking to the people in their neighbourhood and then choosing to vote with the majority, in a sort of self-fulfilling way. As these examples illustrate, the motivation to vote was strongly fuelled by the desire to vote for a particular person or party, which in many cases was not in fact the party one necessarily supported. Instead, the calculation of choice depended as much on which party the voter wanted to punish or warn or indeed thumb one's nose at. As NES results show, only 30 per cent of respondents mentioned leadership as an issue that decided whether they voted for a particular party, indicating that several other factors were taken into consideration.

Affectivity

We also found in some sites that anger towards the party one normally supported led to a full-fledged 'vote boycott' (vote *bahiskar*), with people refusing to vote altogether.[1] In our research site in Bihar, people had decided to use their right to abstain as a political statement. To mark their dissatisfaction with the poor performance of their party, the RJD, two-thirds of Yadavs chose not to vote at all rather than transfer their vote to some other party. Recognising that a boycott was meaningless unless organised as a collective action, they said, 'What will one person's abstention achieve!' (*Ek insaan se kya hota hai, kya milega bahiskar se*). So despite the complications that inevitably arose in organising such an effort, it was done and the results showed up duly in the NES survey data as a low turnout among the traditional supporters of RJD and Lalu Prasad Yadav.[2] But what was notable was how regretful people were of having to take this step. We talked

---

[1] The colloquial term was the pun *matdan* which meant 'to vote' but when disaggregated to *mat dan*, it meant 'do not vote' (*mat* = do not *dan* = give).

[2] On the other hand, the traditional supporters of the JD(U) — the Kurmis, Koeris and Muslims — voted in high numbers thereby ensuring the convincing victory of the incumbent state government at the national elections.

to some people in two other villages where they had done something similar during the previous elections and they made it clear that their action was not something they were proud of and described it as an act of desperation (*majboori*). They had decided to boycott the polls in the hope of exerting pressure on the party to build a bridge across the river that passed through their village. One of the villages had got their bridge, but the other one did not. So the action seemed to not guarantee the desired outcome and instead intensified the feeling of shame. Using an analogy of maternal attachment, one person said, 'For us not to vote is like a child to be separated from its mother' (Vote *na diye toh aisa laga jaise maa se baacha bichad jata hai na*). In the 2009 elections too, we saw people begin to waver in their decision not to vote as the polling day came closer and without declaring it revoked, several people in the *baniya* caste and among the Bengali community, i.e., those who were not OBC, quietly went and cast their votes.

A further range of explanations offered for voting was out of loyalty to a community, an issue that both the earliest and current studies of elections in India had identified as important (Chandra 2004; Kothari 1970; Weiner 1957). As a local in Rajasthan puts it neatly, 'A Jat gives his daughter in marriage and his vote in an election to only another Jat' (*Jat apni beti aur apna* vote *sirf Jat ko dete hain*). With a nod to these local sentiments of electoral endogamy, the Congress, BJP and CPI(M) duly selected Jat candidates to maximise their chances of winning among this numerically dominant caste group. When other parties such as the BSP nominated a Rajput candidate instead, this was with the express purpose of reflecting their alternative policy of putting up higher-caste candidates in order to expand the social base of their support. It was no surprise that they did not win. The need for such loyalty and its translation into votes was inevitably affected by community leaders (*samaj ke bade, gaon ke mukhiya*) and directed in particular towards women. For women in turn, such as those we also met in Bihar, voting was often seen as an extension of their marital (*pativrata*) responsibilities. This is not to say that they didn't have political opinions or were hesitant to discuss politics.[3] Women almost everywhere were able to speak quite eloquently about their

---

[3] As Oldenberg points out 'less than 2% of electorate got direct advice on whom to vote from caste and community leaders' (Krishna 2010).

demands such as BPL cards, schooling and hygiene, and were able to keep sight of the issues that were going to affect their daily lives despite the cacophony of voices from various parties. But in a number of cases their marital, kin or community loyalties determined whom they actually voted for.

The relationship between community and vote though, as we know from Rajni Kothari's prescient remarks, can be more a complex than straightforward match between the caste of the candidate and that of the community of the voter. As he put it, 'politics is affected by caste but the reverse is also true' (in Yadav 2010). One significant way in which we can see how caste is affected by politics is by observing how much the act of voting *together*, as a group, was valued by people. Regardless of whom they were voting for or whether they were using their votes instrumentally or not, the elections marked an important moment to express and make manifest a generic collective identity. The vote in these cases became a modern extension of older rules surrounding marriage and commensality that were practised to express group solidarity. It was as much an expression of a general sense of collectivity as it was an assertion of any particular identity. As a middle-aged man put it, 'We need to stand by each other together' (*Hum agar hamare log ke saath hi nahin khade honge toh kis ke saath honge*).

Thus, interestingly, and perhaps surprisingly, such positive feelings towards group solidarity for voting were not always about *whom* people were voting for but *why* they were voting at all. Several people remarked on how the mere fact of having their name on a voters' list itself created a sense of community. Consequentially, those whose names were missing from the list felt left out (*samaj ka hissa nahin hain*) from the pre- and post-poll discussions. People who were not a part of the buzz of the elections felt it acutely, and an informant in Bihar put it thus: '*Log ja rahe hain, ho halla ho raha hai,* police *yahan bhag rahi hai, log yahan bhag rahe hain, toh hum bhi saath ho lete hain, hum bhi* vote *daal aate hain kabhi kabhi, par jab dhoop tej hoti hai toh, toh nahin jate hain*' (Everyone goes to vote, there is excitement, the police is running around, people are rushing around, so we also join in the melee, we also go along and cast our vote, but not of course when it is too hot!). People participated in elections as much as they would in any other communal activity, and 'being there' in a performative way was valued. 'I vote because everyone does it', as someone put it simply. Evidence from our Delhi site also showed that while not everyone was persuaded by others about their choice of candidate, they were certainly affected by a general peer pressure to vote. Another expressed this feeling of being swept along with others by a wave thus: 'If all sheep and goats are going to the well then why not us too?' We might therefore rightfully ask for the reason behind such a feeling of compulsion. Can India's high turnout rates be put down to a herd mentality?

Peer Pressure

The issue of peer pressure to vote needs further examination. Our data consistently showed that people in India voted because they thought it might look bad if they didn't do so. This came as something of a surprise given that in most other democracies no one is ever able to establish whether you have voted or indeed cares very much. However, as research has shown, such a desire to be seen to be voting is not confined to India alone. Some years ago, in Switzerland, for instance, an experiment with postal voting was abandoned after it revealed that despite the greater logistical convenience of a postal ballot, turnout figures actually dropped. The reason was that in the small world of Swiss cantons, people knew each other and wanted to be *seen* to be publicly performing this act of civic participation. In Indian elections, we came across similar peer pressure which was in fact somewhat unwittingly further enhanced by a small procedural detail. During his term in the 1960s, India's third Chief Election Commissioner S. P. Sen Verma had introduced the use of indelible ink to avoid voter fraud. As a result, since then, the left index finger of every successful voter's hand is marked with a short line in this ink. While its primary function is to prevent the same person from being able to vote twice it has also emerged over time as a sort of electoral stigmata that was coveted by Indian voters. To not be able to display it once polling had started led to endless solicitous enquiries from neighbours and others and as a result many preferred to go and vote if only to avoid those awkward questions and even a potential social boycott by the majority who had bothered to vote.[4]

---

[4] Schaffer (2007) reports that in many countries such as Kenya, Mexico, Pakistan, Djibouti, Sri Lanka, Panama, Namibia, Guatemala, Afghanistan,

This humble ink mark also had a curious levelling effect. One young woman in Tamil Nadu said proudly as she emerged from the polling station, waving her left hand: 'After this mark we are all the same'. The experience at the polling station where everyone, regardless of any other social identity, had been counted simply as a voter and nothing else reinforced this extraordinary feeling of equality. As a young Dalit law student in Chhattisgarh said, 'I enjoy the identity of being equal with everyone at least for one day' (George FR: 11). This sentiment was echoed in a wide variety of ways across the country. 'Priya in Tamil Nadu said, "I am happy I have voted — it gives me some pride"' (Carswell and De Neve FR: 20).

For everyone, without exception, the source of this pride lay in being counted as a citizen of the country. As one person explained, 'Once we vote then our name gets recorded in the government's register (book) and because of this we are accepted as the citizens of this village by the Government. And then only will everyone in the wider society (*samaj*) know that we are the citizens of this Sardoi Village'. Being registered to vote and successfully having one's name recorded on an electoral register gave people a sense of legitimacy of being fully accredited members of the Republic of India. That the electoral roll was a public document and available to anyone to consult made this legitimacy even stronger as it proclaimed people's citizenship without them having to lay claim to it. As a young woman Hiral, a first-time voter said, 'I wanted to feel that experience [of voting], I wanted to press the button on EVM and I wanted to see how it functions. I am very happy because from now on I will be considered the citizen of this country'. Such bureaucratic existentialism was therefore another crucial factor that motivated people to vote.

Perhaps more curiously, such official recognition also led to a more general existentialism as voting seem to lend people's lives greater meaning. Consider the statements in the next section regarding voting and citizenship by a cross section of Allapuram's population in the days before the election.

---

and Papua New Guinea, there have been allegations of 'removability of ink marks with bleach, abrasives, or just soap and water' (ibid.: 187). But such allegations are rare in India, no doubt less for the lack of effort than for the quality of the ink.

Voting for Citizenship

'Vijay, who came from a family where everyone votes, said: "We are nothing if we don't vote, we are not worth anything if we do not vote". And his father added: "Only dead people will not vote. If you don't vote, it means you are not living". The implication of these statements was that voting not only concretised one's identity as a citizen, but also as a living sentient being. A lower-caste woman in the main village similarly stated: "It is our right to vote; if you don't vote, then it means you are not alive. Only those who have died will be removed from the list. There is no meaning to life if you don't vote". Her statement further clarifies that rather than the expected causality of "I am alive therefore I vote", these Tamil voters were in fact stating the opposite.' Even Gurusamy, a Gounder farmer with no particular party loyalties or interest in politics had this to say:

> There is no respect for us if we don't vote. There is no meaning in life if you don't put a vote. If I don't vote, it's like I am dead. It isn't that we vote for a good person or a bad person, but it is our duty to put a vote. They [i.e., the politicians] earn lakhs and crores and we don't benefit but still we vote (Carswell and De Neve FR: 19).

In these statements, a strong sense emerges of how voting in an election is life-affirming and to not vote is to be as good as dead. What the people here are implying of course is that the ECI regularly purges electoral rolls of dead voters and so to be inactive and not vote is equivalent to being like a dead voter. This idea was reiterated by a middle-aged man from Gujarat who said:

> A person who votes is considered as a human being. If we don't vote then we will not be considered part of the community called 'human'. If one wants to live a proper life then he has to prove himself to be part of it. And if we don't vote then what is the difference between human beings and the animals? I vote because I am a human being and I have the right to choose a government of my choice. Have you heard of animals going to vote? (Jani FR: 9)

Thus, as we can see, far from being driven by a herd mentality, the ability to vote was one that several Indians saw as their defining human quality. At the heart of this pride in asserting citizenship was the foundational right of universal franchise that qualified every adult Indian, without exception, to vote. Thus when people were asked why they voted, some expressed surprise. *'Kahe nahin dalenge vote, hamara adhikar hai. Janam siddah adhikar hai,* vote *toh dalenge hi'* (Why wouldn't I vote? It is, after all my birthright) is how people put it. However, when asked what would happen if they didn't vote they replied: 'The only consequence of not voting is that one has not utilised the right to vote, that's all. Each person has this right, so of course we take it, but we don't worry about the consequences' (*Vote na dene se kya hoga, adhikar ka prayog toh karenge hi na . . . Aab apna adhikar hai toh le lete hain . . . par sahi kiya ya nahin, ye kuch nahin dekhte hain*). And several people put it in emphatic terms: 'Vote *toh debe hi karo'* (Of course I will vote), because exercising this important right was an end itself.

One of the most striking findings of this study was that even people with little or no education were aware that the right to vote was universal and available to all. 'We heard more than one illiterate person say to us, *Bote hamar maulik adhikar hai* (Voting is my fundamental right). Dhankunwar Pankaj is one such example. A Dalit mother of four, she is also an active member of the Dalit movement in her area in the state of Chhattisgarh. She outlined two reasons why she voted: "It is my right to vote. It is part of my fundamental rights embedded in the Constitution and also it is my right to get my rights". When asked to elaborate on her rights, she answered quickly: "the right to development, the right as a woman, the right to live, the right to work, the right to see that my village and community is properly developed, and the right to have a safe and secured future for my children". She was clear that by exercising her right to vote she could activate the other rights that she had enlisted. But she also clarified that she wished that the right to vote for a candidate could also be linked to calling back a non-performing representative. As she put it:

> We believe that the elected representative should work hard for the people. If we can't call back the elected representatives who doesn't work for the people, then there is no meaning of democracy as such, we must have the right not only to vote and elect but also to remove the person from his power and position so that he or she understands the one singular fact of being accountable and responsible towards the masses.

To this end, she had along with her colleagues prepared a pamphlet during the election with a charter of demands which included: (*a*) the right to call back the elected representatives through a plebiscite and (*b*) the addition of an extra switch on the EVM with the heading "None of the Above".

Later in the day, while talking to one of her colleagues, she clarified the point further: "vote is my fundamental right and it is also the way I could express my power and politics. This is not like other means of *andolan* [movement]. Voting is a different *andolan* expressing the power to throne or dethrone someone to or from power'" (George FR: 10). What was interesting about Dhankunwar and her compatriots was that they were aware of their constitutional rights. Second, they did not see voting for someone as a passive activity whose performance they had to live with but were also actively engaged in thinking about modifying the system to make it even more reflective of their demands. Further, they also made a distinction between foundational rights of franchise and other rights. In their clarifications they explained that they in fact had no right to make further demands on the state if they did not exercise the one right that the state facilitated so effectively. As noted before, the credibility of the ECI runs high among the electorate and elections are considered to be genuinely free and fair. Thus, by availing of this rare efficiency of the state, voters could enter into agitations for more elusive demands easily and with enthusiasm.

We had similar discussions in Tamil Nadu too, with people with more education. 'Karpagam, a first-time voter studying at a teacher training college when asked why she votes replied: "It's our right, so why should we give it up? The only right of Tamil people is the vote, so why should we give it up?" When we saw her again a few days later she added, "I'm very happy [to be voting]. This is the first time I've been given this responsibility. This is my right and no one can interfere with that". When we asked another woman, Priya, what she would do if she didn't get leave from the factory on Election Day, she exclaimed: "I will just go! I have to vote! It is our right (*urimai*) to vote. The government gives us no other benefits, it only respects us in that regard, this is the only place where they respect us!"' (Carswell and De Neve FR: 17–18) Thus, across a fairly wide ranging demographic of people from different social and educational backgrounds, the importance of availing of the foundational right to vote seemed to be well established. The fact that the right existed whether or not people exercised it further enhanced the importance of the duty of exercising it.

Voting for Recognition (*Bote se hamar pehchan banthe*)

An important finding in the NES data has been the high voting figures among the poorest and most deprived castes in India. The reason behind this was never fully clear until we heard a large number of voters drawn from these sections in society who emphasised how important it was to vote in order to be recognised as equal. As Biharilal Sarthi, a young man of 35 years, from the Ghasia (Dalit) community put it, 'I vote to establish my identity and let the government know that there is someone with so-and-so name living in so-and-so village. Another reason for voting is that I carry a dream of a good and healthy government that supports the poor people'. His 60-year-old father Rammani Sarthi added, 'it's to have an identity and also to keep my citizenship alive'.

Most of the young Dalit voters repeated similar concerns of identity. Here are a few examples. Khemchand Banjare (24 years old), a second-time voter says, 'When I vote, it gives me an identity and recognition. My voter ID establishes my identity and no one can change it'. Gayatri Banjare (19 years old), a young Dalit woman and a first-time voter, said, 'I get a feeling that I would get myself identified in the village, particularly when I walk to the booth and cast my vote, people notice me and I feel great about it'. Mohan Nirala (22 years old), a young Dalit law student says, 'It is my right to vote according to human ethics and according to my understanding, to cast your vote means to become conscious of being a citizen and being counted as equal before law'. Sunita, another young woman said, 'I realise that it is my fundamental right and I would get a new identity as an equal citizen of my village'.

It is interesting that a similar expression was echoed by members of non-Dalit OBC communities such as the Painkas. 'Although there are many OBC communities in Chhattisgarh, Painkas are mostly Kabirpanthis (the ones who follow the principles of the saint Kabir) who have suffered severely from the stigma of untouchability in the past. To the present day, most of the upper-caste groups practise untouchability with them. Even some of the OBCs stay at a distance and keep them away from all socio-cultural and religious functions. Tiratdas Mahant (20 years old) said, "It is my right to vote, but it also gives me a feeling of being identified as a citizen with equality rights".

Similarly Mangli Mahant (25 years old), a young woman from the same community, said, "It is to make an able and stable government whereby I take part and get myself recognised"' (George FR: 11).

Voting as a Duty and as a Right

In fact, the idea of duty was inextricably linked to the idea of voting as a right. People used the words interchangeably and together: *adhikar/ kartavya* in Hindi, *urimai/kadamai* in Tamil and *kortobbo/odhikar* in Bengali. For those who emphasised a narrative of 'duty' it appeared to be a deliberate move away from an understanding of the vote as a naked instrument for material gain or a vote given in expectation of reciprocity from politicians and the state. On the contrary, giving one's vote was expressly defined as a form of giving without any expectation of return. In fact, people talked about giving their vote almost with a sense of fatalism, of resignation tinged with hope, in the same manner as they talked of God's presence in the face of their own poverty: *Umeed paar daal dete hain, bharosa hai ki kuch badlega . . . aage peeche ka nahin sochte hain, daal dete hain* (we vote in the hope and faith that things will change . . . we don't think about it too much, we just vote). But the frustration also came through: *Hum toh yahan se aacha hi bhejte hain, ab aage ja kar kuch aur hota hai* (we send our mandate with positivity, but it seems to end up the other way). A short exchange between two groups of women in Gujarat expressed this very well. One of the Pandya women teasingly asked the Vanker women as they saw them emerging from the polling station, 'So, did you get *aam ras* [mango pulp] or *shrikhand* [a well-known Gujarati sweet] from the machine? Or did the Party workers deliver these to you last night itself?' In response, the women from Vanker community got angry and one of them retorted, 'We have not come to take anything from here but to give something very important for our country. We have come here to fulfil our responsibility towards the country'. People tried to express this sense of giving without any expectation of return in various ways, but the most often used concept was one of *dan*. Given the importance of pure intention in any *dan* as discussed in Chapter 3, voters across India treated the voting process with the solemnity they felt it deserved, regardless of the virtue (or the lack thereof) of the recipient. Therefore, it should not be a surprise to learn why, in a small polling station in Gujarat, women were seen to leave their shoes outside, before entering the voting chamber, just as they would when entering a temple or mosque.

In Chapter 4, we discussed the example of a lady in Kerala who used the metaphor of the atom to describe the potency of her vote: 'It may be small but it has a lot of power'. This idea of one vote having enormous value was an idea that was shared by many in all parts of India. This has partly to do with the experience of people having voted in Panchayat elections, where the scale was much smaller and winning margins could indeed be very small. Everywhere, people cited examples from the past where someone had won by just one vote. But there was also a reason that went beyond arithmetic, as Rukmini Bai's explanation in Chapter 1 showed. 'She was one of three women who worked in a grain market. It was a male-dominated world of traders, farmers and officials but the women had the job of sweeping up all the grain that was scattered on the floor, which they could collect and sell at the end of the day and keep part of the earnings. On Election Day we found her literally in tears because she had been turned away at the polling booth, unable to vote because she did not have the correct ID. When we asked her why it was so important to her she first said, "Why?! Because we can vote for a better government, one that helps the poor. All these programmes, wheat for three rupees, employment guarantee, it makes a difference for poor people like us". But we pointed out that she had only one vote in the end and asked if she really felt that one vote could make such a difference to the outcome. To this she said, pointing to a small grain of lentils next to her, "You see me every day, sweeping the *mandi*, collecting the grain that has fallen. Every day I run after each *daana*, collecting each and every one. Why do I do this? Because I know that one grain can change the weight (*thol*) of the heap. It is the same with votes. Every single vote means something and one vote can make or defeat a government (*sarkar*)"' (Krishnamurthy FR: 5). Rukmini Bai's statement was a particularly poignant expression of how the very poor, who have nothing to give away, value enormously what they do have. What is striking is that much like Rousseau's ideal citizen, they have the imagination to see a common good that is larger than themselves and that can only be made up by an aggregate of individual contributions. By drawing parallels between her work and not wasting a single grain, Rukmini Bai made this vision as vivid as it could be.

Urban and Middle-Class Voting Trends

In an article entitled 'Why Should We Vote?' Christophe Jaffrelot (2008) examines the reasons behind India's unusual record of middle-class urban voters voting less than their rural counterparts.[5] He shows that unlike the US, UK or France, the proportion of rich voters who voted in India (56.7 per cent) is lower than that of the proportion of very poor voters who voted (59.3 per cent). This is also a recent trend, for until 1977, a smaller proportion of rural voters voted than urban ones (57.2 per cent *vs* 61.4 per cent). After 1977, however, the trend reversed and by 2009, urban voters voted 7 per cent less compared to their rural counterparts. In 2005, John Harriss published the results of a survey (2005) conducted in the National Capital Region of Delhi which indicated considerable difference in electoral participation across the wealthy and poor, such that the least well-educated and poorest seemed to be the least likely not to vote. Jaffrelot's explanation for this decline in interest in elections among the prosperous urban middle classes is the growing 'plebianisation' of Indian politics — a result of the 'silent revolution' of the entry of low-caste actors and political parties into the electoral arena. He argues that the ensuing rise of 'caste politics' and the fact that a sizeable proportion of the population (70 per cent) consists of Dalits and OBCs means that upper castes feel largely alienated from parliamentary democracy. Given the coincidence of upper-caste and urban voters, the lower number of urban voters at elections can be thus explained. No wonder then that in the SDSA report (Lokniti 2008), 80 per cent of urban voters felt that the important decisions for the country should be taken by experts and not elected representatives. This trend was confirmed again in the 2009 NES data in which 40 per cent of respondents supported the rule of experts who would not be accountable to elected representatives and 40 per cent endorsed the statement that it was desirable for the country to be governed by a strong leader who did not have to bother about winning elections (Bora 2009: 107). Further, and less surprisingly, the growing Dalit middle class does not share the same apathy as their upper-caste counterparts. In fact, Jaffrelot (2008: 47) notes, 'the difference between the electoral participation of upper castes and Dalits is even more significant than the difference between the electoral participation of the rich and poor'. Thus, a combination of the growing electoral assertion of the lower caste and their sheer numeric advantage has resulted in a retreat of the middle classes from participating in elections, and their growing mistrust of parliamentary democracy. Further, in 2009, we also saw the emergence of small-town voters as the most enthusiastic voters, drawing our attention to an increasingly complex urban Indian scenario (Falcao 2009). By disaggregating the category of 'urban', we see from the NES 2009 data that the most disinterested voters in India lived in metropolitan cities and formed the majority (10 per cent) of the 40 per cent of the electorate who did not vote.

---

[5] This trend changed somewhat in 2009 and was no longer as dramatically low as before (Kumar 2009).

Conclusion

At the end of this chapter, we are able, finally, to solve the mystery of why poor people in India vote with such enthusiasm. We have seen that people vote because they are animated by a variety of reasons, some expected but also some not so much. Most of all, the articulate expressions of the importance of citizenship, rights and duties from illiterate voters who would struggle to write their own name come as a surprise. When these same people explained the importance of their own participation in making India's democracy work or revealed their awareness of universal suffrage in India or demonstrated through patient argument that rights and duties were inextricably linked, that without discharging their duty as citizens they could not hope to assert their rights as citizens, they effectively flouted all our received wisdom about the linkages between education and voter awareness. The vociferous assertion of their identity as citizens above all other identities was notable and was akin to what Holston (2008) calls 'insurgent citizenship' in the context of urban Brazil. Holston uses the notion of insurgent citizenship to define the character of popular challenges to persistent inequality and attempts to renegotiate forms of belonging and participation in a democratic polity. He has argued that intermingled with older conceptions of citizenship that regarded rights as privileges, insurgent citizenship has equipped the working classes with a new found confidence to claim their text-based rights and participate in the city. Further comparative ethnographic research between Brazil and India needs to explore whether the assertion of citizenship in these two countries by the poorest citizens are comparable phenomena. Indian citizens, especially those who otherwise felt ignored by the state, were clearly motivated to vote to remind the state of the importance of the sovereignty of ordinary people in a democratic country. As some put it, politicians might hold power for five years at a time, but for the 15 days of campaigning, the voter was the king. Often people remarked that they felt important during the elections, because the powerful people who were usually remote and inaccessible had to come to them during a campaign, shake their hand and ask them how they were doing. As one man put it, 'It is because I have a right to vote that I feel I am valued in society' (*samaj main hamari bhi* value *hai*). For those members of society who belonged to the lowest sections, such as those from the ex-untouchable communities, who continue to be discriminated against, this momentary glimpse of feeling valued was hugely significant. As a Dalit man who belongs to the *bhangi* caste said, 'At election time even if the candidate is from an upper caste he still has to come to my doorstep to ask for my vote'.

As I have shown throughout this chapter, our findings confirm results and trends identified by surveys and studies conducted by political scientists and other scholars. For example, the political scientists Ahuja and Chhibber (n.d.) explain the motivations for voting with people's relationship to the state, which varies according to class. According to the results of their research on focus groups, they propose that the marginalised groups at the bottom of the social hierarchy vote to gain a sense of empowerment by exercising their right to vote as well as out of fear of losing their rights or the benefits that the state gives them. This is the social group that is often most neglected by the state and therefore, such fears and assertions are entirely understandable. Those who are better connected to the state and its officials — the 'state's clients' — are seen to vote mainly on account of the ties of patronage. And finally, the elite, who have otherwise turned their back on the state and depend on it only minimally on an everyday basis, vote out of a sense of civic duty. While we can confirm these findings on the basis of our own, we can also provide a further nuance to their conclusions, namely that while we might ascribe different motivations to specific socio-economic groups, a variety of different motivations can also be held by the same socio-economic category of people. Thus, as we have seen, while poor and illiterate people use the vote to gain a sense of empowerment, they can also be conscious of their civic duties and the importance of voting as an end in itself. As Rukmini Bai's poignant statement demonstrated in Chapter 1, even a lowly daily wage labourer who earns a few rupees from sweeping up the grain on a market floor has the rhetorical and philosophical sophistication to draw parallels between her work of chasing every stray grain and the importance of each person casting their vote.

I. **West Bengal: CPI(M) and Trinamool Congress**

Source: All photographs by Benjamin Dix.

II. West Bengal: Trinamool

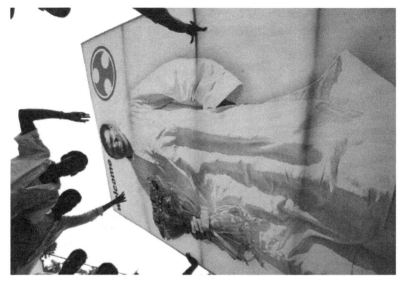

III. The Upside Down World of Elections

IV. Chhattisgarh: Bahujan Samaj Party

V. Chhattisgarh: Bahujan Samaj Party Office

VI. Party Branding

VII. Tamil Nadu: Flag Printing Factory

VIII. Chhattisgarh: Rahul Gandhi's Public Meeting

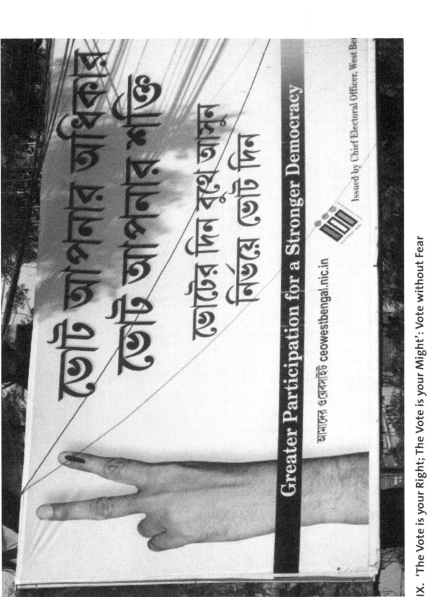

IX. 'The Vote is your Right; The Vote is your Might': Vote without Fear

X. An Electronic Voting Machine

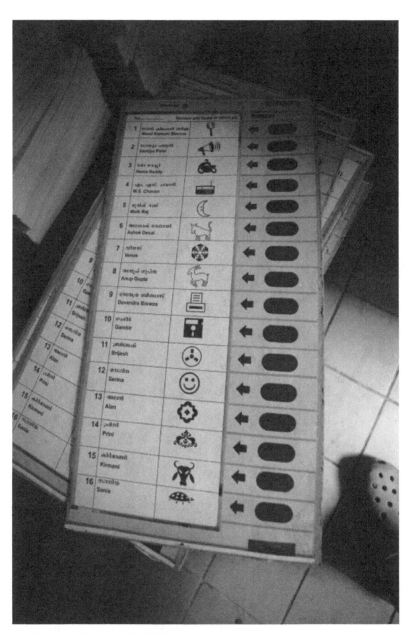

XI. Kerala: Ballot Paper for EVM

XII. Madhya Pradesh: Polling Document

XIII. Kerala: The Day before Polling

XIV. Polling Officers Waiting to be Transported to their Polling Stations

VEHICLE ARRANGEMENT
124 KOLLAM

VEHICLE NUMBER	POLLING STATIONS	
	TRIP-I	TRIP-II
1	1, 2, 7, 8, 9, 10	
2	3, 4, 5, 6, 11, 12	
3	13, 14, 15, 16, 17	
4	18, 19, 20, 21	
5	22, 23, 24, 25, 26	
6	27, 28, 32	
7	29, 29-A, 30, 31	
8	33	
9	34, 35, 41, 42	54, 55, 56, 57
10	36, 37	38, 39, 40
11	49, 50, 51, 52, 53	43, 44, 45, 46, 47, 48
12	58, 59, 62, 81, 82	63, 64, 65, 66, 67
13	60, 61, 68, 69, 70	71, 72, 73, 74, 75
14	76, 77, 78, 79, 80	83, 84, 85, 86, 87
15	88, 89, 90, 91, 92, 93	94, 95, 96, 97, 98
16	99, 100, 101	102, 103, 104, 105
17	106, 107, 108, 109, 110, 111, 112	113, 114, 115, 116, 117, 118
18	119, 120, 121, 122, 123, 124	125, 126, 127, 128, 149
19	129, 130, 131	132
20	135, 136, 137, 137-A, 138, 147, 148	
21	139, 140, 141, 142	
22	133, 134, 143, 144, 145, 146	

XV. Kerala: Transport Arrangements for Polling Officers

XVI. Kerala: Off on Duty

XVII. Kerala: Polling Booth Queues

XVIII. Kerala: Finger Marked with Indelible Black Ink Just before Polling

XIX. The Proof of Having Voted

VI
Conclusion

The question 'why India votes' is provoked by two facts. First, India's poorest and most marginalised citizens vote in high numbers. Second, India's performance on eliminating poverty has been abysmal, and the country has higher levels of chronic poverty than sub-Saharan Africa even though its economic growth rates are among the highest in the world. These two facts when taken together raise an important question — why do poor people bother with voting when elected governments don't seem to be making their lives any better?

In this book we have provided a set of answers that focus on the meaning that elections hold for ordinary, impoverished and neglected voters. Elections are meaningful and significant for a large number of Indian voters because they think that ultimately it is better to choose (and dismiss) the devils who will govern them than have to suffer an autocrat; because Indian voters understand that unless they come together and participate in elections, the whole edifice of political democracy will collapse; and because the act of voting itself is seen to encode principles of equality, fairness, efficiency, rights, and duties, all of which are valued ideals.

We have been able to provide such an understanding of elections in India by studying voters across the country ethnographically. As a result, our conclusions are the result of what people said to us and what we observed on the ground. The sites in which research was carried out during the parliamentary elections of 2009 were diverse enough to provide a comprehensive national picture, as there was a healthy mix of regions, rural and urban, rich and poor, across our sites. We had no prior explanations for why Indians vote — instead our conclusions are genuinely inductive. Through our extensive reporting of people's own formulations of their ideas through direct quotations, we have made an attempt to trace the 'social imaginaries' of democratic ideas in the Indian electorate (Taylor 2004).[1] I have also tried to show through the analysis in this book that it is the research question 'why India votes' that dominated this study rather than any disciplinary chauvinism. I have therefore demonstrated how, in designing the ethnographic studies of this project, we were constantly informed by other disciplines and methods, most notably the surveys of the National Election Studies (NES). It is a great vindication of our methodological rigour and open-mindedness that on a number of issues, our findings converge. The respect for the Election Commission, the rising trends in middle-class voter turnouts and the increase in door-to-door campaigning by political parties are examples of our similar findings. In each case, our ethnographic probing of the very same questions asked by the NES has provided greater insight into the reasons behind some of the macro-trends in voter attitudes in India as revealed by the NES surveys.

In the remainder of this conclusion, I wish to take a step back from the rich data that the Comparative Electoral Ethnographies project generated during the 2009 elections to reflect on how what we have learnt may alter and add to what we think about the nature of democratic politics in India. The people we spoke to said a great many things, some of which were astonishingly profound, and this makes it imperative that we give their ideas and opinions serious theoretical attention.

Let us start by casting our mind back to 1950, when India's democratic journey began. On the occasion of inaugurating India's constitution as a democratic republic, B. R. Ambedkar, the chairman of the Constituent Assembly that drafted the constitution, made some cautionary remarks amidst the euphoria. He pointed out that in order for India to truly realise its potential as a genuine democracy, it needed to build on the constitutional provisions of universal adult franchise and the principles of liberty, equality and fraternity. Guaranteeing individual liberty, he reminded his audience, was a necessary but not a sufficient condition of democracy, for the three values had to be realised as a whole. Uday Mehta (2007: 26) notes that the Indian Constitution provoked an alternative vision to be formed and marked a rupture with

---

[1] See the Introduction (Taylor 2004) for a longer discussion of 'social imaginaries' and Ruparelia (2008, especially pp. 51–54) for a discussion of Taylor's ideas in the context of Indian politics.

the past and that 'it's from this rupture or distancing from history that sovereignty and the political as an expression of a capacious political will comes to be formed'. As Ambedkar pointed out in his speech to the Constituent Assembly, political democracy and the new electoral system recognised 'the principle of one man one vote and one vote one value' (cited in Guha 2010: 323). However, in the face of deep social divisions and hierarchies, the idea of 'one man one value' was a much harder ideal to realise, for hierarchy implied that some people were inferior to others, both in rank and in substance. It was, therefore, imperative, Ambedkar argued, that this contradiction be done away with at the earliest, for not to do so would threaten the very idea of political democracy itself. 'We must remove this contradiction at the earliest possible moment or else those who suffer from inequality will blow up the structure of political democracy which this Constituent Assembly has so laboriously built up' (Ambedkar 1948, in Guha 2012: 323). Further, the principle of fraternity required the imagination of a nation and a sense of belonging that was based on shared solidarity and unity among people, but once again caste and class divisions stood in the way of this vision. For a Dalit intellectual such as Ambedkar, who had experienced untouchability and discrimination first hand (Jaffrelot 2005), any vision of a fairer society of the future *had* to imagine an alterity that was different from what had gone before and this was summed up in the principles of equality, liberty and fraternity. Under his leadership, the writers of the Indian Constitution as a body tried to put in place structures and institutions that would enable the creation of such an alterity in a post-colonial India, one that was distinct from the immediate colonial past but also from the older and equally iniquitous pre-colonial past. The hope of democracy lay not in just independence from foreign rule, but also in using the opportunity to create a new society that would be able to transcend the traditional divisions caused by caste and class.

Sixty-two years after he made the speech, we can appreciate the prescience of Ambedkar's caution. While it is true that India's record as a political democracy has been exemplary and laudable, the same cannot be said of its record as a social or economic democracy. Old social inequalities between rich and poor have persisted and in some cases have gained renewed salience through new economic regimes. Caste-based discrimination continues in everyday life and tribal and rural communities face an ever-growing assault on their land and resources. Female foetuses continue to be killed, brides continue to be burnt for inadequate dowries, and women and children continue to be raped and abused by family and strangers despite legislations against all these crimes. Thus, the status of the most vulnerable sections of society has remained unstable in modern democratic India, despite her constitutional commitment to social justice and equality. And yet, we learn that it is the same vulnerable sections of the Indian population who are among the most enthusiastic voters. Why is this so? What is so special about elections that even though they legitimise a system that ultimately fails the vulnerable, people invest such faith in them? Do elections mean anything more than a system of procedures and arrangements to elect politicians to power? Is there something about participating in them that makes the experience a special one and unlike all other experiences in life? Is there something about elections that elicits hope such that people continue to invest meaning in them every time they come around?

As we have seen, elections are carnivalesque moments in Indian public life. Alongside the colour and noise, elections also brought with them a reversal of social order, when the powerful had to beg for votes, arrogance could be punished, officials were polite and solicitous, and ordinary people were made to feel that they were important. Elections therefore emerged as aesthetic and ritual moments that allowed for the inversion of the rules of normal social life, as classic anti-structural liminal moments that lie betwixt and between everyday states of inequality. As Victor Turner (1969: 119) noted in his discussion of the nature of liminality, such moments of reversal are also characterised by a mode of social relatedness that he calls 'communitas', which is a community of feeling that is tied neither to blood nor locality and instead tends to be undifferentiated and egalitarian. As the evidence in Chapter 4 demonstrates, this is the nature of the shared feeling among voters at a polling booth during their participation in the act of voting. An Indian election thereby creates a heightened awareness of what is missing in everyday hierarchical life while simultaneously providing a glimpse of democracy's ideals of egalitarianism and cooperation, of equality and fraternity. Thus, people participated in elections in the hope that this extraordinary and visceral experience of egalitarianism and communitas would in turn infuse into everyday time and eventually bring genuine social change. This is the radical message that Indian elections encode by creating temporary moments of radical rupture that provide a vision of an egalitarian future. In this, Indian elections are, as John Dunn (1993: 2) defines for all elections, 'a happy synthesis of liberation and revenge, secured in the ideal case without either bloodshed or massive public disorder: all the conveniences of revolution, without any of the inconveniences'. And it is because they serve this radical function that elections have become sacrosanct in India and continue to keep India's democracy alive.

But contrary to such a radical reading of electoral participation, there is a widely held view, especially among those who are moderately well off and middle class, that the reason why poor people vote in large numbers is because they *get* something from elections, namely, material benefits disbursed during the campaign or favours from victorious candidates as *quid pro quo* for votes cast for them. The English-speaking middle classes and those who support the recent anti-corruption social movement led by Anna Hazare alike see themselves above such nakedly instrumental politics partly because candidates rarely offer material incentives to their class and also because their assumption is that they can be less easily bought off. Such benefit-maximising activities are seen to be the hallmark of poorer, and by implication, less educated and sophisticated voters, whose only concern, it is assumed, is to use every opportunity to get something for what they give. The data collected from across India presented in this volume shows that there was indeed widespread disbursement of material incentives by political parties during election campaigns and that in many cases people admitted to accepting these incentives. At the same time, however, they thought it absurd to assume that it would be possible to *buy* their vote with these incentives. In a large number of cases, people pointed out that the vote was a precious resource and that the bribes offered by politicians were incommensurate with its value. While these incentives were welcomed by people, especially those who had very little, the reasons why they actually voted were the result of a complex combination of rational, instrumental and expressive reasons that displayed a combination of pragmatism and a sophisticated understanding that had something but not everything to do with the material incentives offered to them.

This understanding was perhaps the reason why enthusiastic voters invariably responded with the counter-question: 'Why would you *not* vote?' when asked why they did vote. Thus, the posing of the question 'why do you vote?' seemed an absurdity, the result of an incomprehension and failure to understand something quite fundamental and important. This should, therefore, lead us to question the very epistemology that poses such a question. Is the question 'why do you vote?' the result of a certain set of assumptions about social action that are based on an understanding of the world in which all actions are meant to achieve something concrete? Is the posing of this question, and the middle class assumptions about the poorer citizens of India, the result of two different 'universes of common sense' as Kaviraj puts it (Kaviraj 2011b: 314)? In his analysis on Gandhi's trial held in August 1922, he shows how Gandhi's triumph in the trial was not because he was acquitted (he was not) but because he effectively and uniquely was able to communicate simultaneously with both the educated middle classes and the illiterate peasantry. This was a triumph, Kaviraj argues, mainly because class not only separated these two constituencies but they also displayed different and conflicting rationalities.

> For the Western-educated middle class, often speaking in English while discussing grave and complex things like politics or historical possibilities, the world was a realm of causal and instrumental processes . . . Peasant groups did not share this entirely secularised, profane, disabused view of political rationality. To them the world appeared as not a realm of causality alone, but also of meaningfulness; and since they lived in a world in which significant things are invested with meanings, even causally efficient acts could contain an indelible aura of mystery, of something larger of the world's inscrutable design expressed through the small and finite acts of ordinary people (ibid.: 314–15).

This depiction of peasant ontology of the political, as outlined in greater detail by Shahid Amin (1987) and Ranajit Guha (1983), is certainly persuasive for the colonial period when the mutual incomprehensibility between languages also encoded a deeper ontological incomprehensibility. This continues in contemporary India. As a result, the subalterns think it absurd to be asked to justify why they vote and the educated middle classes find it impossible to attribute any other motivation but naked greed to 'poor people'. But as the voices presented in this volume show, the ontology of the political that exists among those who vote is a complex one. Not only is it not a simple case of 'getting' something in exchange for one's vote, but the play on the word *dan* discussed here also shows how people genuinely believe that they are in fact giving something without expectation of material return when they vote and that thereby they are giving something back to the system in order to sustain it.

The Individual Citizen

An enduring subject of discussion in Indian democratic behaviour has been the tension between individual-citizens and those dominated by group loyalties. The source of this tension has been the view that democracy increases individualism, especially following a democratic revolution. Tocqueville argued that a democratic system detaches individuals from their ancestors and companions such that they 'owe nothing to any man, they expect nothing from any man; they acquire the habit of always considering themselves as standing alone' (Tocqueville 1945: 99, in Hauser and Singer 2001). In India, as we know, the trajectory has been different, especially in the last two decades. The importance of the collective bargaining power of group identities has been felt most acutely in the silent revolution caused by lower castes opting to form their own political parties to fight electoral battles rather than remaining within the larger and older national parties. This change has evolved over two decades to create competition between various caste-based parties, with each one staking a claim to represent a particular coalition of caste groups. Given that numerically lower-caste groups together form the majority of the electorate, much of the political competition has been dictated by this kind of politics. A further consequence of such collective bargaining on the basis of shared identity has been the *quid pro quo* that gaining electoral victory brings. Parties have had to repay their voters and constituencies with goods and benefits as a reward for their support. Such a process has been dubbed 'patronage democracy' to explain why ethnic parties have succeeded (Chandra 2004). Some people consider the undermining of a liberal notion of citizenship to be the most damaging outcome of such a development. As Pratap Mehta (2003) notes, for instance, one of the failures of Indian democracy has been its inability to produce a citizenry that is bound by a sense of reciprocity. In a strong *demos*, the argument goes, citizens should make responsible moral choices in the public sphere in their capacity as autonomous individual agents, rather than as individuals dominated by strong group identities that curtail such autonomy. But whatever the model, the question that remains with us is whether collective bargaining practices do result in the loss of autonomy of the voter as identified by liberal theorists.

Yogendra Yadav's argument is that the mechanism of formal political representation in India, namely elections, serves the important function of acting as a hinge that connects two very different areas which otherwise remain unconnected (Yadav 2010: 354). One is the how, where and what of representation — that is to say, the mechanics of elections itself and the pool from which the representatives are drawn. This is also the arena of the political structures of liberal democracy that were introduced to India through its adoption of the model of democratic republicanism after Independence. Second is the relationship between people and their representatives, that is to say, what the representatives do on behalf of and for the people they are trusted to represent. The paradox of Indian democracy, Yadav argues, is that there have been two simultaneous but opposite tendencies in each of these realms (ibid.). The first has seen the flowering of the democratic principle with a steady improvement in the conduct of elections as well a deepening and widening of the social base from which politicians are drawn. But at the same time, in the second, 'political understanding and practices have thinned precisely when more people have got involved' with new entrants failing to set new agendas of governance that do justice to their enthusiastic supporters (Yadav and Palshikar 2009: 425). If anything, the governments formed by the (relatively new) representatives of the backward caste communities have had only delivered inefficiency and non-performance (ibid.). This has led to a narrowing of choice for the voter rather than the provision of genuine alternatives.

In many ways, as the material presented in this book illustrates, it is during elections that this paradoxical nature of Indian democracy and political representation is most apparent. As we saw in our account of the election campaign, the leaders who draw the largest crowds at mass rallies are often those who have, in fact, created populist messages of direct appeal. These leaders are also often responsible for creating an upsurge in voter turnouts among the 'backward castes'. Clearly, for these marginalised groups, voting is a politically meaningful act as it enables them to be represented by those who are 'like them'. Over time, however, older patterns of representation in which family and kin determine political succession have come to prevail. Lalu Yadav installing his wife as Chief Minister in his place when he was sent to jail and Mulayam Singh Yadav nominating his son as his political heir are but just two examples of this trend. They seem to confirm Béteille's despairing conclusion that 'millions of Indians continue to believe that the natural succession to high office lies within the family. It is neither individual nor institutional charisma, but the charisma of the family that prevails' (2008: 39). These kin-based leadership structures have in turn further harmed the organisation of the very parties that the leaders had built their support on. Ramachandra Guha (2010) identifies this as the 'conversion of charisma into authoritarianism', a tendency that many successful politicians have shown, from Indira Gandhi to Bal Thackeray, Lalu Yadav, Mayawati, Mulayam Singh, and Jayalalitha, all of whom 'used their personal charisma to gain control over the apparatus of their parties' (ibid.: 297). This trend combined with the lack of performance of the governments led by these new representatives provokes ordinary citizens to depict the world of politics and politicians as demonic with an ability to co-opt and corrupt any new entrant.

We also need to note that while this might be true for identity-based politics, newer processes have evolved in the older political parties and the governments led by them, and there has been a further evolution in electoral bargaining practices leading to newer ones. In the 1980s, in urban areas, we saw the emergence of the 'dadas' who are often persons from the popular world itself, with less social distance from those they claim to protect. It is a style of assertion which appeals particularly to young men from the popular world (Hansen 1998: 158). Their emergence was both the cause and effect of a

> democratic revolution that gradually undermined Ma-Baapism [the state as a paternalistic force]: it has undermined the authority of politicians, government institutions . . . Ordinary political clientilism could no longer absorb the growing resentment . . . and so a new type of popular discourse which emerged most clearly in Bombay in 1980s was the so-called *Dada culture* or *dadaism* [protection by the elder brother] (ibid.).[2]

The increasing number of Panchayati Raj institutions (PRIs) in rural areas has brought a huge number of new actors into the electoral arena who had hitherto encountered the state or 'seen it', as Corbridge and Harriss (2010) put it, only through 'vertical and highly mediated exchanges with its members'. The PRIs have created what they call the 'constitutional sarkar' that now encounters the more entrenched 'permanent sarkar'. Furthermore, in the past decade in particular, India has witnessed the rise of the figure of the *naye neta* (new leaders) who have become the crucial mediators between ordinary rural

---

[2] Paul Brass's 'Kala Bachcha: Portrait of a BJP Hero' (1997: 204–59) describes the role of one such character in the management of an institutional riot.

Indians and the Indian state (Krishna 2010: 307). These new actors in local politics are often drawn from among young educated men in rural India who also often belong to lower classes and castes. In the absence of sufficient job opportunities, they have deployed their education and knowledge of the world to help ordinary people with different engagements with the state that invariably entail paperwork and conversations with officials. Through their consistency and reliability, they are able to build trust and networks both within their communities and in the world of offices, banks and development projects. It is no surprise then that in a changed scenario of greater education and altered caste dynamics, it is these new leaders who have replaced older village strongmen as the mediators between the village and the state (ibid.: 302). But unlike the mediators of the past, who were actively cultivated by political parties and given access to state officials in exchange for votes, the *naye neta* have no such guaranteed access. Instead they have to act as political entrepreneurs to create, nurture and invest in relationships with the official world. Krishna identifies the variety of little and big tasks that are involved in this kind of, what I call, 'political work' (Banerjee 2010b).

> To scurry around from office to office; to fill out forms and lobby government officials; to supervise construction labour on behalf of officials; to fill out forms and keep accounts; to arrange elaborate 'site visits' when officials or politicians come to the village . . . To do all this and also attend to villagers' everyday concerns — taking a sick person to the hospital, often in the middle of the night, and keeping up one's contacts among doctors and hospital officials; to have someone's government pension approved and paid out in time . . . to get someone a loan from a bank . . . To badger, pester, entreat, implore, threaten, cajole and bribe if necessary — and to do these things everyday and also be accessible at night — does not add up to a comfortable life (Krishna 2010: 307).

It is no wonder that much of this group of middlemen consists of young men drawn from the less-privileged categories of people who need to create a stake in the system. Election campaigns provide the ideal opportunity for these actors to consolidate and take stock of the influence they have been able to garner. Mediators, by definition, act as a hinge to connect different parts of the political world. But unlike the intermediaries of the past, these new leaders are less clients and more political mercenaries, making their connections available for the most beneficial arrangements. Political parties eagerly seek out these actors in order to reach the voters and to gain votes at the forthcoming polls, especially as they have failed to invest and maintain their party organisations. Harvesting the goodwill created by these leaders among ordinary people, therefore, has emerged as an economical solution. The 'new leaders' on their part are able to use their accumulated capital of goodwill to go for the highest bidder or the most promising party to form new ties, nurture old ones, eliminate competitors, and create opportunities for attracting and 'being seen' with powerful people, thereby generating potential for their personal growth in the future. This association with the powerful is crucial to bolster their credibility with ordinary people for whom such proximity to power promises easier and quicker access to getting their aims accomplished in the future.

But they also know that their local leader expects them to reward all the help they receive with their votes. Campaigning thus becomes less a battle between ideologies of different political parties because they are often indistinguishable (Hasan 2010; Krishna 2010). Instead, as we saw in Chapter 2, an election campaign becomes an arena for a number of different games being played by everyone. For political parties it is about reaching out to the electorate and convincing them to vote for them; for the voters it is about making a judgement as to which party is likely to make their lives better and easier in the future; and for the *naye neta*s a campaign is an opportunity to accumulate and expand their social capital. In a recent discussion, Sanjay Reddy (2005) shows how the degeneration of party organisations in parties such as the Congress since the early 1970s has marked a shift from a mobilisation mediated through stable party structures to one of populist 'direct appeal'. By bypassing established structures, the latter mechanism subverts and avoids entrenched patron–client relations and appeals directly to the voters themselves, and it has been enthusiastically embraced by caste-based parties who need to reward their support bases materially. This type of populism has been facilitated and made necessary largely due to the 'massified mobilisation' of caste and ethnic identity politics. Of course, such mobilisation has taken place mostly at the state-level in India and has been facilitated by an enormous increase in the discretionary development funds allocated to MPs and MLAs.

However, this scenario is also constantly evolving. With an increasing loss of control over state governments while remaining in power at the centre for two parliamentary terms, the Congress has countered this trend by using its clout at the central government to bypass local structures and make governmental development schemes directly available to voters. Discussing this move as an arguably important factor in creating the incumbent Congress's return in the 2009 national elections, James Manor (2012), has argued that such 'post-clientilism' might be the way forward. By making goods and services available to people without requiring the mediation of local (and rival) parties, the Congress has endeavoured to implement its social developmental policies, particularly in the case of the National Rural Employment Guarantee Scheme (NREGS). This can be said to have paid off as a strategy, for people seemed to recognise the provenance of such schemes in their responses to NES surveys. Further, it remains to be seen if the introduction of the Unique Identification Number (UID) Scheme across India (from 2012) will also have the intended effect of empowering poor and marginalised citizens further by making access to information interfaces easier. Manor argues that several of the UPA programmes were demand-driven in order to draw poorer people more fully into the public sphere as actors — in part to enhance their political capacity, which he defines as 'political awareness, confidence, skills and connections' (ibid.: 17). We can only speculate about the impact that such an enhancement of political capacity and empowerment within the electorate will have on electoral participation. The results are far from predictable and will require future research.[3]

Elections as a Site of Constitutional Morality

I would like to conclude this book by examining whether elections in India are a site for the cultivation of the otherwise increasingly elusive 'constitutional morality', a value that lies at the heart of popular participation in a democratic republic. In his article on this subject, sociologist André Béteille (2012) examines the importance of this essential value for a successful democracy and concludes that its fate remains precarious in contemporary India. He reminds us that at its very inception, in 1950, the authors of the Indian Constitution had warned of the need to cultivate and preserve this quality for the

---

[3] I propose to study this in a new three-year study from 2012 to 2015 as part of a network of institutions across Europe and India.

safeguarding of the constitution. B. R. Ambedkar in particular had said, 'Constitutional morality . . . is not a natural sentiment. It has to be cultivated. We must realise that our people are yet to learn it. Democracy in India is only a top-dressing on an Indian soil, which is essentially undemocratic' (Constituent Assembly Debates 1989: VII, 38; quoted in Béteille 2008: 36). There were three main reasons for this caution. First, the transition from being subjects of the British Empire to becoming citizens of independent India would require asserting the importance of the individual over any group identity, a move that was complicated both by the experience of colonial dominance as well as the structures of community and hierarchy. Second, the traditional structures of caste did not allow for an equal consideration of individuals without regard to caste, religion or gender. 'The Constitution itself could provide a legal framework . . . [but] it could not by itself conjure into existence the attitudes, dispositions and sentiments without which the transformations could be hardly effective' (Béteille 2008: 36). Third, the deployment of civil disobedience as a method of protest during the anti-colonial struggle had left a lasting legacy in the repertoire of protest against unjust governments in post-colonial India. Béteille's argument is that Ambedkar's prescient misgivings have come to pass as a populist democracy and gradually begun to replace a respect for the constitution and its procedures and prescription of the division of powers between the executive, legislature and judiciary. Several important moments have exacerbated this process but the state of Emergency (1975–77) and the opposition to it were central to this decline. Indira Gandhi's declaration of the Emergency forced the judiciary and legislature to bend to the will of the Executive, thereby demeaning a fundamental tenet of constitutional democracy. The opposition to the Emergency in turn used precisely those methods of civil disobedience what Ambedkar called the 'Grammar of Anarchy' to challenge Gandhi thereby supporting a democracy of populism rather than constitutionalism. As Béteille reminds us, democracy rests on a 'delicate balance between the rule of law and the rule of numbers' and in the Emergency we had a distilled battle between these two opposing tendencies within Indian democracy (ibid.: 40). In the subsequent decades, this tension continues to be played out through various scenarios in which the constitutional state wavers in its commitment to abide by the strict limits on its authority, and populist movements demonstrate an impatience with the 'apparatus of graded authority', regarding these as 'bastions against the immediate and pressing needs of the people' (Béteille 2008: 40). Protests against the government, whether violent or non-violent, therefore, tend to target the functionaries of the state directly rather than following constitutional procedures.

Against this backdrop, if we were to look again at what we have learnt about elections, we could argue that they play an important role in mediating the tension between state and popular politics, and in acting as a pivot in the balance between the rule of law and the rule of numbers. As we have seen in this book, the successful conduct of elections in India is possible largely because of the constitutional authority that backs the ECI. This is not only true in principle, but also recognised by the Indian electorate in very real terms during every election. The imposition of the Model Code of Conduct; the authority of the ECI over politicians, administrators and voters alike; and the hard work of the ECI officials are all palpable evidence of this. This is striking given the danger of the possibility of 'the attrition of bureaucratic hermeneutics', where policies originating in 'one culture and its perception of the social world [metropolitan, central] had to negotiate the boundaries with another [rural, state levels] in its course down the administrative structures. All efforts at rationalisation and democratization had to contend with this subtle but irresistible attack of interpretation' (Kaviraj 2003: 232).

But, the vast scale of the electorate, the awareness that everyone has of the sheer number of voters who participate in an election, and the constant speculation about winning margins and seats to be won serve as a reminder of the importance of numbers to the functioning of electoral democracy. But commentators have also pointed out that '[c]ontrary to the hopes and aspirations of many in the Constituent Assembly, Indian society has not ceased to be a society of caste and communities. Democratic politics has in many ways strengthened collective identities at the expense of the identity of the individual as citizen' (Béteille 2008: 41). But as the testimonies presented in this book show, Indians feel that despite the nature of everyday life in the country, elections provide a rare moment in social life when they are given legitimacy solely on the basis of their citizenship rather than the membership of any caste, community or religion, and are able to exercise the most fundamental of their rights as individual citizens. This, we could argue, goes a long way in realising, if only momentarily, one of the most important requirements of the constitutional state, namely the creation of a universal citizen. Further, in the light of the pressures of community mass mobilisation and patronage structures, people emphasised the importance of the secret ballot in providing a rare space of autonomy in which, at least in theory, citizens could realise the freedom to vote according to their choice rather than the demands of kinship or community. Elections therefore emerge as one of the most important, open and secular institutions that can mediate between the citizens and the state. In privileging the identity of individuals as citizens of India above all others and by obliterating the hierarchies of caste and community and preserving the 'one man one vote' principle, elections go some way in addressing two of Ambedkar's misgivings in 1950.

But what of the third —the need to uphold constitutional morality over the 'grammar of anarchy'? In his essay, 'Ethical Insufficiency of Egoism and Altruim', Rajeev Bhargava (2010) argues for the need of a 'morality' to fight individual and collective egoism (which without doubt lies behind disorder) — one that is an integral part of a larger ethic rather than a self-contained institution of morality. 'Such an ethic must be impartial . . . in short it must be egalitarian. An egalitarian ethic . . . must treat all individuals . . . and all groups as equal' (ibid.: 286–87). It is worth considering whether such a morality is achieved in India, if only temporarily, through the staging of free and fair elections. Here again, Béteille's discussion of 'the virtue of civility as an important component of constitutional morality' is helpful to make sense of what we have learnt from our research into Indian elections (2008: 42). Civility, Béteille argues, 'calls for tolerance, restraint and mutual accommodation in public life' (ibid.). He draws on the writings by Edward Shils, who argues that '[t]he institutional arrangements required for the freedom of expression of beliefs and the representation of interests and ideals — both of which can be divisive — can function effectively in society if those who use them for their own particularistic ends are at the same time restrained by an admixture of civility' (Shils 1997: 3). This is precisely what we witnessed in our field sites all over India during the campaign period. As the discussion in Chapter 2 showed, voters who were otherwise deeply divided by their loyalties to different political parties were able to converse politely, attend each other's meetings and in some cases even offer hospitality to each other's leaders on the grounds of decency. The Model of Conduct imposed by the ECI further encouraged civil behaviour. The suspended nature of electoral time and the rare civility it brought could be contrasted with the everyday nature of disorderly politics. As the former Chief Election Commissioner S. Y. Quraishi put it, '[a]fter the elections end, politics begins' (personal interview). Among the electorate there appeared to be a prevailing common sense that at the end of the day politicians and ideas come and go but people always need to live with each other. The imagination of a harmonious collective in these terms reflected what Shils defined as the 'virtue of civility'. In his essay of the same title, Shils defined this virtue as 'the conduct of a person whose individual self-consciousness had been partly superseded by his collective self-consciousness, the society as a whole and the institution of civil society being the referents of his collective self-consciousness' (1997: 335). For such a collective self-consciousness to be sustained, it is imperative therefore that India's citizenry continue to be able to participate in activities in which the contribution that individuals make and the civility of the manner in which they make it is valued. For at the core of this order is the liberalistic belief in the sacredness of the individual human being, the dignity of the individual's beliefs and the moral value of reason and civil discussion. I hope that this book has persuaded the reader that in their enthusiastic embrace of political participation and the sophistication of their understandings of why they vote, the Indian electorate emerges as the bearers of such civility, at least during elections.

Appendix A
Bihar

Researcher: Priyadarshini Singh*
Champanagar locality (Booth 7),
Bhagalpur AC (156), Bhagalpur PC (26)

Background

Bhagalpur district is situated in the Ganga Basin of southern Bihar, bordering Jharkhand. The total population of the district is almost 2.5 million, with a high population density (approximately 946 people per square kilometre). Out of the total population, 82 per cent resides in rural areas, and the average literacy rate is around 45 per cent. SC and ST populations of the district stand at 11 per cent and 2 per cent respectively. The OBC population is estimated to be 35 to 45 per cent. The total number of electors in Bhagalpur PC stands at 1,433,346, of which Muslims number approximately 350,000; Koeri, Kurmi and Dhanu approximately 300,000; Yadavs approximately 300,000, and Gangotas approximately 200,000.

Administratively, the locality of Champanagar is part of Bhagalpur *nagar parishad* (municipal corporation); electorally, it falls within Bhagalpur AC. However, it lies on the outskirts of Bhagalpur town at the border with Nathnagar AC, with which it shares a number of demographic, electoral and political features. Champanagar is a mixed area with a dominant and politically-crucial Muslim minority. It also has a small Bengali enclave and a few Dalit, Bania and Yadav families.

---

* All Appendices in this book are summaries of longer 10,000-word reports that each of the researchers in the Comparative Electoral Ethnographies Project compiled. The bulk of the data submitted in the reports has been incorporated in the main body of the text. The formal report for the Kerala study was not available and thus not included.

Although the town of Bhagalpur is famous for silk, the significance of this industry is marginal for the district as a whole and the majority of the population is dependent on agriculture. Production has not recovered since the 1989 communal riots triggered by the Ram Janmabhoomi movement. Nonetheless, in Champanagar, the industry continues to dominate the occupational profile: approximately 60 per cent of the workforce is employed as casual labourers in power looms; 20 per cent owns three or four power looms; and 5 to 10 per cent owns more than 10 power looms. Bengali inhabitants of Champanagar are more educated than other groups in the area, and most have government and private-sector jobs.

Delimitation

Following the 2008 delimitation exercise, Bhagalpur PC comprises six ACs: Bhagalpur, Nathnagar, Kahalgaon, Pirpainti, Gopalpur, and Bihpur. Gopalpur and Bihpur had been part of the neighbouring Khagaria PC. The ACs of Mahamgama and Sultanganj were removed from Bhagalpur PC to the state of Jharkhand and the PC of Banka respectively.

The Muslim population of Bhagalpur PC is concentrated in Nathnagar, Bhagalpur and Kahalgaon; delimitation has not affected their representation in the PC. Gangotas have gained most from the exercise, owing to the addition of Gopalpur and Bihpur. Pirpainti AC has been SC-reserved.

Electoral History

Before the riots of 1989 polarised significant areas of the constituency along religious lines, Bhagalpur PC had been represented for five terms by the Congress's Bhagwat Jha Azad. For three terms from 1989 to 1998, it was represented by Chun-Chun Yadav (JD). The BJP gained a hold across the constituency in 1998 but lost in 1999 to Subodh Roy, a CPM candidate backed by the RJD. In 2004, the BJP won the seat, retaining it under Shahnawaz Hussain following a by-election in 2006.

Among Bhagalpur's six ACs, the BJP has a convincing hold only in Bhagalpur, which is dominated by Muslims (32 per cent) while Brahmins and Yadavs together make up 20 per cent of its population. Even there, the BJP only gained significant support post-1989. In

Champanagar, Hindus across castes tend to vote for BJP, and Muslims favour non-BJP alternatives. The presence of a Muslim BJP candidate in the 2009 election complicated the situation.

Contest and Outcome of the 2009 Election

Although 21 candidates stood for election in 2009, the race was essentially between the BJP, RJD, BSP, and Congress. The BJP and RJD candidates were considered frontrunners. BJP and JD(U) contested the polls in alliance with a seat-sharing agreement of 15 seats for the BJP and 25 for the JD(U). The long-standing RJD–Congress alliance collapsed less than a month before the first phase of elections; the RJD entered into an alliance with LJP and SP.

Syed Shahnawaz Hussain is one of only three Muslim leaders of the BJP. The sitting MP since the 2006 by-election, he had also represented Kishanganj, and was a cabinet minister in the Vajpayee Government. Shakuni Choudhary (RJD), an ex-serviceman and well-known leader of the Kushwah community, had been MLA for Tarapur since 1985. He was elected as an MP in 1998. Sadanand Singh, a seven-time MLA from Kahalgaon, senior leader of the Congress and former speaker of the Bihar assembly, was contesting for the second time, having lost to Chun-Chun Prasad Yadav in 1989. The BSP candidate, Ajit Sharma from Bhagalpur, had left Congress when he was denied a ticket. He owns a petrol pump in town. One of four BSP candidates in Bihar, he contested the election entirely from his own resources. Subodh Roy (CPM) from Bhagalpur, considered the leader of the bunker (weaver) community, had won the 1999 parliamentary elections with RJD support, and was greatly respected by candidates and voters.

Shahnawaz Hussain emerged as the early frontrunner, but his lead was precarious. As a Muslim, he faced significant animosity from Hindus who perceived him as favouring his own religious group. They were also angry with the ruling coalition for reopening 27 riot-related cases (closed by Lalu Yadav's government on the grounds of a lack of evidence), which led to the sentencing of Hindu activist Kameshwar Yadav. Further, Hindus saw the administration's reaction to the controversial 'Varun *mudda*' as evidence of minority appeasement — this strengthened their resentment of the BJP's decision to field a Muslim candidate. Meanwhile, some local Muslims accused Shahnawaz Hussain of being a BJP stooge and fake Muslim, criticising his marriage to a Hindu woman, and his lukewarm response to the Varun *mudda*.

Neither Bhagalpur's BJP MLA (denied the MP ticket to the chagrin of many supporters) nor the Nathnagar MLA (JD[U]) offered much support to Shahnawaz Hussain. Some senior members of the Bengali and Bunker communities threatened to vote instead for Subodh Roy. Among the caste associations, voicing displeasure was the Bania Samaj, who initially declared a boycott only to revoke it later, declaring support for Shakuni Choudhary. Nevertheless, Shahnawaz Hussain ultimately won the seat, leading in all ACs except Nathnagar. Turnout was 43 per cent across the PC (in some booths as low as 22 per cent), reflecting a broader trend for low voter participation across Bihar.

Research Questions

The Campaign

The ruling coalition at the state level sought to project a contrast between the *vikas* (development) ushered in by Nitish Kumar's government and the *kushshan* (bad rule) of Lalu Yadav. Unlike other candidates' relatively defensive campaigns, Shahnawaz Hussain's overall tenor was assertive. Except for Nitish Kumar's sabha in Pirpainti AC, there was no high-profile visit in support of the BJP campaign in this constituency. L. K. Advani's planned roadshow was cancelled.

RJD leaders Lalu Yadav and Rabri Devi visited Bhagalpur in support of Shakuni Choudhary. The campaign attempted to recast the election as a vote on secularism rather than development, claiming that communal violence would ensue if Advani came to power. Shakuni Choudhary presented the election as a *chunavi mahabharat* (the big contest). There was no reference to Congress candidate Sadanand Singh, and all speeches drew a distinction between the UPA alliance (presented as standing for secularism, and favoured by Lalu Yadav) and the Congress party, under whose rule the 1989 riots had occurred.

The rather lackadaisical Congress campaign focused on Sadanand Singh's public service achievements, asserting that development in Bihar was only possible owing to funding from Sonia Gandhi and Manmohan Singh's central government, and emphasised the candidate's local roots: *Dharti ke laal ko sansaad mein bhejen, aaj ye din bhi nahin aaya hai ki hum Supal ya Munger ke bete ko bharat ke sansaad mein bhejen* (Today the day has come when we can send the sons of the soil, from our [small] places like Supal and Munger, to the Indian Parliament).

Table A1
Total Votes Polled by Each Candidate in 26-Bhagalpur PC

	Name of Candidate	Remarks	Party	Votes Secured	Total Electors (%)	Total Votes Polled (%)
1	Ajit Sharma	M, 55	BSP	55,387	3.86	8.80
2	Shakuni Choudhary	M, 64	RJD	172,573	12.04	27.43
3	Sadanand Singh	M, 64	INC	52,121	3.64	8.29
4	Subodh Roy	M, 65	CPM	17,087	1.19	2.72
5	Syed Shahnawaz Hussain	M, 40	BJP	228,384	15.93	36.30
6	Daya Ram Mandal	M, 33	BHJAP	6,482	0.45	1.03
7	Deepak Ram	M, 40, SC	BSP(K)	2,361	0.16	0.38
8	Naresh Mandal	M, 48	RPP	5,994	0.42	0.95
9	Md. Izrail	M, 49	LTSD	3,420	0.24	0.54
10	Raman Sah	M, 44	BJJD	4,358	0.30	0.69
11	Ram Vilash Paswan	M, 45, SC	RWS	6,935	0.48	1.10
12	Srinarayan Gauswami	M, 59	IJP	4,165	0.29	0.66
13	Amit Kumar Jha	M, 50	IND	3,420	0.24	0.54
14	Anand Kumar Jain	M, 47	IND	3,555	0.25	0.57
15	Indradeo Kumar Singh	M, 30	IND	5,249	0.37	0.83
16	Dinesh Yadav	M, 30	IND	15,711	1.10	2.50
17	Dr N. K. Yadav	M, 44	IND	8,828	0.62	1.40
18	Ratan Kumar Mandal	M, 25	IND	21,947	1.53	3.49
19	Ravishankar Singh	M, 25	IND	2,628	0.18	0.42
20	Laddu	M, 27	IND	1,902	0.13	0.30
21	Sikandar Tanti	M, 34	IND	6,571	0.46	1.04
	Total			629,078		

Source: Prepared by Priyadarshini Singh.

Note: BHJAP = Bhartiya Jagran Party; BJJD = Bhartiya Jantantrik Janta Dal; BSP(K) = Bahujan Sangharsh Party (Kanshiram); IJP = Indian Justice Party; INC = Indian National Congress; IND = Independent; LTSD = Loktantrik Samta Dal; M = Male; RPP = Rashtriya Pragati Party; RWS = Rashtrawadi Sena.

The unique campaign style of Ajit Sharma (BSP) reflected the priorities of a party trying to establish grassroots support. His two-car convoy travelled mostly through Dalit-dominated areas, and he went from door to door hugging those who recognised him and vigorously shaking those who did not. His campaign message highlighted the development carried out in Uttar Pradesh by BSP leader 'Behnji' (Mayawati). Ajit Sharma also positioned himself as a local 'son of the soil' who would be directly accountable to his constituents. When challenged that as an MP he would be in Delhi, Ajit Sharma replied that his family would still be in Bhagalpur, and he would need to return regularly to look after the petrol pump from which he earns his *dal roti* (livelihood).

Language of Politics

Idioms of local life were enmeshed with those of modern political practices and experiences. Low levels of literacy and poor access to media meant that the use of English words and phrases was rare (although 'vote' had almost become a part of local vocabulary); and even *khadi boli* (the spoken language) Hindi words were not frequently used. When political elites and party workers talked about their support they said: *vote ki banavat hamare paksh main hai* (the result is shaping up in our favour), or *vote bikhar raha hai* (the vote is being scattered). *Karyakarta* (worker) had become *Kajkarta* — *karya* (work) is *kaj* in the local dialect. The EVM is generally referred to as *peti, baksa* (box), and election documents are known as *chunav samagri* (election paraphernalia), *dan dahej* (dowry and prestations exchanged at a wedding) Idioms of marriage, family and agriculture pervade many aspects of elections: almost all political parties compared the process of choosing a candidate to choosing a groom for one's daughter.

Senior members of the *chunav kushang* (election cell) spoke initially of their *kartavya* (duty) towards the country, but later confessed that '*kaam kar rahe hain, job hai toh pete ke liye toh karna padega*' (it's a job; we need to do it to feed ourselves). Junior officers complained more openly about the extra working hours, lack of facilities, and pressures of complying with ECI regulations: *chunav ka matlab bahut hi kasht; bukhar aata hai sooch kar* (an election is a real trial; just thinking about it gives me a fever); '*aagar* DM [district magistrate] *ki hi ye halat hai toh hum kya cheez hain*' (if even the DM can be reduced to such a state, then you can imagine what state we ordinary officials are in).

Polling Station

Booth seven — one of six booths in Mahashay Taraknath Madhya School — had 1,457 voters. The booths had been listed as sensitive on account of a fight that had reportedly broken out between Hindus and Muslims on polling day a few years ago. Though a crowd formed outside the complex before 7 AM on polling day (30 April 2009), no flood of people entered the school when polling opened. The women were generally better-dressed than the men, most of whom wore *lungis*. The atmosphere was lethargic, with the exception of the neighbouring booth where an enthusiastic presiding officer was encouraging *halla* (hullaballoo). The weavers were expected to arrive in droves after 10 AM, but attendance remained low throughout the day. Senior members of the polling party were quite rude to voters, and there was confusion over acceptable forms of identification. While the officials refused the lunch brought by the polling agents, they heartily consumed the cold drinks; the mood of the polling party lifted as voting drew to a close and paperwork was completed.

'Why Do You Vote?'

Voters seemed generally apathetic. Nitish Kumar's much-touted *vikas* was a source of pride only among first-time voters, and while most people agreed that things had changed under the his government, they also pointed out that building roads and drainage systems is not *vikas* — *vikas* is jobs, education, factories, and equal opportunities. Even when people did assert the importance of voting, this was done with a sense of frustration and inertia. Voters may also have felt over-whelmed by the number of well-known candidates.

Narratives of voting frequently began with standard statements: *Nayi sarkar chune ke liye, sarkar bane isliye* (the vote is to elect a new government); *aapne pasand ke neta ko chunene ke liye* (to elect a leader of one's choice); '*Desh ke nagrik hain toh* vote *toh dalenge hi na*' (If we are citizens of the country we must vote). The notion of voting as a right was always tempered with references to the dysfunctional system, the *netas*' lack of concern and the largely static standard of living: for many, the right was also a burden, grudgingly accepted. In this narrative, voting is not a contract with the system for the delivery of goods and services ('Vote *na dene se kya hoga*' [what would happen if we did not vote]; *adhikar ka prayog toh karenge hi na* (we would obviously exercise our right to vote); 'Vote *toh debe hi karo*' [that's all, we will vote]). Others cited the indispensible value of a single vote — a view expressed adamantly during sabhas and on polling day, often by the same people who on other occasions articulated strong displeasure with the system, politicians and the state.

At the very minimum, voting allows people to prevent the unilateral dominance of principles, policies, candidates, ideologies, or parties that they oppose. For example, some Muslim bunkers explained that by voting they could at least make some dent in the BJP support base. By not voting, one loses the opportunity to express displeasure towards a particular candidate. Among Muslim voters, voting was considered important because otherwise, *kanooni karvahi kari gayegi hum par* (we could be taken to court for this). Having one's name on the voters' list was proof that one counts as part of the system, owes allegiance to India and takes it as one's own country.

Appendix B
Chhattisgarh

Researcher: Goldy M. George

*Chotte Katekoni village, Chandrapur AC (36),
Janjgir-Champa PC (SC) (3)*

Background

Separated from Madhya Pradesh on 1 November 2000, Chhattisgarh covers an area of 135,194 square kilometres. In the 2001 Census, the population of the state was 20,833,803, of which approximately 80 per cent lived in rural areas. The state's SC population is 12 per cent, of which 79 per cent live in rural areas. The ST population is 32 per cent, of which 95 per cent live in rural areas. Chhattisgarh comprises three natural regions: the Bagelkhand plateau, where abundant mineral resources have attracted large-scale industry; the plains (the state's rice bowl); and the forested Bastar plateau. A low Human Development Index in the region indicates extreme poverty, which is largely a result of highly skewed landholding in rural areas — a remnant of the erstwhile *zamindari* and *malguzari* (land tenancy) systems. Only 44 per cent of the available land is used for cultivation, and of this only 12.5 per cent is irrigated.

Situated at the centre of the state, the district of Janjgir-Champa is a major producer of grains. The district's population in 2001 was 1,317,431 (22.5 per cent SC; 11.6 per cent ST). The Satnami, Suryavanshi, Ganda, and Ghasi are the major SC communities, and the three largest STs in the district are Gond, Kawar and Sawar. The literacy rate is 66 per cent.

Chotte Katekoni village is a panchayat headquarter within Janjgir-Champa district. It has a dependent village named Turkapali, and lies approximately 75 km from the district headquarters; its nearest township is Dabhra, 5 km away. The village population is 1,968, and includes Satnami (SC), Chandra (OBC), Kurmi (OBC), Ghasia (SC), Saura (ST), Ganda (SC), and Muslim. Social and political spheres are dominated by Satnamis and Chandras. Almost 42 per cent of village residents are SC, 49 per cent are OBC, one family is Muslim, and the remaining residents are ST.

Delimitation

Before the delimitation exercise, the area was covered by two separate PCs: Janjgir and Sarangarh. The delimitation exercise removed Saranghar PC from the map; the new PC of Janjgir-Champa consists of Akaltara, Janjgir-Champa, Sakti, Chandrapur, Jaijaipur, Pamgarh (SC), Bilaigarh (SC), and Kasdol ACs. Some of these ACs have also been reshaped or renamed. Before delimitation there were two ST-reserved ACs and one SC-reserved AC in Janjgir, and four SC-reserved ACs in Saranghar. There are now two SC-reserved ACs in Janjgir-Champa PC.

Delimitation has also reduced the number of SC-reserved Lok Sabha seats in the state. Prior to 2008, Bilaspur and Saranghar had been SC-reserved. Bilaspur is now a general constituency; Janjgir-Champa is the only SC-reserved PC in Chhattisgarh.

Electoral History

In undivided Madhya Pradesh, the Congress won regularly from Janjgir even when the party lost many seats in the 1998 Lok Sabha election. Janjgir has acted as a laboratory for many different social and political forces over several decades; the region's sizeable Dalit presence has made it difficult for other caste groups to ignore their socio-political aspirations and needs. In the late 1970s and early 1980s Dalits throughout the area supported the BSP, though the late 1990s saw a backlash against BSP, remnants of which are still apparent, particularly in the village of Chotte Katekoni.

Janjgir PC had an exceptionally long history of being dominated by Dalit-OBC politics, despite being a general constituency before delimitation. From the first elections in 1951, Congress candidate Minimata Agam Dass Guru, a Dalit woman, remained the MP until the Emergency. In 1977, a non-Congress candidate (Madanlal Shukla of the Janata Party) won the seat for the first time, marking the emergence of upper-caste candidates. In 1980 and 1985, the Congress candidate won. In 1989, the BJP's Dilip Singh Judev won the election; but in 1991, the Congress wrestled the seat back only to lose to the BJP in 1996. In 1998, Charandas Mahant won the seat for Congress, retaining it in 1999. The 2004 election was won narrowly by Karuna Shukla of the BJP.

Sarangarh remained an SC-reserved constituency since the reconstitution of constituencies in 1977. The first election was won by Govindram Miri of the Janata Party. From 1980 to 1998, Parasram Bharadwaj of the Congress held the seat continuously. In 1999, the BJP, represented by P. R. Khute, won for the first time. The 2004 election saw another BJP victory under Guharam Ajgalle, who secured 41.3 per cent of the vote, followed by Congress (31.2 per cent) and BSP (19.2 per cent).

Chandrapur AC had been held by the Congress until 1990 when BJP won the seat. In 1993, the Congress won it back, but it was reclaimed by the BJP in 1998. The 2003 election saw a split in the Congress: when former winner and 1998 runner-up Novel Verma was denied the Congress ticket, he stood for the NCP and won the election. However, he lost his seat in 2008 to Dilip Singh Judev's son Yudhivir Singh Judev of the BJP.

Generally, Panchayat elections in Chhattisgarh are contested on a non-party basis. However, many of the elected representatives have some kind of political affiliation. In the past this was usually with the Congress, but of late many have shifted towards the BJP or joined the NCP with Novel Verma. The current Sarpanch is an Adivasi and BJP supporter.

Contest and Outcome of the 2009 Election

A close race was expected, but ultimately Kamladevi Patle of the BJP won comfortably by 87,211 votes. Turnout in Chotte Katekoni was 48.4 per cent (across the PC it was 48.6 per cent). NCP decided not to contest these elections; it also openly opposed Congress in this constituency on the grounds of negative voting practices in the 2008 Vidhan Sabha election.

Table B1
Total Votes Polled by Each Candidate in 3-Janjgir-Champa PC (SC)

	Name of Candidate	Remarks	Party	Votes Secured	Total Electors (%)	Total Votes Polled (%)
1	Shrimati Kamla Devi Patle	F, 43, SC	BJP	302,142	19.90	40.96
2	Dauram Ratnakar	M, 51, SC	BSP	175,979	11.59	23.86
3	Shivkumar Dahariya	M, 45, SC	INC	214,931	14.15	29.14
4	B. R. Chauhan	M, 59, SC	RPI(A)	5,256	0.35	0.71
5	Neelkanth Ware	M, 59, SC	CSP	2,303	0.15	0.31
6	Prem Shankar Mahilange Urf Prem India	M, 39, SC	LJP	1,959	0.13	0.27
7	Sanjeev Kumar Khare	M, 26, SC	CGVP	2,231	0.15	0.30
8	Anandram Gilhare	M, 35, SC	IND	3,720	0.24	0.50
9	Chattram Suryavanshi	M, 62, SC	IND	2,979	0.20	0.40
10	Chhavilal Ratre	M, 55, SC	IND	4,278	0.28	0.58
11	Mayaram Nat	M, 50, SC	IND	6,455	0.43	0.88
12	Ramcharan Pradhan Adhiwakta	M, 51, SC	IND	15,345	1.01	2.08
	Total			**737,578**		

Source: Prepared by Goldy M. George.

Note: CGVP = Chhattisgarh Vikas Party; CSP = Chhattisgarh Samaj Party; F = Female; IND = Independent; LJP = Lok Jan Shakti Party; M = Male; RPI(A) = Republican Party of India (A).

Research Questions

The Campaign

Gorelal Ratnakar — once a BSP campaigner and currently an active member of a Dalit movement — spoke of his campaign experience:

> the atmosphere in the village is very heated when the election nears. All of a sudden there is a greater mobility of people, vehicles, discussions, debates, arguments, etc. Sometimes there are fights also. In such cases the existing family dispute or caste rivalry is converted to political rivalry. Nevertheless the village looks very colourful.

He noted too that the festivities were greatest around a Panchayat election — Lok Sabha elections attracted much less interest. Mohan Nirala described the Panchayat campaigns thus:

> the mobility of people is visibly much higher. Lots of colourful banners, wall writings, all canvassing methods, cajoling with things, liquor, chicken, distribution of money, flow of money . . . For nearly a month it is like the biggest festival of our village. Everywhere people would talk about it.

Role of the Media

In Janjgir, the newspapers *Navbharat* and *Dainik Bhaskar* carried interviews and analyses concerning the candidates and their campaigns. Caste analysis was seen as particularly crucial, owing to Chhattisgarh's high OBC population. The media also exercised power to expose public figures; for example, after press reports claimed that the Director General of Police had misused his power to influence the Vidhan Sabha election, he was forced to go on leave until the elections were over. One story regarding the seizure of liquor from a Protestant church in Bilaspur made the front page in most leading dailies on the day of polling: that it was a story created to target Congress candidate (and ardent Christian) Renu Jogi was not mentioned. The incident reflected the saffron inclination of newspapers in Chhattisgarh.

This trend was also noticeable in electronic media (local and state channels are either run by BJP cadres or their supporters). Many channels ran a week-long telecast of Yogpeeth-II, ignoring questions of hunger, poverty and discrimination. Chhattisgarh-based channels focused mainly on 'Raman Singh's Roadshow', the 'Modi Effect', and 'Hema Malini's jan sabhas'. The major Congress story was the visit of Sonia Gandhi and Rahul Gandhi.

Language of Politics

People in Chotte Katekoni understand the political situation much better now than in the past, and many express frustration about corruption and broken promises. According to Reshamlal Ratre (44 years old), a migrant worker at a kiln in Jharkhand:

> If the government for all these years had fulfilled even half of the promises they made, then I wouldn't have been a migrant labourer for the past 20-odd years. I am landless and today I don't have any identity either . . . Whenever the election nears all the political leaders come forward and place these fake promises before us. I was promised twice or thrice that I would get land. At least they could have given me homestead land or sanctioned an *Indira awas* [housing loan scheme]. But these promises are just endless and never to be fulfilled.

Shankardeo Mahant (65 years old), who said he refused to vote any 'fake leaders' to power, claimed not to be bothered by party affiliations, asking: 'Why should I waste my time to decide which snake is the most venomous?' He opined that politicians used to have more sincerity, but that the language had changed, and now money is all-powerful. He called politics 'the most abominable subject' — and elections as merely an extension of the same thing.

According to Sundar Pankaj (22 years old), a young Dalit activist:

> Today politics is one of the most hated words in rural areas. If you are an honest man, then you should keep away from politics. Sometimes I also feel that we can't stop it, we may have to live with it as long as possible. When election nears, I think it is our chance to take revenge and show our power. I vote and also promote people in my village to vote. The lone reason is to keep the hopes and aspiration of our community growth and development alive.

Polling Station

On the day of polling, people lined up outside the school from about 7.15 AM. The first to arrive were women from the village. Most had brought their voter identification cards, though some had brought NREGA, BPL and ration cards instead. The officials took help from the local booth agents to identify those without voter identification. Among those who voted, 78 per cent did so with their voter identification.

Agents and officers worked together to try to get electrical power to the booths to power the EVM, a bulb and a fan. There was some confusion over timings, as many people were under the impression that the schedule would be from 8 AM to 5 PM. Few arrived before 8 AM and, more problematically, some who arrived after 4 PM were turned away without being allowed to vote.

'Why Do You Vote?'

The vote was commonly seen as a fundamental right (*bote hamr maulik adhikar he*). Dhankunwar Pankaj of the women's organisation and local Dalit movement had, with her colleagues, compiled a charter of related demands, including the right to recall elected representatives and to vote for 'none of the above'. Jalbai Ratre, also active in the women's organisation, explained her reasons for voting:

> I vote to see that the elected leaders take care of the community at large and do not deceive us. It is more a sort of belief, which, in fact, never comes true. Yet I feel that my vote is very important and vital. I value it really highly. It is the only way to express myself. Otherwise they don't listen to my problems before or after the election . . . Vote is an instrument for me.

She said that in some past elections, candidates had won by only one vote: 'Do you think that my vote is not important in such a circumstance? These *panch* [five] aspiring contestants spend more than a lakh [100,000] rupees every round. So my vote values *sava* lakh [125,000]'. Though she expressed disappointment with the current election processes, she saw the act of voting as an important visible expression of citizenship:

> It is my responsibility to vote . . . by casting my vote I will be counted as a citizen of my village, since I will be in the sight of everyone. Further, if I vote, I have a right to demand for the development of my village.

According to Jalbai, the collective decision to favour a particular candidate (this time, the BSP candidate) was reached by discussion and consensus. The Dalit women in this village have a new political approach towards democracy, which emphasises respect for human commonalities, in contrast to mainstream politics as a profession based on the corporate principles of profit.

Many young Dalit voters claimed that voting gave them an identity and let the government know of their existence. One explained that he was also motivated by the 'dream of a good and healthy government that supports the poor people'. Others welcomed the feeling of being 'equal with everyone for at least one day'. Members of non-Dalit OBC communities (Painka) expressed similar views. For some people, including Chudamani Ghasia (nearly 75 years old), voting is a way to express anger and gain self-respect; others stressed the need to keep communal and casteist forces at bay.

Appendix C
Delhi

Researcher: Rosina Nasir

Jafarabad, Seelampur AC (65),
North East Delhi PC (2)

Background

Jafarabad (Ward 92 of the Shahdara North Zone of the Municipal Corporation of Delhi) falls within Seelampur AC. The main thoroughfare of Jafarabad, also referred to as New Seelampur, is a narrow, pockmarked road that resembles a dirt track, yet has to bear heavy traffic. There is no pedestrian pavement, the streets are used as toilets and the clogged drains are blocked with bottles and other solid waste. Though there is little garbage littering the roads, the nearby municipal dump is a towering eyesore, through which child rag-pickers rummage for plastic bags and bottles. The area is characterised by low-income families and high population density. Within Seelampur, the area of Chauhan Bangar houses many migrants from Uttar Pradesh and Bihar, mostly comprising Ajlaf Muslims.

People in Seelampur have few educational or employment opportunities. Although enrolment in formal education is growing, the dropout rate is high. Almost all of the small manufacturing units are engaged in power theft, which has intensified even after the privatisation of electricity. The area had been listed as 'sensitive'.

Delimitation

While the number of parliamentary and assembly seats in Delhi remains unchanged post-delimitation, at seven and 70 respectively, the constituencies have been redrawn considerably. Each PC now covers

10 ACs. While four old PCs remain, at least in name (New Delhi, South Delhi, East Delhi, and Chandni Chowk), former PCs, Outer Delhi, Karol Bagh (reserved) and Sadar Bazar, have been replaced by three new PCs — North-East Delhi, North-West Delhi (reserved) and West Delhi.

Delimitation strongly affected the East Delhi PC, which was divided between East Delhi and North-East Delhi PCs. While the new East Delhi PC has a large presence of Group Housings societies and JJ (Juggi Jhompadi) colonies, North-East Delhi PC is predominantly home to unauthorised colonies. It covers the ACs of Burari, Timarpur, Seemapuri, Rohtas Nagar, Seelampur, Ghonda, Babarpur, Gokalpur, Mustafabad, and Karawal Nagar.

Electoral History

In 1977, East Delhi was won by Kishore Lal of the Bharatiya Lok Dal (BLD). In 1980 the seat was won by H. K. L. Bhagat of the Congress, who held it until 1991 when it was won by BJP candidate B. L. Sharma. The BJP held the seat under Sharma and then Lal Bihari Tiwari until 2004 when Sandeep Dixit (Congress), became the MP.

Ch. Matin has been MLA for Seelampur AC since 1993, when he won on a Janata Dal ticket. In 1998, he stood as an independent candidate, and in 2003 and 2008, he represented the Congress.

Contest and Outcome of the 2009 Election

Over 11 million people were eligible to vote at 11,348 polling booths across the capital's seven PCs. A total of 193 polling booths were identified as 'sensitive' and 32 as 'hyper-sensitive'. Although the political power in the new North-East Delhi PC appears to rest with Brahmins, who are well-represented as legislators and councillors, caste alliances and voting patterns in different areas are also influential, and parties worked overtime to woo the Muslim, OBC and SC voters, who together comprised almost 55 per cent of the PC's electorate.

Contrary to the assembly results, the Municipal Corporation of Delhi (MCD) elections had seen a saffron sweep in the constituency, with the BJP winning 28 of the 40 seats and Congress winning only four. With no clear trend apparent for the new PC, and with sitting East Delhi MP (Sandeep Dixit, Congress) reportedly opting to contest the new East Delhi seat, many aspired to stake their claim in this political green field, including Narendra Nath (MLA, Shahdara) and Jagdish Tytler (MP, Sadar Bazar). The MLAs of Seelampur and Mustafabad were also keen to put themselves forward, as the Muslim vote bank would play a key role.

Eventually, 16 candidates contested the seat. B. L. Sharma's BJP candidacy marked his return to active politics after a decade. He had left the BJP in 1997, joining the Vishwa Hindu Parishad (VHP) and disassociating himself from active politics. Also known as 'Prem Singh Sher', his impressive political experience and VHP connection led people to say: *is haath me jeet ka yog he* (his hand is destined for success). He sought votes particularly on issues of terrorism, rising prices and security concerns.

J. P. Agarwal was selected as the Congress candidate after Jagdish Tytler withdrew from the contest. Agarwal, who had also served in Rajya Sabha, had won his first Lok Sabha election in 1984. At the time of this election he was working as the President of Delhi Pradesh Congress Committee. By giving Agarwal the ticket, the Congress hoped to attract votes from the Vaish/Bania community, who had traditionally supported the BJP but switched camps in the previous assembly elections.

The North-East Delhi PC had 1,677,058 total electors, and turnout was just over 52 per cent. The BSP candidate withdrew three days before the election, which was won by J. P. Agarwal.

Research Questions

The Campaign

The BJP campaign blended logic and sentiment, as speakers at BJP *jan sabha*s enumerated the misdeeds of Congress and berated its record on development. Sharma focused on large issues such as building the Ram Mandir at Ayodhya, repealing Article 370 and bringing the Metro to the constituency. A special effort was made to invite Arif Baig to a BJP *jan sabha* at the Seelampur Chowk; all speeches were put on hold at the time of *namaz* (Muslim prayer). Despite their well-managed propaganda the BJP expressed nothing substantial to attract Muslim voters, and no BJP leader of national stature deigned to visit the constituency. Though Sharma had been sure of victory, the BJP tally suffered a considerable dent following the BSP candidate's

Table C1

Total Votes Polled by Each Candidate in 2-North-East Delhi PC

	Name of Candidate	Remarks	Party	Votes Secured	Total Electors (%)	Total Votes Polled (%)
1	Jai Prakash Agarwal	M, 64	INC	518,191	30.90	59.03
2	Haji Dilshad Ali	M, 36	BSP	44,111	2.63	5.02
3	B. L. Sharma Prem	M, 79	BJP	295,948	17.65	33.71
4	Anis Ahmad Ansari	M, 36	SP	3,476	0.21	0.40
5	Israr Khan	M, 32	RPIE	741	0.04	0.08
6	Kaliram Tomar	M, 48, SC	IJP	1,227	0.07	0.14
7	Ganesh Pal	M, 52	BSKP	2,173	0.13	0.25
8	Pramod Tiwari	M, 45	MBP	636	0.04	0.07
9	Manohar Lal	M, 50, SC	AWD	614	0.04	0.07
10	Sushil Kumar Mishra	M, 35	ABHM	761	0.05	0.09
11	Molana Abdussami	M, 29	IND	1,426	0.09	0.16
12	Manager Chaurasiya	M, 39	IND	1,257	0.07	0.14
13	R. N. Singh	M, 61	IND	1,013	0.06	0.12
14	Mohd. Shear Nabi Chaman	M, 49	IND	1,459	0.09	0.17
15	Santosh Devi	F, 28, SC	IND	1,677	0.10	0.19
16	Mohd. Hasnain	M, 50	IND	3,194	0.10	0.36
	Total			877,904		

Source: Prepared by Rosina Nasir.

Note: ABHM = Akhil Bharat Hindu Mahasabha; AWD = Adarshwadi Dal; BSKP = Bhartiya Sarvoday Kranti Party; F = Female; IND = Independent; M = Male; MBP = Matra Bhakta Party; RPIE = Republican Party of India Ektawadi.

dramatic decision three days before polling to withdraw and declare his support for the Congress. Sharma became insecure and launched an anti-Muslim tirade: *Hindustan Hindu ka, Musalman wapas jao* (India belongs to Hindus; Muslims can go home [by implication, to Pakistan]). For Seelampur and other Muslim-dominated areas, the final three days of the campaign were hugely significant for the swing in favour of Congress: Muslims of these areas had no other option.

The Congress' official election machinery gathered tempo after Agarwal's nomination, but was not as active as anticipated, though Rahul Gandhi attended a rally on the last day. Agarwal came across as a calm person, but was not as convincing a public speaker as Sharma.

At stalls where shopkeepers had arranged for televisions, informal groups of spectators gathered to watch IPL cricket matches. Often, local *paan* and confectionary vendors were also party workers, who used this network to take the pulse of the electorate. These *nukkad* (street corner) agents read newspapers and used their knowledge of party strategy to attract voters and transfer messages while in the guise of the common man.

Role of the Media

The media was important, even though literacy and newspaper readership is low, particularly among Muslim families. Urdu and Hindi language newspapers have wider readerships than their English-language equivalents, and were used by various parties to develop their candidates' personalities. The editors' judgements influenced the views of others; the result was a media consensus that affected the public's sense of the importance of certain issues.

Language of Politics

The less formal the occasion and the likelihood of attracting the attention of the press, the less measured and responsible were the utterances of those making speeches at campaign events. Among the public, words and phrases used in the language of politics included *seva sadgi* (voting is defined as an act of charity for humanity) and *tyuhaar* (the election is compared to a festival). Traditional BJP voters were *Kaccha Dhar*, while *Pappu ban gaya* referred to a 'loser not able to vote'. *Apna Bhai* (our own brother) referred to Muslim candidates, H. K. L. Bhagat was known as *Betaj Badshah* (supreme ruler), and *Chupa hua* (the hidden one) RSS referred to the BJP candidate.

Polling Station

In Seelampur, polling day could be compared to the festival of Eid, and the *netaon ke chehre* (faces of the leaders) with *Eid ka chaand* (Eid's moon). Some respondents described election time as a one-month festival for the poor, who are bombarded with promises, money and liquor. For the candidates, the same month is equivalent to *ramdaan* — a fasting period during which they must work with generosity. The one able to cast their message in front of *janta janadhan* (the public) will succeed.

An election is the only 'festival' when Muslim women also move out in large numbers, some in full *burkha* and a few in *chadder*. After morning cleaning and cooking, women attended the polling station in small groups or with a man from their family. One woman explained: '*hamare miyan ne kaha haath ka* button *dabana, bus hamne kar diya*' (my husband asked me to press the button beside the symbol of the hand, so I did). While most women seemed to vote in accordance with the wishes of male family members, they had many views to share — complaining about rising prices, dwindling business opportunities, and the lack of candidates or parties that worked for their welfare. In the afternoon, when the number of voters arriving at the booth dwindled due to the scorching heat, cycle rickshaws adorned with party symbols were dispatched to spread campaign messages and to transport the handicapped, female and elderly voters.

'Why Do You Vote?'

Initial reactions to this question suggested that people vote because they have been drilled to perform their civic duty. Loyalty to parties and candidates of one's own caste, religion or any other social group was strong, based on a common notion that community affiliation leads to empathy and assistance. For example, one respondent felt that his BPL card had been delayed because his ward's BJP councillor 'knew' him — a Muslim — to have voted for the Congress. Social affiliations were seen as important factors in 'getting work done' (e.g., obtaining licenses, registering land rights, implementing development projects). These practical loyalties were common among the illiterate and poor residents of the slums.

However, people did not readily admit the importance of religion and caste; the majority claimed to vote 'according to the work and capabilities of the candidate'. It thus seems paradoxical that the people of Seelampur have favoured the same MLA for 15 years despite a poor development record. To justify their support, some respondents subtly modified their statements: 'We would favour the candidate because of his work, affiliation and party respectively'. Faithfulness to a party was less pronounced than that to a candidate.

Many people attributed greater value to the act of voting than the vote itself. In these cases, the voter acts not as an individual, but as part of a (somewhat organised) group, based on geography, occupation, caste, or religion. Not every member can persuade other members to vote a certain way — reputation and economic status were among the determinants of an individual's influence. People did not like to waste their vote on a losing candidate, and those whose voting intention differed from the majority view of their group were likely to change their minds in order to conform.

Money and services also became an important aspect of bargaining between certain sections of the electorate — particularly those living in the slum — and the candidate/party. As one respondent stated: *jo dega vo payega* (whoever gives [money] gets the vote); though in some cases, money was taken from all parties, and votes were given not to the highest bidder but on the basis of other considerations. Electricity supply was constant during this time, there were no inspections or evictions, and the sealing drive to close down unauthorised businesses ceased. For people in the slum this was a routine associated with all elections — a business opportunity that arrived with the election period and would soon pass.

Appendix D
Gujarat

Researcher: Mahashweta Jani

Polling station 30, Sardoi village,
Modasa AC (31), Sabarkantha PC (5)

Background

The district of Sabarkantha in North Gujarat covers urban and rural areas, plains and mountains, and is known as one of the backward districts of Gujarat as there has been little industrial development. The roads are good, but groundwater levels have decreased dramatically in the past few years; as a result the three sub-districts of Idar, Meghraj and Modasa have been declared 'dark zones' (farmers in these areas are denied three-phase electricity connections for agricultural purposes). The study site was chosen on the basis of historical research into the caste-orientation of political factions in Modasa undertaken in 1962 by Rajani Kothari and Ghanshyam Shah (Shah 1975).

Sardoi village lies 45 km away from the district headquarters of Himmatnagar, and 18 km from Modasa town, the nearest urban centre. The total population of the village is 3,079, of which 2,314 are registered voters. Polling station 30 had 1,055 voters. Approximately 30 years ago, Sardoi was dominated by the Banias (Khadaytas and Nimas). It was considered the economic hub of Modasa, and an important market for grains and cloth. All the market shops were owned by Banias; they were involved in the money-lending business, and because they controlled the market they also dominated politics. However, as nationalised and cooperative banks arrived, most Banias left the rural areas for cities such as Modasa, Ahmedabad and Mumbai and only a few Brahmin and Bania families remain. The chairmen and directors of the large milk cooperatives and cooperative banks are mostly Patels and Rajputs; the market shops are now OBC- and Kshatriya-owned. Today, Dalits and Kshatriyas are the most populous groups, and almost equal in number; the upper-caste Kshatriyas are the politically dominant caste in the village. In next greatest number are OBCs, which include OBC Kshatriyas, Nayaks, Bhoi, Bharwad, and Rabaris.

Casteism has deep roots in Sardoi. Each caste has its own flourmill, and frequency of access to water is caste-dependent. The hierarchy among the Dalits is also very rigid, distinguishing between Harijan Pandyas (Brahmins of Dalits), Vankars, Chamars, and finally Valmikis, who interestingly all had government jobs, and were economically and educationally well-to-do. People in the Vankar Vaas described significant changes since the village was dominated by the Banias, and explained that though the upper-castes, or 'Sahukars', still held power, the Kshatriyas had to keep the lower castes informed before taking action. Yet from the perspective of the Kshatriyas-Rajputs; 'To rule the people is in our blood and that's why now we are in politics in big numbers'.

The main occupation in Sardoi is cattle farming. The village has two separate cooperative dairies, and produces 2,000 litres of milk every day, which go to Sabar cooperative dairy — one of Gujarat's largest. Some people are also involved in cultivation, though few own agricultural land. They grow cash crops including vegetables, groundnut, potatoes, wheat, and *bajri* (millet). The village is surrounded by forested hills, and many villagers pick leaves to make *bidi* and traditional leaf plates.

Delimitation

Before delimitation, this PC included the ACs of Danta and Vadgam (SC), which are dominated by the tribals and the Dalits. Following delimitation, these segments were moved to the Banaskantha and Patan PCs. The ACs of Prantij and Bayad, formerly part of the Kapadvanj PC, were added to Sabarkantha. As the delimitation exercise replaced Congress-dominated ACs with BJP-dominated ACs, the BJP was expected to easily win this seat.

Electoral History

Sabarkantha PC covers seven ACs: Modasa, Bhiloda, Idar (SC), Khedbrahma (ST), Himmatnagar, Prantij, and Bayad. The PC has traditionally been a Congress stronghold, even though the majority of the ACs is now held by the BJP (only Bhiloda and Khedbrahma are Congress). Past elections have often involved a clear contest between these two parties; no other party has a presence here. This parliamentary seat had been won by the BJP only once, in 1991, when the actor Arvind Trivedi — who played Ravana in the famous epic serial *Ramayan* — was elected. It was a great challenge for the BJP to win this seat.

Politically, Sardoi village has been divided between BJP and Congress, and it has active political workers from both parties. The Sarpanch is Jyotsna Pandya, a Dalit.

Contest and Outcome of the 2009 Election

There were 12 candidates who contested the election, but the race was effectively between the BJP and Congress. The sitting MP, Madhusudan Mistry, had been the whip of the Congress in the previous parliament. He belongs to the lower strata of society, and is a social activist who had been working for tribal rights in the Khedbrahma area for the past 20 years; he also runs an NGO. The BJP candidate Mahendrasinh Chauhan — an upper-caste Kshatriya and an Ayurvedic doctor — had been actively associated with the BJP since being youth-wing *taluka* president in 1980, though this was his first time contesting a parliamentary election. He was chairman of the District Education Committee when he was selected by Narendra Modi, and the campaign focused on his local roots.

Much has changed since Kothari and Shah's study in 1962: the shifting demography of the village has changed the castes' characters, and the OBCs have become conscious about their political power. In this election the BJP candidate was Kshatriya, so the politics of 'KHAM' (Kshatriya, Harijan, Adivasi, Muslim) did not work for any party. Instead, the Harijan, Adivasi and Muslims created one bloc, with the Kshatriyas (both upper-caste and OBC) on the other side. For the public, politics is still very much divided along caste lines: Congress is the party of Dalits, Muslims and Adivasis, while the BJP is the party of the upper castes. The OBC remain a floating bloc, and the result of their shift towards the BJP in this election was a BJP victory, with a margin of over 17,000 votes.

Of 1055 electors listed at polling station 30, only 369 voted — a turnout of 35 per cent. The Deputy Sarpanch explained that the voting rate in Panchayat elections is almost 90 per cent, while in Lok Sabha elections the maximum turnout is 45 per cent. People in the rural areas are more interested in Panchayat and Dairy elections than those of the Lok Sabha, and the younger generation in particular is highly apolitical. Turnout across Sabarkantha PC (1,452,240 electors) was 49.4 per cent.

Research Questions

The Campaign

Both Congress and BJP held roadshows and public meetings. As it was such a challenge for the BJP to take this seat, Chief Minister Narendra Modi held six public meetings in the constituency. His use of media and technology made 'Modi mania' effective in Gujarat: after polling, he used print and electronic media to thank the people of Gujarat for voting in large numbers. Modi knows his audiences and his language of profit and development (with a little touch of communalism) is popular in the business-oriented society of Gujarat.

Campaigns also involved music, dance and drama. There was a cricket tournament, a small door-to-door campaign, lunch and dinner parties for different castes, and distribution of leaflets, scarves, pens, liquor, masks, and badges. Congress candidate Madhusan Mistry visited the villages with a dummy EVM, demonstrating to the villagers how they could vote for his party.

Role of the Media

People waited eagerly each morning for the newspaper — the major source of news in Sardoi. The main regional newspapers *Divya Bhaskar* (circulation of 200 in Sardoi), *Gujarat Samachar* (110) and *Sandesh* (90) each published one main edition, with a four-page local supplement. Circulation of English newspapers in Sardoi village was zero. Throughout the month of the election, the deadly Hepatitis B outbreak captured much of the space of political news — rallies,

Table D1
Total Votes Polled by Each Candidate for 5-Sabarkantha PC

	Name of Candidate	Remarks	Party	Votes Secured	Total Electors (%)	Total Votes Polled (%)
1	Chauhan Mahendrasinh	M, 55	BJP	337,432	23.24	47.02
2	Mistry Madhusudan	M, 63	INC	320,272	22.05	44.63
3	Ramlavat Vikramsinh Laxmansinh	M, 31	BSP	8,246	0.57	1.15
4	Kadari Molana Riyaz	M, 46	SP	1,614	0.11	0.22
5	Parmar Minaba Dipsinh	F, 30	IJP	1,066	0.07	0.15
6	Sinhali Dashrath Chandulal	M, 55	CPI(ML)(L)	1,151	0.08	0.16
7	Chauhan Mahendrasinh Padamsinh	M, 36	IND	1,765	0.12	0.25
8	Trivedi Balkrushn Pranlal	M, 71	IND	3,176	0.22	0.44
9	Patel Kantibhai Khushalbhai	M, 73	IND	2,201	0.15	0.31
10	Patel Danabhai Becharbhai	M, 65	IND	3,052	0.21	0.43
11	Rathod Sabirmiya Amirmiya	M, 51	IND	9,504	0.65	1.32
12	Solanki Chhaganbhai Kevalabhai	M, 63, ST	IND	28,135	1.94	3.92
	Total			717,614		

Source: Prepared by Mahashweta Jani.
Note: F = Female; IND = Independent; M = Male.

roadshows and public meetings were reported only if they had been addressed by 'star campaigners' such as Narendra Modi, Rahul Gandhi or Sonia Gandhi, whose visit to nearby Patan was a front-page story. Two stringers for *Sandesh* explained that during elections no political news was accepted from them.

There was no cable connection in Sardoi, but people had access to Dish TV and Direct to Home (DTH) satellite dish. The popular (and generally neutral) 7 PM report on Doordarshan covered major political events in Gujarat; like other private channels, Doordarshan also showed party advertisements. The BJP advertisements of *Majboot neta Nirnayak Sarkar* (strong leader, decisive government) were broadcast in Hindi, and addressed national issues such as security and Ladli Lakshmi Yojana (a welfare scheme for young girls); but while many people remembered the memorable slogan, few agreed that Manmohan Singh was a weak prime minister. Congress advertisements, broadcast in Gujarati, focussed on local issues such as incidents of rape and suicides of farmers and diamond workers. When covering political speeches, the reporters sent catchy and satirical statements in 30-second sound bites. People listened to film songs on the radio, but it was no longer a major news source.

Language of Politics

Language travelled very effectively from Narendra Modi to the people in the villages. At his sabha in Bayad taluka, he contrasted the Congress' 'politics of the vote bank' with the BJP's 'politics of development', and emphasised the BJP candidate's roots in Sabarkantha. A few days later, local leaders spoke the very same words at the Vijay Vishwas Yuva Sammelan in Modasa taluka. From there, Modi's words travelled to the villages, carried by the young people — almost 20 from each village — who had attended the meeting. Modi's famous slogan — *Hun khato nathi ane khava deto nathi* (I am not corrupt and I won't let other be corrupt) (neither am I corrupt nor do I allow corruption to flourish) — remains popular. One executive member of the village dairy, in a conversation about corruption, broke suddenly into a repetition of words Modi had used in his address: *ame khaie nahi ne khava daie pan nahi* (I am not corrupt and I won't let others be corrupt). The Congress party lacks a similar structure to effectively transmit language from top to bottom, as one party member stated: 'There are no workers but all leaders in Congress'.

Modi involved his audience by asking questions, mimicking his opponents, and playing up his 'macho' image (particularly when addressing the issue of terrorism), eliciting shouts of *Jai Shri Ram* (Hail Lord Ram). He carefully matched his language to his audience, addressing local people in Gujarati but turning to the camera and speaking in Hindi to address a television audience. He made effective use of figures and statistics, and remembered to acknowledge the sarpanch by name in Vatrak village, a gesture that touched the local people.

Polling Station

Polling Station 30 was set up in the village primary school — a site that had also recently acted as a Hepatitis B vaccination centre. The EVMs arrived the evening before polling, accompanied by the zonal officer. The gates of the campus (one of which opened toward the Dalit *basti* and the other towards the Kumhar *basti*) were then locked. The candidates' names and details were posted outside in Gujarati. Owing to a history of clashes during polling, Sardoi was regarded as a sensitive polling booth. The ECI had appointed an observation officer, and a cameraman to record important incidents at the polling station.

The only apparent difference between the day of vaccination and the day of voting at the site was that people came in fewer numbers to vote. There were no long queues. Women mostly came in groups of three or four, some with their friends and neighbours and others with the other women of their household; men came alone or with their wives. Widows arrived with other widows. Many elderly people and some first-time voters did not know how to use the EVM machine. The polling officer taught them politely, making use of a dummy EVM chart. However, almost 25 women were turned away because they did not have any photographic proof of identity — a common issue as most women do not hold any property or bank accounts in their name.

'Why Do You Vote?'

For some in Sardoi, voting was like a sacred ritual, arousing sentiments similar to performing *dan* at the temple. Many people expressed eagerness to experience the election mechanism. Some described the happiness of being considered a citizen and some raised issues of equality. Among the lower castes — women in particular — there was a sense of the consciousness of power and of individual freedom of choice, though in certain castes that have maintained a patriarchal structure, the final say of the *mukhiya* is decisive. Some associated voting with a cultural process by calling it a tradition; for many, the process of voting was expressed as an outlet for the creation of one's identity.

D1. Election Campaigns involved Music and Dance

Source: Courtesy of Mahashweta Jani.

Appendix E
Madhya Pradesh

Researcher: Mekhala Krishnamurthy

Mandi Polling Station,
Harda Town, Harda AC (135), Betul PC (ST) (29)

Background

The bustling agricultural market town of Harda (population: 64,497) is the administrative headquarters of Harda district in the Narmada Valley of central Madhya Pradesh. Harda district has two ACs (Timarni and Harda), and is part of the Betul PC. The region has undergone a significant agrarian transformation over the past three decades, beginning in the early 1980s when the Tawa Dam brought irrigation to the area. This coincided with the introduction of soybean in many parts of the state, which overtook the previously prevailing cotton crop. Wheat also made a comeback as the second *rabi* (spring harvest) crop.

The *mandi* (agricultural grain market) is at the heart of Harda's local economy, and is also an institution that breeds politicians and leaders among its traders, farmers, *mazdoor*s, and functionaries. It brings together diverse income groups and communities, and serves as a hub for the circulation of all sorts of information. The 2009 Lok Sabha elections were held during the most intense period of government wheat procurement. As a state-regulated institution, no political campaigning is allowed in the mandi, and any signs of political affiliation or advertisement are covered up with black cloth or newsprint (though discussions of the elections — and their impact on market prices — continued). The proliferation of political aspirants and activities led one trader to exclaim: 'These days children are not born in

Harda, we give birth straight to netas!'; it has also earned Harda the administrative status of a 'politically sensitive' district.

Harda is well-known for its industrious, aggressive and politically active farmers. The major agricultural castes are Gujjars, Rajputs, Jats, and Bishnois. SC and ST populations constitute around 32 per cent. Local politics is dominated by the Jats, whose rise to power began in 1993 with the election to the Vidhan Sabha of Kamal Patel (BJP), a Jat farmer who began mobilising his political base from within the market yard. Jats occupy key positions within the mandi, cooperative societies, the public distribution system, and the police. In the villages, small farmers often narrate tales of land encroachment by Jats, while in town tensions have been blamed on an influx of Jat families seeking education for their children and new business opportunities.

If Kamal Patel represents the newly-prosperous Jat farmer, a political history of the town must also acknowledge the old *Nagar Seth* (trader), a veteran Congress Party figure named Eknath Agrawal (known as Eknath Seth). He personifies the economic and political capital of the old trader: though he has never contested an election, he is said to have influenced all major political outcomes in Harda, often according to personal or factional, rather than party, interest. Against these two figures of rural political power, there have been attempts to create an alternative political space. A few months before the Vidhan Sabha election, in the peak wheat procurement season, Mumbai-born lawyer and social worker Shamim Modi led the mandi's *hammals* (labourers) in a successful month-long strike for higher rates.

Delimitation

For the 2009 Lok Sabha elections, Betul PC was declared an ST seat.

Electoral History

At the time of the Vidhan Sabha election in November 2008, Kamal Patel was revenue minister in the Shivraj Singh Chouhan government, a position he subsequently lost after the Central Bureau of Investigation (CBI) initiated an inquiry into a murder case in which

Patel's son was accused. While Kamal Patel ultimately retained his seat, it was commonly said that his victory had been secured by cash and the splitting of Congress votes, while acknowledging that his years of fieldwork continued to pay off. The losing Congress candidate Hemant Tale, a Gujjar, was the president of the *nagar pallika* — an important local institution controlled by the Congress. Having led the *hammals*' strike a few months previously, Shamim Modi stood for the Samajwadi Jan Parishad (SWJP). However, she lost her deposit, and was later arrested and detained for 15 days in connection with old cases. The SWJP fielded a candidate in the Lok Sabha election, but had a negligible impact. Nevertheless, the episode did trigger debate about the challenges of converting social struggle into votes.

At PC level, the outgoing MP for Betul was the Hemant Khandelwal (BJP), who had been elected in a by-election in April 2008 after the death of his father Vijay Khandelwal, a popular figure who had held the seat for BJP since 1996.

Contest and Outcome of the 2009 Election

Sixteen candidates contested the 2009 election for Betul PC, which was won by BJP candidate Jyoti Dhurve. By the end of polling day, the turnout reported across the town was around 46 per cent — and in the mandi polling station it was only 42 per cent. The PC had 1,286,761 electors, of whom just under 50 per cent cast their votes.

Research Questions

The Campaign

During both the Vidhan Sabha and Lok Sabha elections, the general conversation around town concerned the distinct lack of *maahol* — the colour, energy, noise, and expectation of political campaigns — as a result of the EC's *Adarsh Aachar Samhita* (Model Code of Conduct). While the EC's strength was broadly admired, there was also a sense that the Aachar Samhita was being misused by candidates who traded alleged violations.

As soon as the Aachar Samhita came into force, it transpired that Shivraj Singh Chouhan's government had not been able to process the necessary papers for the season's wheat bonus before new policy actions had to cease. Farmers worried that the government would not

Table E1
Total Votes Polled by Each Candidate in 29-Betul PC (ST)

	Name of Candidate	Remarks	Party	Votes Secured	Total Electors (%)	Total Votes Polled (%)
1	Ojharam Evane	M, 54, ST	INC	237,622	18.47	37.33
2	Jyoti Dhurve	F, 43, ST	BJP	334,939	26.03	52.62
3	Rama Kakodia	M, 50, ST	BSP	13,586	1.06	2.13
4	Sukhdev Singh Chouhan	M, 42, ST	SP	5,857	0.46	0.92
5	Kallusingh Uikey	M, 59, ST	GMS	1,660	0.13	0.26
6	Kadmu Singh Kumare (K. S. Kumare)	M, 59, ST	GGP	1,226	0.10	0.19
7	Gulabrav	M, 53, ST	RDMP	976	0.08	0.15
8	Mangal Singh Lokhande	M, 51, ST	SWJP	3,534	0.27	0.56
9	Sushilkumar Alis Balubhaiyya	M, 39, ST	RPI(A)	1,379	0.11	0.22
10	Imratlal Markam	M, 58, ST	IND	1,316	0.10	0.21
11	Kamal Sing	M, 45, ST	IND	1,643	0.13	0.26
12	Kadakshing Vadiva	M, 27, ST	IND	2,044	0.16	0.32
13	Krishna Gopal Parte	M, 35, ST	IND	2,739	0.21	0.43
14	Motiram Mavase	M, 48, ST	IND	4,343	0.34	0.68
15	Adhivakta Shankar Pendam	M, 66, ST	IND	9,779	0.76	1.54
16	Sunil Kumar Kawde	M, 27, ST	IND	13,912	1.08	2.19
	Total			**636,555**		

Source: Prepared by Mekhala Krishnamurthy.

Note: F = Female; GGP = Gondvana Gantantra Party; GMS = Gondwana Mukti Sena; IND = Independent; M = Male; RDMP = Rashtriya Dehat Morcha Party; SWJP = Samajwadi Jan Parishad.

be able to fulfil its promise to buy wheat at ₹1,130; traders, meanwhile, dared to hope that wheat would be available to them at a lower price. After a period of confusion, Chouhan himself obtained clearance from the ECI, much to the farmers' relief.

During this time, political and bureaucratic relationships that were usually expressed openly were heavily disguised, if not entirely suspended. The Collector madam and the secretary could respectfully request that the Mandi Samiti president, a BJP man, leave a meeting about government procurement; wedding invitations extended by local political figures to district officers were turned down. One district officer compared the effect of the Aachar Samhita to a curfew or emergency situation: 'nobody needs to say anything, one just starts to respond differently, bring oneself under control'. While a collectorate functionary expressed that it should be a time to push through pending works unencumbered by political interference, to others it was a 'big *bahaana*' — an excuse — to not complete important work. An officer whose leave application had been rejected remarked: 'What is the idea, you can't do any work, but you can't go on leave either!'

Language of Politics

A strong, proactive ECI also meant the introduction of new terms and processes, including a detailed 'vulnerability assessment' of all polling station villages and neighbourhoods. The district team in Harda took this very seriously. However, the term 'vulnerability' itself was a source of considerable confusion, in terms of both pronunciation and meaning. The officers understood that the exercise involved identifying local *bahubali*s (people providing the muscle power in politics) and *dada*s who use violence, bribery and intimidation to seize votes in their communities, but the question remained: who is 'vulnerable' — those at risk of intimidation, or the perpetrators? According to one election officer, the lack of clarity was intentional: 'they are deliberately sending us words that the local *dada*s and *neta*s can't understand. That way they won't be able to follow what is actually being done and will not be able to interfere with the arrangements!'

Polling Station

The day before the polls involved the *samagree vitaran* — the distribution of election materials to the polling teams. The incoming officers arrived at the Polytechnic College with carefully packed bags — they did not yet know where they would spend the next two days. Inside the College, the atmosphere combined that of a *mela* (fair), a school examination, and a boot camp. Representatives of the collectorate and nagar pallika were enthusiastic: 'This is no ordinary mela. This is our *maha kumbh*! [largest peaceful gathering in the world when 100 million pilgrims come together]'

Colleagues and friends discussed destinations and the team members with whom they would share the space and pressures of a polling booth. The officers' nervousness was palpable: 'They will never let us forget that you can't afford to make a mistake'. Some teams appeared stressed, their materials in disarray; others cracked jokes as they ticked off their tasks. A stall manned by the chief medical officer and compounder was busy, as officers presented cuts and bruises, nausea, headaches, weakness, and received freely distributed tablets. The compounder observed: 'This is what you call election fever!'

The scene drew endless comparisons with weddings; indeed the election was taking place in the midst of a relentless summer season of marriages. 'The *baaraat* [wedding procession] is getting ready to leave!'; 'Look, we have collected the *dehej* [dowry]!' someone exclaimed, explaining that possession of the *samagree* grants power (another officer pointed out that returning with the *dulhan* [bride] — the EVM complete with votes — would be even more auspicious).

Teachers are always well-represented in election duty. One Jat headmaster explained: 'We have to read, write and record all day anyway. Even bank managers make errors, but not teachers!' Other teachers also reflected on their suitability, describing themselves as *darpan*s (mirrors) of society, *kumhar*s (potters) shaping society, 'real netas', and 'lamps that light society, although many of them feel a darkness inside themselves'. A young teacher preparing for his first election as a polling officer declared: *Mujhe lag raha hai ki yeh prajatantra ka maha yagya hai aur mujhe ek havan karvane ka mauka mil raha hain* (This feels like a great ritual is about to take place and I have been given an opportunity to conduct one of the small rites that constitute it). The team's Presiding Officer was delighted with his young colleague's eloquence and enthusiasm. Overhearing the words, the experienced mandi superintendent Yadavji offered his own memories:

> Two days before I had to report, I concentrated and concentrated to focus on the job ahead . . . It is like you are doing a great act of *tapas*

[meditation]) and like a *tapasvi* [hermit] you concentrate very deeply, and it is like another *praan* [spirit] enters your body, another form that protects you from making any errors . . . Here, you know that if you make a mistake, it is a very big crime [*bahut bada apraadh*] . . . there is no mercy, just straight suspension.

Yadavji was renowned as a meticulous administrator in his everyday work, which he described as akin to daily routine of waking and washing; election duty demanded more care. For Yadavji, both the mandi and the elections have ritual properties, but these belong respectively to the domains of the everyday and the extraordinary.

On polling day, voters arrived at the booth in two main waves, between 7 AM and 10 AM, and from 3.30 PM to 5 PM, when polls closed. Turnout in the mandi polling station was only 43 per cent. Perhaps because this was a Lok Sabha election in a large constituency with its centre in Betul, people in Harda felt quite disconnected from the candidates, unlike during Panchayat elections, when the *saap* and *nevla* (snake and mongoose) battle directly in every single booth. Further, the reservation of the seat for an ST candidate was reported to have reduced interest. The scorching heat also kept people away, and one of the most noted features of election day was an uninterrupted supply of electricity — some farmers explained that they had not been able to bring themselves to leave the cool environs of their homes. Finally, a few people remarked on the poor quality of the field, explaining the low turnout as a protest against a politics bereft of meaningful issues.

'Why Do You Vote?'

Along with two other women, Rukmini Bai collects grain that is spilled on the auction platform, sorts it and then sells it to a trader. Rukmini had been unable to vote in the Vidhan Sabha election as her name had not been on the list. She explained her distress: voting meant so much, because she could vote for a better government to help the poor; even one vote could make a difference:

These days, people are winning and losing by only one or two votes! Look at this grain . . . Every day, I run after each *daana* [grain], collecting each and every one . . . Because I know that one grain can change the weight of the heap. It is the same with votes.

Four Bais who mixed grain in the market yard had quite different reasons for voting. Matter-of-factly, they explained that they vote only because 'people come, round us up in rickshaws and trucks and tell us that we must vote'. They went on to say that voting does not really mean anything to them, as no one gives anything to the poor. These two contrasting narratives of poor women voters, one influenced by the pain of being denied a vote, the second by the frustration of being 'rounded up to vote', captured why voting can seem at once to mean so much and so little.

Appendix F
Maharashtra

Researcher: Abhay Datar

Chanda Village, Nevasa AC (221),
Shirdi PC (SC) (38)

Background

Chanda village is located in the Nevasa *taluka* (subdistrict) of Ahmednagar district in western Maharashtra. The population of the village is approximately 12,000–13,000. Like most villages in western Maharashtra, it is Maratha-dominated. Among the Marathas, the Dahatonde clan is numerically the largest. The other major caste is the Malis (OBC), while Muslims and Dalits also form a significant section of the population. Many of the Dalits have converted to Christianity and there is a small church in the village. All three major Dalit castes of Maharashtra — Mahars, Charmakars and Matangs — have a presence in the village. The Marwadi community, whose main occupation is trading, is numerically insignificant in the village but is considered politically influential.

The village consists of the main *gaothan* (portion of the land ordinarily used for settlement) and its surrounding settlements, most of which are located 1–2 km from the main village area. Agriculture is the main occupation, and the Mula Right Bank flows through the village, providing irrigation. Sugarcane is one of the main cash crops, and a crucial component of the local political economy. Politics in western Maharashtra revolves to a large extent around the cooperative sector, which includes banks, sugar factories and credit societies. Elections to these and to local self-government institutions form the building blocks of many political careers, and their results are regarded as indicators of how the political wind is blowing. Their political significance means that at least every alternate year sees an important election.

Delimitation

Prior to delimitation, Chanda village was located in Ahmednagar North AC and Ahmednagar PC. After delimitation, the Nevasa taluka became a separate Nevasa AC, part of the new Shirdi PC (SC). However, this had not sunk into the consciousness of all voters by the time of the election campaign, and any discussion of the election began with talk of Ahmednagar PC.

Post-delimitation, the Shirdi PC consists of six ACs: Akole (ST), Sangamner, Shirdi, Kopargaon, Shrirampur (SC), and Nevasa. The addition of the tribal-dominated Akole AC (formerly part of the Nashik PC) marginally changed the social profile of Shirdi PC.

Electoral History

The cooperative sector exercises considerable political influence owing to its potential for exercising patronage and commanding economic resources. During elections, employees of these institutions are required to work as campaigners and polling agents for their employers. There are two cooperative sugar factories in the taluka — the first controlled by Yeshwantrao Gadakh, the dominant Maratha leader of the Nevasa taluka; the other by the Ghule-Patil family (also Marathas), whose political base lies in neighbouring Sheogaon taluka. Gadakh has a considerable political presence in Chanda itself. Two months before the elections he switched his allegiance from the Congress to the NCP, taking his followers in the village with him. The only other party with a presence in the village is the Shiv Sena.

The northern part of Ahmednagar district has historically been a Congress stronghold. From 1971 it was identified with veteran Congress figure Balasaheb Vikhe-Patil. In the last decade, he joined the Shiv Sena, and served as a minister in the Vajpayee-led NDA government at the centre before rejoining Congress in 2004. The legendary organisational strength of his Congress faction rested on his control of a host of cooperative institutions in the district. The Congress party in the area has historically been a conglomeration of competing factions, and since the emergence in the 1990s of the Shiv Sena–BJP alliance, some of these factions have chosen to join the Sena–BJP rather than fight it out within the Congress.

Contest and Outcome of the 2009 Election

The main contest in Shirdi PC was between Republican Party of India (Athawale) (RPI[A]) leader Ramdas Athawale and Bhausaheb Wakchoure (Shiv Sena). The third candidate was Premanand Rupwate, a Congress rebel. Initially, many people believed that Athawale could win — one of the leading figures of Dalit politics in Maharashtra, he also had the support of Congress and NCP (partners in the state and central governments). Although by the time of the contest it was widely expected that Athawale might lose, Wakchoure's victory margin was unexpected. The Shiv Sena led in all six ACs in Shirdi PC. The PC had a total number of 1,317,890 electors, and turnout was a little over 50 per cent.

Four factors may have led to Ramdas Athawale's defeat. The first was the relatively late announcement of his candidature compared to Wakchoure's (Athawale had reportedly declined a request to contest as an official Congress candidate). Second was the unspoken unwillingness of Congress and NCP leaders, and local party activists, to exert themselves for Athawale. Balasaheb Vikhe-Patil, retiring as Kopargaon MP, was reportedly annoyed that a candidate not to his liking was being foisted upon him, and reportedly requested the Congress ticket for Ahmednagar PC, in return for his acceptance of Athawale. However, that constituency had already been allotted to NCP in the seat-sharing agreement. Vikhe-Patil was placated by being made chairman of the Congress' campaign committee; only in the final two weeks before polling did he actively begin campaigning for Athawale.

Third, Athawale was perceived as an outsider. He had been elected to the Lok Sabha from Pandharpur PC, which had earlier been reserved for SC. Following delimitation, the constituency was dereserved and renamed Madha, and Athawale was shifted to Shirdi. Wakchoure, however, was a former state government official who had served as chief executive of the Shirdi Temple Trust. Some inhabitants of Chanda also knew him for his tenure as the local block development officer.

Table F1
Total Votes Polled by Each Candidate in 38-Shirdi PC (SC)

	Name of Candidate	Remarks	Party	Votes Secured	Total Electors (%)	Total Votes Polled (%)
1	Kacharu Nagu Waghmare	M, 60, SC	BSP	8,408	0.64	1.27
2	Wakchoure Bhausaheb Rajaram	M, 59, SC	SHS	359,921	27.31	54.21
3	Athawale Ramdas Bandu	M, 52, SC	RPI(A)	227,170	17.24	34.22
4	Dhotre Suchit Chintaman	M, 25, SC	KM	6,052	0.46	0.91
5	Satish Balasaheb Palghadmal	M, 26, SC	PRCP	1,567	0.12	0.24
6	Adhagale Rajendra Namdeo	M, 39, SC	IND	1,923	0.15	0.29
7	Kamble Ramesh Ankush	M, 32, SC	IND	1,690	0.13	0.25
8	Gaikwad Appasaheb Gangadhar	M, 64, SC	IND	1,584	0.12	0.24
9	Bagul Balu Dasharath	M, 34, SC	IND	2,249	0.17	0.34
10	Medhe Prafullakumar Muralidhar	M, 46, SC	IND	1,889	0.14	0.28
11	Rakshe Annasaheb Eknath	M, 43, SC	IND	2,040	0.15	0.31
12	Rupwate Premanand Damodar	M, 65, SC	IND	22,787	1.73	3.43
13	Londhe Sharad Laxman	M, 42, SC	IND	4,626	0.35	0.70
14	Wagh Gangadhar Radhaji	M, 60, SC	IND	6,295	0.48	0.95
15	Vairagar Sudhir Natha	M, 38, SC	IND	6,326	0.48	0.95
16	Sable Anil Damodar	M, 40, SC	IND	1,480	0.11	0.22
17	Sandip Bhaskar Gholap	M, 29, SC	IND	7,874	0.60	1.19
	Total			663,881		

Source: Prepared by Abhay Datar.
Note: IND = Independent; KM = Krantisena Maharashtra; M = Male; PRCP = Prabuddha Republican Party; SHS = Shiv Sena.

Ultimately, the most important factor was the fear that an Athawale victory would lead to false cases being brought against caste Hindus under the Scheduled Castes and Scheduled Tribes (Prevention of Atrocities) Act, owing to allegations that Athawale had been responsible for 'misuse' of the Act in the Pandharpur area. Though this was never made an explicit campaign issue, it was constantly discussed by voters in Chanda.

Research Questions

The Campaign

The public or explicit level of campaigning consisted of public meetings and rallies, leaders' statements (in turn publicised through the media), campaign literature, and so on. At a subterranean or implicit level, issues were discussed through relatively invisible means, including gossip and informal face-to-face campaigning (often by lower-level activists). This level of campaigning includes factors such as caste, which often sway elections but are rarely visible in formal campaigns.

In Chanda, the usual campaign pamphlets and leaflets were distributed by all candidates. All three leading candidates also broadcasted campaign slogans and appealed to voters from vehicles. The Wakchoure campaign truck carried a group of professional entertainers singing campaign songs to the tune of popular folk songs; the star attraction appeared to be a dancing dwarf.

Role of the Media

All major Marathi daily newspapers are available in the village. However, very few individuals purchase their own copy; most people prefer to borrow. While there are many DTH connections in the village, viewing television is not easy: the main village area experiences nearly six hours of load shedding every day (even more in outlying settlements). In any case, as the Indian Premier League (IPL) was in progress, attention was focussed on cricket.

News items were rarely discussed with interest, and the main sources of election information were networks of relatives across the Ahmednagar district, and individuals who travelled outside the village and brought back news (perceived to be more reliable than newspaper reports). Most villagers were more interested in the complex triangular contest between well-known BSP, BJP and NCP candidates in Ahmednagar PC than the Shirdi election. Although the influence of the media appeared minimal, many residents opined that the arrival of television had enhanced the political consciousness of the village, and the people could no longer be taken for granted by politicians.

Language of Politics

The general consensus was that politics was of minor consequence to people's everyday lives, and that the outcome of the election was largely irrelevant. There appeared to be a mutual disconnect between local political activists and voters; each expressed irritation at the other's behaviour. Politicians were regarded as crooks who were more interested in enriching themselves; meanwhile activists and some who had stood for, or held, political office lamented that the voters were swayed by money and caste considerations, rather than *vikas* (development).

Politics is regarded by many as an inherently corrupting activity. Stories were told of well-regarded individuals who became 'spoiled' after taking office in the local multi-purpose credit society. Another popular story about the leader of the village's Gadakh faction, who belongs to an artisan OBC caste, was that he had been a close associate of Gadakh's local rival, a former MP, for whom he had taken out a loan; when the former MP refused to pay it back, Gadakh reportedly agreed to bail out the associate in return for a switch of political loyalties.

Polling Station

The field site had seven separate polling booths, each with approximately 1,000 voters, grouped into two polling stations — one in the primary school and one in the high school. A short distance from each station, political parties set up their own booths, from which activists coordinated the mobilisation of voters, for example by telephoning 'sure-shot voters' to ensure their attendance, dispatching vehicles to collect them, and taking continuous stock of the turnout.

The Athawale booth outside the primary school was manned throughout the day by an elderly employee of Gadakh's cooperative factory and the middle-aged secretary of the local multi-purpose cooperative credit society. The two men sat on a large rubber sheet, surrounded by voters' lists. The leading political activists of the village had gathered at the other Athawale booth outside the high school. The actual work was largely done by second-rung workers. The activists of the Gadakh faction did not seem particularly interested in the election, and were present more as a matter of form. Indeed, by miming the action of shooting an arrow (the Shiv Sena symbol), one Panchayat member indicated to a couple of voters that they should vote for the Shiv Sena (whose booth was relatively quiet and undermanned). Late in the afternoon, Athawale arrived in a convoy, accompanied by Gadakh's youngest son and a few activists, to enable his aide to cast his vote. The leaders stepped out and were surrounded by the enthused local activists; a quick round of introductions allowed the people gathered to display their political loyalties before the vehicles departed.

'Why Do You Vote?'

One of the main features of this election in Chanda was an extremely low turnout. According to the figures made available after voting closed on 23 April 2009, only 33.5 per cent of the eligible voters exercised their franchise. Various factors were cited by those who voted, as well as the leading political activists in the village, to explain this lack of enthusiasm: the insistence by polling staff that voters supply official election identity cards or other photographic identification; the unusually warm weather; the Lok Sabha elections being regarded as largely remote from villagers' everyday concerns; minimal efforts made by the political actors to mobilise voters, for example by arranging transportation; and the lack of money being distributed to voters.

Appendix G
Rajasthan

Researcher: Vanita Falcao

*Booth 19 of Dodhsar village,
Chomu AC (43), Sikar PC (5)*

Background

Dodhsar village lies along a 2-km stretch of National Highway 11, 50 km from Jaipur City, within the Govindgadh Panchayat Samiti and Chomu *tehsil*. Although Dodhsar is located in Jaipur district, it is part of Sikar PC, and falls within Chomu AC. Over the years, several minor settlements known as *dhani*s were established around the village, each centred on a well. Many families have now sought further convenience by moving to live on their own fields; the village has expanded considerably since Anand Chakravarti of Delhi University conducted a study in this site in 1964–65 (Chakravarti 1975). The 2001 Census recorded a population of 4,949; local people stated that figure was likely to have reached 6,500. The village has a large population of Raegars (SC — approximately 350 families) and Boonkars or Balai (SC — approximately 300 families), Kumawats (OBC — approximately 300 families), and Jats (approximately 300 families). Other castes include Yadavs, Rajputs, Brahmans, Banias, Kir, and Gujjars.

As was the case throughout most of Rajasthan, Dodhsar was dominated by the Rajputs until the Rajasthan Land Reforms and Resumption of Jagirs Act, 1952 dealt a severe blow to their power and landholdings. Generally, the Rajputs continued to exercise substantial political control over the lower castes; in Dodhsar, however, the SCs claimed many rights under the guidance of Chavand Singh, who went on to be Sarpanch from 1961 to 1972. However, the economic status of the Dalits (if this can be separated from their social status) is still the lowest in the village. Some have become teachers or clerks; some have migrated abroad to work; but most continue to do *mazdoori* (daily wage labour). Alcoholism appears to be relatively widespread amongst this community.

In terms of natural resources and the standard of living of most villagers, Dodhsar is fairly prosperous. It has paved roads, a reasonably well-maintained drainage system, and access to government and private healthcare. Government schooling up to the senior secondary level is available within Dodhsar, and there are several private schools. The village boasts of superior water quality, and has never suffered a drought, though water levels have dropped significantly over the last 20 years. Most people are still dependent on the agricultural sector as their main source of income — wheat, onions, groundnut, garlic, and watermelon are grown here. There is also a dairy cooperative.

Delimitation

Dodhsar village was not affected by the recent delimitation of PCs. Elsewhere in Sikar PC, reorganisation of boundaries resulted in some votes of the general category and the Yadav community being redistributed. This may have marginally affected the PC-level outcome, but had little influence on Dodhsar.

Electoral History

Dodhsar has for several years been a Congress stronghold. Until the previous assembly election, Congress regularly garnered two-thirds of the votes. The Panchayat elections were until recently particularly influenced by a wealthy Rajput, Narendra Singh Shekhawat, known to have far-reaching political contacts.

Sikar PC had been represented since 1998 by Subhash Maharia (BJP). Hari Singh (Congress) won in 1996, Balram Jakhar (Congress) in 1984 and 1991, and Devi Lal (Janata Party) in 1989.

Contest and Outcome of the 2009 Election

The incumbent MP Subhash Mehriya (BJP), a wealthy Jat businessman of Sikar block, had served three terms in office. The Congress candidate was five-time Khandela MLA Mahadev Singh Khandela, a Jat from Khandela village (30 km from Dodhsar). The contest was initially expected to be between these candidates; however, a third also entered the fray: CPI(M)'s Amararam, the sitting MLA of Data Ramgadh AC. Amararam, a Jat, had previously represented Dodh AC, and had led farmers' movements for water and electricity in the area. Initially, there were rumours that his candidacy had been partly financed by the BJP in an attempt to split the Congress vote. A fourth candidate, Bharat Singh Tanwar (BSP), was also discussed, although he was not considered capable of winning. A Rajput businessman from Mumbai, he was often referred to as a 'readymade politician'.

The election witnessed a victory for Congress at village and PC level. Turnout across Dodhsar on polling day (7 May 2009) was 47 per cent. At Booth 19, turnout was 42.5 per cent. Across Sikar PC (1,507,740 electors), turnout was 48 per cent.

Research Questions

The Campaign

Conforming to national party lines, the local BJP campaign was loaded with criticism of the Congress, including personal attacks on Manmohan Singh's apparent indecisiveness and Sonia Gandhi's foreign background. The Congress largely concentrated on NREGA and the Farmers' Loan Waiver; they promised to address all pending electricity applications within six months, and highlighted the party's basic principles: *tyaag, ballidaan aur parishram* (austerity, sacrifice and hard work). They also attempted to placate the disgruntled Yadav community, who were displeased that Bhagwan Sahay Dahsil of their community had been denied the Congress ticket in the 2008 assembly election.

Amararam's CPI(M) campaign was relatively small-scale (with the exception of one large rally), and relied primarily on his previous work for water and electricity provision. For the BSP, Mayawati and Bharat Singh Tanwar spoke of reservations for the socially and economically backward, and for religious minorities, and emphasised their efforts to elevate people from poverty. The party was also attempting to save face after all six BSP MLAs joined the Congress in April 2009.

Table G1
Total Votes Polled by Each Candidate in 5-Sikar PC

	Name of Candidate	Remarks	Party	Votes Secured	Total Electors (%)	Total Votes Polled (%)
1	Amararam	M, 54	CPM	161,590	10.72	22.28
2	Bharat Singh Tanwar	M, 34	BSP	30,374	2.01	4.19
3	Mahadev Singh	M, 66	INC	324,812	21.54	44.79
4	Subhash Maharia	M, 52	BJP	175,386	11.63	24.18
5	Acharaya Devendra Kumar Pauranik	M, 54	SP	3,559	0.24	0.49
6	D. P. Kumawat	M, 48	RJVP	812	0.05	0.11
7	Bhagyan Sahay	M, 47	LJP	558	0.04	0.08
8	Makhan Lal Saini	M, 31	JGP	728	0.05	0.10
9	Sita Devi	F, 41, SC	BHBP	786	0.05	0.11
10	Hemchand Agrawal	M, 38	BCP	1,246	0.08	0.17
11	Ajaypal	M, 52	IND	1,847	0.12	0.25
12	Jugal Kishor Meghawal	M, 31, SC	IND	1,394	0.09	0.19
13	Mahabeer Parsad	M, 53	IND	3,466	0.23	0.48
14	Maheshkumar	M, 29	IND	8,163	0.54	1.13
15	Ramesh Sharma	M, 53	IND	2,785	0.18	0.38
16	Hanuman Sahai	M, 50, SC	IND	7,759	0.51	1.07
	Total			725,265		

Source: Prepared by Vanita Falcao.

Note: BCP = Bhartiya Chaitanya Party; BHBP = Bhartiya Bahujan Party; F = Female; IND = Independent; JGP = Jago Party; LJP = Lok Jan Shakti Party; M = Male; RJVP = Rajasthan Vikas Party.

Role of the Media

Almost all the men in the village read a newspaper first thing in the morning. The two most widely-read papers, the *Rajasthan Patrika* and *Dainik Jagaran*, reported on national and local campaigns and constituted the only source of current affairs for some people (television was more popular for entertainment). Towards the end of April, a newspaper article described the Sikar PC election as a three-way contest between Congress, BJP and CPM. While Amararam was known to have support in three of the ACs, he had not previously been seen as a significant contender. He experienced a sudden wave of popularity after the article was published, leading to speculation about whether he would in fact be the runner-up.

Language of Politics

Men in Dodhsar are outspoken about politics, and they engaged in discussion in a range of spaces: Parsa Ram's tea stall, with its in-depth election forecasts; the particular street corner in the Raegar *mohalla* (neighbourhood) where Chottu Ram would speak about the exploitation of the Dalit vote banks; and the grocery where people of the 'opposition' would criticise the incumbents. The absence of such discussions among women was absolute, possibly on account of lack of time (many women do both housework and wage labour), limited access to information and restricted scope for political discussion. The language ranged from English medical terms to words from everyday parlance. Some examples include: 'actual *zindagi*', used by a Raegar man talking about the difference between constitutional rights and the rights people enjoy in real life; 'neglect *karenge*', to describe what politicians will do when they take power; *raj palta nahi hain*, a Raegar man's description of the role of the Rajput kingpin in maintaining a divide between the Raegars and Boonkars; *desh ka kodh rog rajniti hain*, which describes politics as leucoderma plaguing the country. The BJP was referred to as '*poonjipatiyon ki* party' (party of capitalists); and at a campaign speech in Jaipur, Ghanshyam Tiwari described the UPA alliance as the '*Ulta Pulta* [upside down] Alliance'. The English 'vote' was used more commonly than the Hindi *matdaan*, and the influence of English on broader vocabulary was notable, though largely restricted to the more educated. A more general tendency when speaking of politics was to make reference to folklore or other traditional anecdotes.

While the verbal language used to describe the political system and its various components did not differ significantly across caste or class, body language varied considerably. SCs in particular communicated a pronounced sense of helplessness when speaking about local politics.

Polling Station

The boys' and girls' higher secondary schools acted as the polling stations in Dodhsar. There were three booths (17, 18 and 19). The officers arrived the evening before polling, accompanied by a micro observer, appointed because booths 17 and 18 had been demarcated *atti-samvedansheel* (very sensitive) on account of their particular caste/community composition, and because Booth 19 had a large number of electors (1,628). Voters started to arrive in small groups as soon as polling started. At first, most were men; the women came after doing housework. Party stalls distributed *parchi*s (chits with the voter's details) and leaflets showing the placement of the party buttons on the EVM. These stalls were set up at a distance from the polling station on account of the observers' presence.

'Why Do You Vote?'

A number of factors may have contributed to the dismal turnout of 47 per cent in Dodhsar. First, the Lok Sabha is perceived to be somewhat divorced from people's everyday reality — an outcome of constituency size, physical distance from central government, and the fact that people rarely approach their MP for assistance (turnout is much higher in Vidhan Sabha and Panchayat elections).

While a general distrust of politicians was widespread, some people were so repulsed by the political system that they desired to remove themselves from it altogether: *Rajniti mein hone ke liye logon ko jhooth bolne ki shapath leni padti hain* (to be a politician one has to take a vow of dishonesty); *Humara uske saath koi lena dena nahi hain. Humain bas apne dhande se matlab hain* (I have nothing to do with it. I am only bothered about my business). Others viewed voting as an inconvenience: it was too hot; there was housework to complete and money to be earned. Also, the season was auspicious for marriages (six were scheduled to be solemnised in Dodhsar on polling day). Party workers predicted a 10–15 per cent decrease in turnout as a result, and candidates tried to persuade voters: *pehle matdaan, phir kanyadaan* (first cast your vote then partake in giving away the bride).

Asking the direct question, 'why do you vote?', initially elicited a standard response: voting is the duty and responsibility of a citizen. Women on the whole do not participate in the campaigns, and most vote according to the orders of male family members. The Bawariyas, an ST community residing on the outskirts of the village, explained that they used their vote only because: 'If we have it we might as well give it to someone'. Caste identity has far-reaching influence, as summarised by a former political kingpin: *Jati ke samne sabkuch bauna hai* (everything else is dwarfed in front of caste).

Following the redistribution of their land to the cultivators (mostly Jats and Yadavs), the Rajputs felt further let down when the Yadavs (in 1994) and Jats (in 1999) were classified as OBCs in Rajasthan, entitling them to quotas in government employment. As the Jats were given OBC status under BJP rule, there is sizeable support for the party amongst the Jat community whereas Yadavs have largely supported the Congress (in 1984, the BJP's Ghanshyam Tiwari led a *Yadav Hatao* — 'Remove the Yadavs' — campaign). One Yadav shopkeeper compared their rivalry during elections to Hindu–Muslim tensions.

The majority of SCs in Dodhsar are either Raegars or Boonkar, both groups which have traditionally supported Congress. While this is still largely the case, their votes are now also split between BJP and BSP. Kanhayalal Raegar expressed his frustration that voting choices are often subject to the power dynamics of rich politicians: *Oonchi jaat ke log hamare samaaj me phoot peda karte hain. Woh doodh mein kanja ke tapka jaise hain* (The upper-caste people create divisions in our community. They serve the same purpose as *kanja ka tapka* [acidic ingredient used to curdle milk]). This election suggested a return to traditional patterns: in Booth 18, which mainly covers the Raegar *mohallas*, Congress received almost 70 per cent of votes.

Some people will vote for a particular party irrespective of a candidate's caste, reputation or criminal record. However, some who had proclaimed unconditional support for a party admitted that they had changed their preference temporarily, on the grounds of caste or personality. One man spoke of switching allegiances to vote for a fellow Rajput the first time the opportunity arose. A candidate's proximity to potential voters can also be influential; some claimed that this worked in favour of Mahadev Singh Khandela — a well-known 'local' person, with relatives in the village. The fact that few people voted for Amararam, despite viewing him as a good candidate, was somewhat attributable to a lack of influential CPM supporters. People are also aware that the coordination of work and funding may suffer if an MP and MLA are of different political parties. Material incentives also played a role: it is a given that liquor is distributed the night before elections (though few people admitted to receiving any), yet since all parties distribute it, it is difficult to determine who will receive the 'beneficiary's' vote.

Appendix H
Tamil Nadu

Researchers: Grace Carswell and Geert De Neve[1]
Allapuram Polling Booth (SI 194; Polling Station 154)
Allapuram Hamlet, Palladam AC (115), Coimbatore PC (20)

Background

The polling booth was located in the Allapuram hamlet of Allapuram panchayat, Pongalur union, and covered 356 households across four hamlets: Allapuram, Perumaalpalayam, Thottampalayam, and Pallipalayam. The land-owning Gounders (Backward Caste [BC]), constituting 28 per cent of the population, are the dominant caste in Allapuram, Perumaalpalayam and Thottampalayam in terms of numbers, economic wealth and political voice. There are approximately equal numbers of Matharis (SC, also known as Arunthathiyars) (22 per cent) and Adi Dravida Christians (23 per cent). Adi Dravidas are officially categorised as BC; however, many are still grouped as Hindu — thus SC — on their community certificates, and are socially perceived as SC by others in the village. There are also BC castes (15 per cent) including Nadars and Mudaliyars, and Most Backward Castes (MBC) (8 per cent) including barbers. A wealth-ranking exercise grouped households into four locally-defined groups: rich (9 per cent); medium (26 per cent); poor (48 per cent); and very poor (17 per cent).

---

[1] This research would not have been possible without the help of S. Gayathri and Adele Fash, to whom we extend our thanks. All mistakes remain our own.

Until 20–30 years ago, most inhabitants of Allapuram would have been landowning farmers (Gounders), agricultural labourers (Adi Dravida and Mathari), or engaged in service occupations (e.g., barbers and potters). However, the booming textile industry in nearby Tiruppur has led to dramatic changes in the village economy. While men from Gounder households are the most likely to have started a business of their own, or worked as a supervisor in a garment company, men and women from other castes also commute daily to work as tailors, ironing/cutting masters, checkers, and helpers. The majority of women remain employed in agriculture, but while Gounder women are unlikely to work outside the village, some Christian and Mathari women commute to Tiruppur, though in smaller numbers than men, and some non-SC women carry out house work. The high demand for labour means that Matharis no longer rely exclusively on low-paid, seasonal agricultural work for Gounders.

Agricultural crops include maize, chollam, coconut, onion, tomatoes, and other vegetables irrigated by wells, boreholes and the Parambikulam Aliyar Project (PAP) canal. While falling water tables and limited access to canal water meant that for years the 'water problem' was the main issue for agriculturalists, today it is the 'labour problem' that dominates. Gounder landowners have responded by offering higher wages, contracting labourers from further afield, and introducing crops with low labour requirements, such as coconuts.

Delimitation

Following the delimitation exercise, Allapuram falls within Coimbatore PC. It had previously been part of Pollachi PC (SC), represented by C. Krishnan (MDMK). The exercise also led to changes at AC level: Allapuram had been within Pongalur AC, represented by A. S. Mani (DMK). However, while Allapuram still belongs to Pongalur union, it now falls within Palladam AC. Moreover, Allapuram has shifted from Coimbatore district to the new Tiruppur district, formed in January 2009. Given Tiruppur's relative proximity, and the fact that most people from the Allapuram work there, villagers were generally more exposed to campaigning in Tiruppur than in the village or in Coimbatore; indeed, many initially assumed they were part of the Tiruppur PC.

Electoral History

The continued domination of the two major political parties in Tamil politics (AIADMK and DMK) was evident in the village. The hamlets covered by the Allapuram polling booth are located at the heart of a region with a historically strong AIADMK presence. Even after A. S. Mani (DMK) won the Pongalur AC seat in 2006, the party remained popular among villagers of all castes. It is no exaggeration to say that Allapuram is an AIADMK village. However, it is just one hamlet of the Panchayat, whose current president is B. Kamalan (DMK). The political division between the hamlet and the Panchayat leadership has caused the villagers of Allapuram to feel rather marginalised.

At PC level, the Pollachi PC (under which Allapuram used to fall) had been represented for two terms by C. Krishnan (Marumalarchi Dravida Munnetra Kazhagam [MDMK]). Coimbatore PC had been represented by MPs from the CPI and BJP during the preceding decade.

Contest and Outcome of the 2009 Election

Changing alliances, rather than party manifestos, dominated election discussions. Of particular interest was the shift of the PMK and communist parties from the DMK–Congress to the AIADMK alliance. The launch of a new party less than three months before the election also triggered policy debates and speculation about shifting vote banks. The regional Kongunadu Munnetra Peeravai (KNMK) emerged from the Kongu Vellalar Gounder Peeravai (Kongu Vellalar Gounder Association), and was formally launched on 15 February 2009. Despite activists' efforts to convince the public that it was established for the 'upliftment' of all communities, KMP was widely seen as a Gounder party. It seemed unlikely that many Gounders would be prepared to abandon their current loyalties, or that non-Gounders would vote for KMP; yet a good deal of scepticism about this party was misplaced: 11 KMP candidates stood, and although none gained a seat, several gained around 100,000 votes, split the vote in their constituency, and thus influenced the overall outcome.

The Congress, DMK, Viduthalai Chiruthaigal Katchi (VCK) and Indian Muslim League contested the election as one alliance

Table H1
Total Votes Polled by Each Candidate for 20-Coimbatore PC

	Name of Candidate	Remarks	Party	Votes Secured	Total Electors (%)	Total Votes Polled (%)
1	Ramasubramanian K.	M,41	BSP	2,937	0.25	0.36
2	Selvakumar G. K. S.	M, 47	BJP	37,909	3.26	4.60
3	Natarajan P. R.	M, 59	CPM	293,165	25.19	35.58
4	Prabhu R.	M, 61	INC	254,501	21.87	30.88
5	Eswaran E. R.	M, 48	KNMK	128,070	11.00	15.54
6	Kathirmani P.	M, 36	SP	1,396	0.12	0.17
7	Selvam M.	M, 51	SHS	2,007	0.17	0.24
8	Pandian R.	M, 52	DMDK	73,188	6.29	8.88
9	Rajan S. K.	M, 60	PPOI	2,340	0.20	0.28
10	Stephen Ganeshan S.	M, 45	AIJMK	859	0.07	0.10
11	Arunchalam K. V.	M, 55	IND	1,237	0.11	0.15
12	Eswaran G.	M, 38	IND	1,677	0.14	0.20
13	Kathiresan C.	M, 38	IND	1,333	0.11	0.16

No.	Name		Party	Votes		
14	Sivaraj V.	M, 40	IND	1,747	0.15	0.21
15	Natarajan L.	M, 43	IND	913	0.08	0.11
16	Noormuhamad A.	M, 51	IND	4,172	0.36	0.51
17	Prem Anand J.	M, 31	IND	3,872	0.33	0.47
18	Markandan N.	M, 72	IND	1,274	0.11	0.15
19	Murugan M.	M, 50	IND	3,424	0.29	0.42
20	Murugesan K.	M, 33, SC	IND	1,690	0.15	0.21
21	Ramasamy P.	M, 43	IND	1,833	0.16	0.22
22	Rajappan N.	M, 49	IND	1,088	0.09	0.13
23	Rajkiran	M, 52	IND	1,069	0.09	0.13
24	Vijayakumar C.	M, 38, SC	IND	907	0.08	0.11
25	Venkatachalam A.	M, 69	IND	1,439	0.12	0.17
Total				**824,047**		

Source: Prepared by Grace Carswell and Geert De Neve.

Note: AIJMK = Akhila India Janayaka Makkal Katchi; DMDK = Desiya Murpokku Dravida Kazhagam; IND = Independent; KNMK = Kongu Nadu Munnetra Kazhagam; M = Male; PPOI = Pyramid Party of India.

(represented in Coimbatore by R. Prabhu of Congress and in Tiruppur by Karventhan of Congress); the AIADMK, CPM, CPI, PMK, India National League, and MDMK formed another (represented in Coimbatore by P. R. Natarajan of the CPM and in Tiruppur by Sivasami of the AIADMK). The AIADMK alliance was successful in both PCs.

In Coimbatore PC (1,163,781 electors); turnout was 70.8 per cent. In the Allapuram booth, party activists recorded a total of between 654 and 665 votes (depending on which list was consulted). At 78 per cent, turnout was well above the Phase V average of 62 per cent. The activists recorded 270 votes for CPM (AIADMK alliance), 170 for Congress (DMK alliance), 129 for KNMK, 47 for DMDK, 15 for BJP, three for BSP, and approximately 20 for various independent candidates.

Research Questions

The Campaign

Protracted alliance negotiations delayed the major parties' campaigns until about three weeks before polling. Parties that were not part of an alliance (notably DMDK and KMP) were better-organised — their symbols were the first to be painted on walls; their candidates the first to visit. Party leaders spoke to large rallies in the major towns, attended by crowds of between 3,000 and 10,000 people — mainly men, but sometimes including women, as was the case when AIADMK leader Jayalalithaa visited Tiruppur. Local candidates also embarked on tours, accompanied by small convoys (the number of cars was restricted under ECI rules). The processions were often greeted with firecrackers and a small *puja*, and the candidate would speak briefly from the open roof of a vehicle. Evening meetings in towns, addressed by candidates and local politicians, were attended almost exclusively by men. Finally, there was door-to-door campaigning in the evenings. In the weeks before the election, professional signwriters traversed the region with party activists, painting walls with the names and symbols of relevant candidates, parties and alliances.

Role of the Media

Local television channels are owned by politicians: Karunanidhi (DMK) owns Sun TV, Sun News and Kalaignar TV; Jayalalithaa owns Jaya TV; and the PMK owns Makkal TV. Yet the widespread availability of television news (most households own a television) does not necessarily translate into people watching large amounts of election coverage. Many voters — especially women — have little time to watch the news, and few newspapers circulate in the village. One teashop always carries a newspaper — some male customers read it, but they are relatively few in number.

Language of Politics

Politicians are described as corrupt ('they take half of our tax for their personal use') and, in the case of DMK, highly nepotistic. People talked about how different politicians earned lakhs or crores from corruption, citing cases such as T. R. Baalu (Minister of Shipping and Road Transport and Highways [2004–09]) and A. Raja (2G spectrum case). Some informants almost excused the politicians, saying that they were taught to be corrupt by government officials. In contrast, the ECI was held in high regard for its strict overseeing of this election.

Polling Station

In contrast to everyday accounts of caste relations in the village, polling day saw men of many different communities cooperating to procure votes. One group of women voters explained that they do not discuss voting choices in the queue: 'It would create competitiveness . . . we don't want to create a bitter relationship with people from other parties. We just make jokes!' This sentiment was echoed by the men, some of whom said that AIADMK and DMK activists visited each other's houses to canvass.

While polling day was deemed to have passed without incident (the atmosphere of the booth was described by voters as 'quiet'), there are times when rules might have been bent and local power muscles flexed; for example, allegations of bribery and counting errors, and issues with the forms of identification accepted or refused at the polling booth. In Allapuram, enthusiasm for the elections was rather muted, and anything but festival-like. This may be explained in part by the shifting politics of alliance-building in Tamil Nadu, and in part by this being a national rather than local election.

'Why Do You Vote?'

There were several reasons why some people may not have voted, including the difficulty of returning to one's 'native place'. For many — including labour migrants and women who had moved for marriage — the costs of returning to vote were prohibitively expensive.

One widow, who said she had never missed a vote but does not always vote for the same party, said that she looks for who will 'help people', particularly in terms of increasing the old-age pension, providing water facilities and bringing down prices. A man from the Christian area, who works as an ironing master in Tiruppur, explained:

> Last time, they gave us a government loan to build this extension [to our house], that was under the AIADMK, so I voted for them. Now the DMK has given us roads and street lights. Whoever is giving something at the time of election, that's whom I will vote for.

Similarly, a Gounder man favoured Congress in central elections on account of its agricultural loan waivers, and DMK at state level because Karunanidhi has provided farmers with free electricity. A group of Congress leaders in Tiruppur stated that people in other countries whose basic needs are fulfilled have lost interest in politics, while 'here, people still have lots of needs, so people keep voting to get a government in place that will do something for them'.

Many voters have strong family traditions, and would not dream of swapping party allegiances. Yet, there are limits, and many women admitted to voting differently from their husbands. Secrecy regarding voting decisions was particularly valued by women who felt passionately about their right to make personal voting choices. Some people's loyalties rest on historical identification, for example, the Matharis who stated: 'Our people have always voted for two-leaf' (*irettalai* — the AIADMK symbol). A Mathari mother explained her love for AIADMK founder MGR thus:

> We used to have to stand up when [Gounders] passed our house . . . [she bowed deeply to demonstrate] . . . Because of [MGR] we haven't got that fear anymore. He said all our children should go to school, and he started free school meals and introduced eggs for the children . . . What MGR did, Amma is now following . . . Whether I die tomorrow or live another 50 years, I won't change the party I vote for!

Allapuram's Mathari voters offered examples of how 'Amma' continues MGR's legacy, keeping prices down, supplying water and street lamps; they even attribute good rainfall to her ('Whenever Karunanidhi comes we don't get proper rains, but when we have Jayalalithaa we have good rains!') Moreover, the party and its leaders are perceived to have given low-caste and poor people like them a sense of dignity and self-respect, and to have been instrumental in the transformation of social relations in the village and beyond. The Adi Dravida Christians in the village closely identify with the DMK, which they consider takes care of them in several ways, including good support for government staff. As a minority group, they see voting for AIADMK as risky, given the party's earlier alliance with the BJP.

People often asserted that they vote because it is their right (*urimai*) or duty (*kadamai*) as citizens of India. Though these terms are often used interchangeably, some people made distinctions. This was most clearly expressed by a group of female first-time voters and trainee teachers: 'The right to vote is an individual right, it's a right given to us by the state. But it is our duty to use it, it is our duty to select a good leader'. Several informants described voting as not only a matter of being recognised by the state as a person and citizen, but also an act that gives meaning to their life.

Appendix I
West Bengal

Researcher: Dolonchampa Chakrabarty

*Sunil Nagar Colony (Part 49),
Kasba AC (149), Kolkata Dakshin PC (23)*

Background

Sunil Nagar colony falls within Kasba AC and Kolkata Dakshin PC, and within the jurisdiction of the Kolkata Municipal Corporation. Refugees from Bangladesh settled here after partition in makeshift huts, later obtaining the land from the West Bengal government. The area now consists of brick houses and multi-storey apartment buildings. Some people own their houses but a major portion of residents live in rented accommodation. Area residents are employed in government service or private firms. This is a typical middle-class neighbourhood in Kolkata with mostly Bengali *bhadralok* or gentry in residence. The area is quite developed, and its residents are accustomed to the benefits common to urban life, such as brick houses, electricity, televisions, refrigerators, and internet access at cyber cafes.

The voters of Part 49 live in the Picnic Garden area, which lacks any parks or open fields. The majority of residents are Bengali and Hindu by religion; there are also some Anglo-Indian Christians and one or two Bihari and Sikh families. Being located within the main city, caste prejudices are largely absent. According to the last published voters' list, the area's electorate numbers 844.

Delimitation

The number of seats in West Bengal remained the same following delimitation, though their distribution was changed. Before delimitation, 32 of West Bengal's 42 PCs were general, eight were reserved for SC and two for ST; now 30 are general, 10 are reserved for SC and two for ST.

Kolkata's 21 Vidhan Sabha seats were reduced to 11. Its Lok Sabha seats were reduced from three to two: Calcutta North-East and Calcutta North-West ceased to exist, and Kolkata Uttar was created instead; South Calcutta was replaced by Kolkata Dakshin, which includes three ACs from South 24 Parganas district (Kasba, Behala Purba and Behala Paschin) and four from Kolkata district (Kolkata Port, Bhabanipur, Rashbehari, and Ballygunge). There were also changes to the part numbers. The study area was initially in Part 85, but later in Part 49, within Ward 66 of the Kolkata Municipal Corporation.

Electoral History

The influential political parties here are the CPI(M), All-India Trinamool Congress (AITC — popularly known as Trinamool) and Congress. As in other parts of Kolkata, the influence and popularity of Congress has receded since the emergence of AITC under Mamata Banerjee. CPI(M), the ruling party in West Bengal, had secured 35.6 per cent of votes (and 21 seats) in 1999 and 38.6 per cent (and 26 seats) in 2004.

The CPI(M) enjoyed the trust of the majority of voters in this area until 1995, when Javed Khan won the local council elections as an independent candidate under the 'watch' symbol; he had served as a councillor for Ward 66 since 1995. Javed Khan later joined the AITC, and served the area as both councillor and MLA. Since 1995 the majority of people have voted for AITC, from corporation to parliamentary level.

Contest and Outcome of the 2009 Election

Thirteen candidates stood in the Kolkata Dakshin election, though the real contest was between Mamata Banerjee (the AITC chief, in alliance with Congress) and Rabin Deb (CPI[M]). Mamata Banerjee's participation attracted a great deal of media interest. She had represented South Calcutta PC for some time; however, many CPI(M) leaders were hopeful of a better performance in the city following delimitation and the withdrawal of the Tata Nano factory from West Bengal to Gujarat. According to the CPI(M), Mamata Banerjee's movement against the land acquisition had been planned according to Narendra Modi's advice; now the people of Gujarat would benefit from the factory. The CPI(M) tried to prove that Mamata had alliances with divisive elements, and claimed that AITC might form an alliance with BJP in future.

Conversations with local CPI(M) workers made it clear that Rabin Deb had acknowledged that there was no hope of winning in Ballygunge. He focused on campaigning in areas that had been added to the PC after delimitation; however this strategy was ultimately unsuccessful.

The Left Front fared badly across the state — their worst showing since 1984 — despite the CPI(M) securing the largest number of votes as a single party (33.1 per cent *versus* AITC's 31.2 per cent). While the AITC increased their seat count from 11 to 16, the CPI(M)'s decreased from 26 to nine: voting trends suggested that CPI(M) had lost its support base in at least 10 districts, and all 11 seats in Kolkata and its suburbs went to the opposition. Bengal, predominantly 'red' until 2009, had started showing signs of turning green (symbolic of AITC) (see Map I1).

There are several possible reasons for CPI(M)'s poor performance. Voters may have been more aware of the administrative failures of the ruling Left Front than its achievements, and more concerned with drinking water and roads than foreign policy and nuclear deals. Some have become exasperated with party dominance in rural areas, and with leaders who are seen to have drifted from the public, distracted by internal factionalism. CPI(M) leader and State Transport Minister Subhas Chakraborty expressed his own disillusionment live on television with the decision to withdraw support from the government — comments which influenced the public and demoralised party cadres. Conversely, media reports attributed AITC's success to the alliance with Congress, the Singur Nandigram movement, the image of Mamata Banerjee, and the party's organisational strength.

Turnout across West Bengal rose from 75 per cent in 1999 to 78 per cent in 2004, reaching 81.5 per cent in 2009. Turnout was highest in the second voting phase (83 per cent), and lowest in the third and final phase (79.5 per cent), during which the CPI(M) did

Table I1

Total Votes Polled by Each Candidate for 23-Kolkata Dakshin PC

	Name of Candidate	Remarks	Party	Votes Secured	Total Electors (%)	Total Votes Polled (%)
1	Jyotsna Banerjee	F, 58	BJP	39,744	2.64	3.95
2	Mamata Banerjee	F, 54	AITC	576,045	38.26	57.19
3	Paresh Chandra Roy	M, 60, SC	BSP	6,745	0.45	0.67
4	Rabin Deb	M, 60	CPI(M)	356,474	23.68	35.39
5	Asif Md	M, 36	MUL	5,896	0.39	0.59
6	Leela Hans	F, 46	IJP	1,472	0.10	0.15
7	Arun Biswas	M, 78	IND	1,984	0.13	0.20
8	Barnali Mukhopadhyay	F, 36	IND	2,623	0.17	0.26
9	Jayanta Datta	M, 43	IND	1,512	0.10	0.15
10	Nishat Khan	M, 50	IND	2,923	0.19	0.29
11	Pijush Banerjee	M, 33	IND	1,674	0.11	0.17
12	Ram Chandra Prasad	M, 65	IND	4,091	0.27	0.41
13	Yusuf Jamal Siddique	M, 34	IND	6,042	0.40	0.60
	Total			**1,007,225**		

Source: Prepared by Dolonchampa Chakrabarty.

Note: F = Female; IJP = Indian Justice Party; IND = Independent; M = Male; MUL = Muslim League.

Map I1
Colour-Coded Map Showing Winning Parties in West Bengal

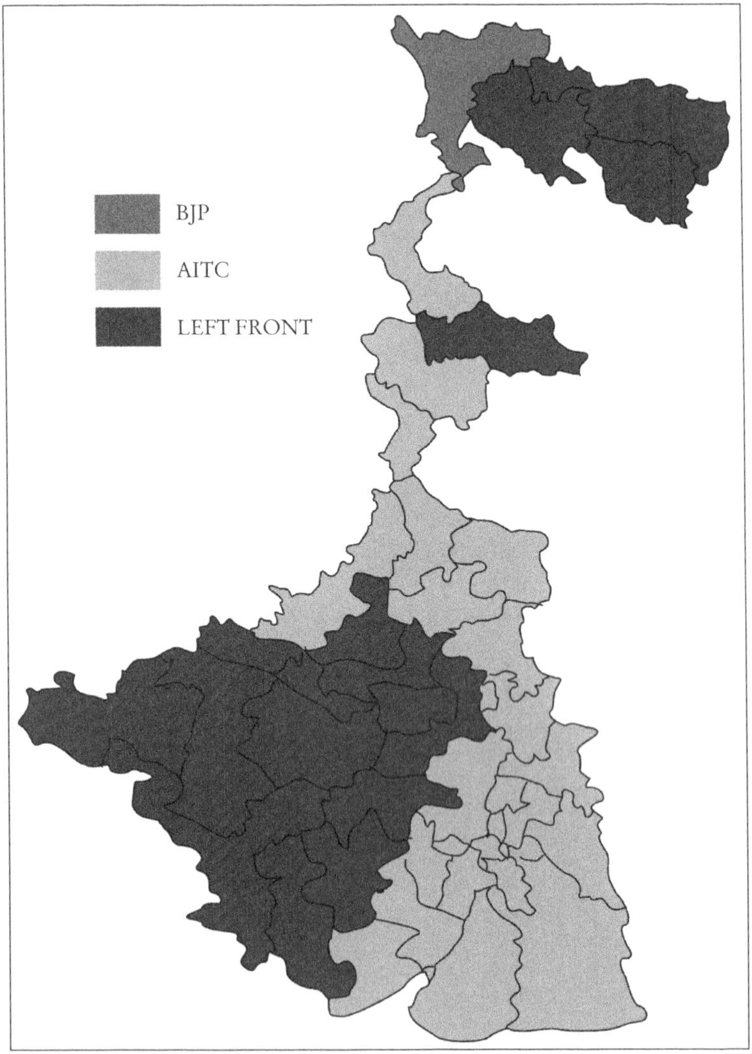

Source: Prepared by the author.

not win a single seat. In Kolkata Uttar PC and Kolkata Dakshin PC, turnout was 64.5 per cent and 67 per cent respectively. In this polling station, turnout exceeded 80 per cent.

Research Questions

The Campaign

Until the end of school examinations on 13 April (2009), the use of microphones for campaigning was banned by official decree; after this date Kolkata experienced heat waves the likes of which had not been seen in the previous three decades. As a result, campaigning in daylight hours was almost non-existent, although close to the election date, all parties held meetings during day and night. Wall graffiti — previously a unique feature of election campaigns in West Bengal — was on the wane, and for the first time flex hoardings flooded the city, with AITC and Left Front banners outnumbering those of other parties. BJP candidates failed to draw much attention.

The CPI(M) used various wings of its party organisation to canvass among voters of varied social status. All party members, from the lowly booth committee to the politburo, had designated duties, and the leaders were asked to visit various localities whenever required. The AITC's procedures and methods emulated those utilised by CPI(M), which was not surprising given that a large number of AITC supporters had once supported CPI(M). The AITC now boasts of area campaign committees, election booth committees, training for members, and a fixed itinerary for leaders.

Both AITC and CPI(M) used the Sachar Committee report and Arjun Sengupta Committee report for their own benefit. The AITC was arguably more successful in using the Sachar Committee report, citing its assessment of the abysmal condition of Muslims in West Bengal to secure the Muslim vote bank.

Role of the Media

The 2009 campaigns used Bengali television and radio (popular in the suburbs of Kolkata) to air party advertisements to the masses. Some heavyweight candidates even hired PR agencies to run attractive audio-visual campaigns. The majority of people relied primarily on television for election information; they trusted visual media more than the press, saying that there is less scope for covering up information. Politically conscious people enjoyed the 'spice' of the campaign news as much as they enjoyed the IPL, or 'K' serials. The traditionally Left-leaning population followed the '24 hours' and

Akash Bangla TV channels, which featured programmes including the satirical *Jhontudar Jhanda* ('Jhontu's Flag') and 'Vote Café'. Star Ananda, the most popular channel among people opposing the Left Front government, aired *Moharone Moharothi* or 'Stalwarts in War', and 'Vote Rongo' (parody on voting), which featured reporters from *Anandabazar Patrika*, which is one of the oldest newspapers opposing the Left parties and has become increasingly popular by adopting an anti-establishment agenda. *Ganashakti* is considered to be the voice of CPI(M) and was particularly critical of the AITC–Congress alliance, claiming it was based on opportunism, not ideology.

Language of Politics

The AITC leaders used simple colloquial language to promote their election theme of *ma, mati, manush* (mother, land and people). They highlighted the misrule of the CPI(M), and claimed that the ruling party had rigged results and used the delimitation exercise to fragment Kolkata. Their speeches included lines from great poets including Kaji Nazrul Islam, Sukanta and Rabindranath Tagore. Outside the city, the hero was Mithun Chakraborty.

The language of the ruling party was different: their messages focused primarily on opposing American interference in India and pushing for job creation; they also pointed out inconsistencies in AITC campaign materials, either ridiculing the claims or offering counter-arguments.

Polling Station

The voters of Part 49 cast their votes at the Sunil Nagar Primary School, which served as a polling station for two parts. It is also used for other government programmes including polio immunisations and ID card photography. The school's leaders were evidently less than pleased about the premises being used as a booth: in the past polling agents had left the school dirty and students had been caught smoking the agents' leftover cigarettes. The school has had to pay for the agents' use of lights and fans.

The paramilitary forces had arrived the day before polling. Shops were closed, banners and posters near the polling station removed, and the party stalls — set up at a distance from the polling station — were decorated with large umbrellas rather than banners. Only voters were allowed to enter the school premises, within which two separate rooms were marked out for the two parts. Only after the polling agents of all parties had confirmed the identity of a prospective voter was a slip provided, the voter's finger marked with ink, and the EVM prepared.

As the day progressed, celebrations in the AITC camp increased as people passed by to declare that they had cast their vote for 'Didi' (Mamata Banerjee). Enthusiasm in the CPI(M) camp was considerably lower, and leaders instructed the cadres not to allow themselves to be provoked into any kind of trouble.

Although voters had to stand in line for a long time, there were no quarrels or complaints — everyone seemed happy that they had been able to vote for their chosen candidate. Many in Kolkata call the process a 'vote *puja*' (vote worship), and throughout the day people were in a holiday mood. After voting early in the morning, most voters chatted in the alleys and neighbourhoods, then had lunch and a nap. Many had made plans to visit relatives. For the average middle-class Bengali population, election day is an ideal holiday, provided there is no violence.

'Why Do You Vote?'

West Bengal is one of the highest-polling states in India, and rural areas typically have higher turnout than urban areas. This is perhaps because a sizeable proportion of the voters migrated to the area after partition; since their citizenship and voting rights were recognised by the Indian government they have sincerely executed their moral responsibility as Indian citizens to vote. It was also noted that the three Communist-governed states have high polling percentages, possibly a result of the Communist parties' attempts to mobilise the grassroots level.

While party leaders emphasised their view that common people are rational and politically aware and exercise independent choice when they vote, the electors themselves had a range of reasons for voting. One voter from the Picnic Garden area said that voting is a right, and failing to vote might lead to anarchy, while another man speculated that it might not be long before people did not vote at all — they would lose their faith in the democratic process if things did not change. Others cited moral responsibility, the need for a voice for the poor, and fears that someone else might vote illegally on one's behalf. One woman said that people would call her mad were she not to vote, while others were resigned to the formality of the process. Overall, people were tight-lipped about their motivations and preferences in the 2009 elections compared to similar events in the past.

Appendix J
Uttar Pradesh (East)

Researcher: Badri Narayan

Shahabpur Village (Booths 226,227, 228),
Phaphamau AC (254), Phulpur PC (51)

Background

The tiny village of Shahabpur lies approximately 20 km from Allahabad, 5 km north of Hathiganh Chauraha on the Allahabad–Lucknow highway in the Doab area of the Ganga River. The village is divided into 13 *pattis* (hamlets and subhamlets, also called *poorvas* and *tolas*). Shahabpur's residents are from a variety of castes, mostly from the lower strata of the caste hierarchy. Patels, Pasis, Mauryas, Kumhars, Chamars, Turks (Muslims), and Dhobis are mostly settled in their own pattis, while other castes with smaller populations, including Yadav, Darzi, Lohar, Nai, Bhuja, Dafali, and Churihaar, live in the Shahabpur Bazaar or scattered throughout other pattis. The hamlets are connected by recently-constructed narrow pitch roads, *kutcha* (unpaved) roads or furrows (*chauri aris*) through the agricultural fields that surround each patti, in which crops such as rice, wheat, mustard, pulses, and vegetables are grown.

People of the Patel caste, or Kurmis, are mostly engaged in agricultural work. Although they are categorised as a backward caste, they link themselves with the Kshatriya lineage. They are mostly settled in the Inara patti, which has 55 households and is named after a large well (*inara*) in its centre, constructed by Sangram Singh, the respected feudal landlord of the village, said to have been killed by the British and collaborators at the time of the 1857 Rebellion. Mauryas live in the gated Maurya Nagar (30 households). They cultivate vegetables, which would have been exchanged under the barter system but are now sold in the village market (*haat*). Like Patels, they link themselves with the Kshatriyas. Pasis or Saroj (SC) live in the secluded Pasiyapur patti of 125 households. They are among the lowest castes in the Hindu hierarchy, and worked as guards for the erstwhile feudal landlords (they claim to have served in Sangram Singh's army). Today they are mostly agricultural labourers. There are 16 Kumhar (potter) households in the Kohran patti, though availability of plastics has led them to diversify into other occupations, such as rickshaw-pulling in Allahabad and seasonal agricultural labour.

Chamars, or Harijans, belong to the lowest rung of the caste hierarchy. Most live in the Godam patti (45 households) and have embraced either the Kabirpanthi or Raidasi sects. They have given up skinning and tanning animal hides to practise agriculture instead, or to work as rickshaw pullers or labourers. Their sense of injustice about their past treatment has motivated them to become the most politically powerful community in the village. They tend to vote for the BSP.

The Muslims of Turkan patti (six households), commonly known as Turks, are relatively affluent. They own small shops in the Bazaar and small plots of land. Most are Qureshis. Other Muslim groups including Dafali, or Darvesh (who remain part of the *jajmani* patron–client system and follow their traditional profession — making musical instruments) and Manihaar or Churihaar (who sell bangles) are politically and administratively identified as Dalits.

There are only two Brahmin households in the village, and they do not have much voice in village politics. The power tilt is in favour of the Patels and Mauryas, and the Dalit castes. Most Dalit families own some land, and the Patels own the most land in the village.

Delimitation

Some people (including Shiv Bahadur Singh, a Thakur living in the Shahabpur Thakuran) felt that the reconstruction of the Allahabad and Phulpur constituencies would favour the BSP.

Electoral History

The village has a strong political history, and the villagers are politically conscious. Their affiliations are largely caste-dependent: the

Dalits and most Muslims support the BSP, the Yadavs support the SP, the Patels support the newly-formed Apna Dal, and the upper castes support either the Congress or BJP. Prime Ministers Jawaharlal Nehru and V. P. Singh both represented Phulpur PC. Since 1996, the PC has been represented by the SP; Atiq Ahmed won the seat in 2004.

Contest and Outcome of the 2009 Election

The village had three polling booths: Booths 226 and 227 in Shahabpur School, with 1,428 and 880 voters respectively, and Booth 228 in Pasiyapur Primary School, with 319 voters. Phulpur PC (1,426,450 electors) had a turnout just below 39 per cent. The election took place on 23 April 2009. On the afternoon of 16 May, people started to hear via mobile telephone and radio that Kapil Muni Karwariya (BSP) had won.

Research Questions

The Campaign

Traditional forms of campaigning included caste and community feasts held by many political parties, particularly the BSP, who had announced its candidates a year earlier. BSP *pracharak* (campaigner) Srikant Upadhyaya said that he himself had organised six events where Brahmins and Dalits had shared meals together (although he became agitated when asked whether Dalits would be invited to functions in his own house).

The SP organised a Muslim fraternity rally that travelled through the Muslim colonies of Shahabpur on 15 April (2009). Five or six Muslims were present among 60 or 70 Hindus. The Hindus wore tied headbands, beat sticks (as during *tazia* processions) and shouted slogans in Hindi with a sprinkling of Urdu. The rally appeared to be part of a political strategy to appeal to the ethnic memory of the Muslims by imitating dress, language and sounds.

Some women in Shahabpur wore blue saris to display solidarity with Behenji (Mayawati). Meanwhile, other women complained that, in contrast to previous years, no saris and glasses had been distributed.

Table J1
Total Votes Polled by Each Candidate: 51-Phulpur PC

	Name of Candidate	Remarks	Party	Votes Secured	Total Electors (%)	Total Votes Polled (%)
1	Kapil Muni Karwariya	M, 42	BSP	167,542	11.75	30.36
2	Karan Singh Patel	M, 50	BJP	44,828	3.14	8.12
3	Dharmaraj Singh Patel	M, 50	INC	67,623	4.74	12.25
4	Shyama Charan Gupta	M, 63	SP	152,964	10.72	27.72
5	Chandrajeet	M, 28	LD	2,328	0.16	0.42
6	Devendra Pratap Singh	M, 38	RDMP	1,113	0.08	0.20
7	Pradeep Kumar Srivastava	M, 49	AD	1,438	0.10	0.26
8	Lallan Singh	M, 35	RSBP	1,139	0.08	0.21
9	Vijay Kumar	M, 56, SC	GMS	1,156	0.08	0.21
10	Satish Yadav	M, 34	IJP	838	0.06	0.15
11	Sanjeev Kumar Mishra	M, 30	YVP	929	0.07	0.17
12	Krishna Kumar	M, 33	IND	1,003	0.07	0.18
13	Neeraj	M, 43	IND	1,563	0.11	0.28
14	Bharat Lal	M, 52, SC	IND	4,156	0.29	0.75
15	Milan Mukherjee	M, 67	IND	8,357	0.59	1.51
16	Munishwar Singh Maurya	M, 65	IND	6,111	0.43	1.11
17	Radhika Pal	F, 34	IND	4,977	0.35	0.90
18	Radheshyam Singh Yadav	M, 72	IND	1,751	0.12	0.32
19	Ram Janm Yadav	M, 31	IND	1,216	0.09	0.22
20	Ramshankar	M, 47	IND	1,332	0.09	0.24
21	Virendra Pal Singh	M, 66	IND	687	0.05	0.12
22	Shailendra Kumar Prajapati	M, 40	IND	623	0.04	0.11
23	Samar Bahadur Sharma	M, 40	IND	1,544	0.11	0.28
24	Sone Lal Patel	M, 59	IND	76,699	5.38	13.90
	Total			**551,917**		

Source: Prepared by Badri Narayan.
Note: AD = Apna Dal; F = Female; IND = Independent; LD = Lok Dal; M = Male; RSBP = Rashtriya Swabhimaan Party; YVP = Yuva Vikas Party.

Role of the Media

Technology and mass media have become increasingly important in attempts to reach out to the people. Kaka Hathrasi's satires could be heard being played on BJP campaign cassettes at low volume:

> Listen to Kaka
> Select the right government
> Seeing the voters
> Kaka the poet is amazed
> The country's body is skinny
> But even then you are indifferent
> Even then you are different
> This is difficult to understand
> Backbreaking now
> Is the price rise
> Don't select a poor and weak government again
> Press the button on the lotus which is loved by all the people.

Almost all parties composed campaign songs. The Congress had hired the services of Percept, the advertising agency, who composed a song based on 'Jai Ho' from the film *Slumdog Millionaire* (2008). The BJP song's lyrics were: *Saathi saath nibhana ab ke bhaiya phir se tum kamal par batan dabana*, while the SP's declared: *Suno suno Phulpur walon, sun lo bhaiya dhyaan lagaai, ye saikil hai apna saathi, phir se bhaiya diyo jitae.*

Of the two FM radio stations, the more effective reached out to the youth and middle-class voters (already avid radio listeners). However, the medium was more suited to urban areas. In any case, television was not a successful means of communication: of 90 households only 22 had small televisions, most of which were usually out of order, and even those households with working televisions were subject to unreliable electricity supply.

Language of Politics

As soon as news of the result reached the village, heated discussions at the tea stalls in Shahabpur Bazaar gave rise to new strategic discourses about voting choices. SP supporters, for example, could be heard supporting Karwariya's victory, on the proviso that he did something constructive for the village. Many BSP supporters tried to take credit for the party's victory, for example Doodhnath Pasi, the ex-*Pradhan*, who proudly asserted that Karwariya had won owing to his mobilisation of the voters of Pasiyapur. Some people appeared to change their loyalty to the winning candidate.

Many people were not aware that the Congress had won the overall majority of seats and would form the government at the centre with the help of a few allies. Rather than expressing disappointment that Mayawati had not won as many seats as expected, BSP supporters only seemed happy that their local candidate had been successful. In the primarily Patel settlements of Tali and Purai ka Poorva, some were upset that neither their party (Apna Dal), nor the candidate of their caste (Dharmaraj Patel of the Congress), had won; but they did not reveal for whom they had voted. One Dalit woman said that before the elections she had supported Mulayam Singh (former chief minister, SP), who had promised to implement the Kanya Vidya Dhan (an educational scheme for female students), but she had still voted for the BSP. Deepa Patel of Purai ka Poorva was happy with the functioning of the state government under the BSP, but had voted for Apna Dal because of caste affinity.

Polling Station

Rajni (32 years old) had reached her parents' house in Pasiyapur to cast her vote in the blistering heat after completing her household activities in her in-laws' house in Nawabganj. Bhullar, the *Kabirpanthi Mahant* (followers of a sect) of the Chamar patti, had taken a day's leave from work in Allahabad to cast his vote in Shahabpur. Muslim women went in large numbers to vote, accompanied by their husbands and other men of their families. The mud-streaked hands of Ram Bharose, a 65-year-old Pasi, showed that he had left his work in the fields half-done to come and cast his vote. After 10 minutes of standing in line, he was turned away because he had not brought his voter identification card. Ram Bharose wanted to know why it was needed when he was there in person, but he eventually fetched it from home.

Itwari (28 years old) of the Patel community had come on her husband's motorcycle to vote, wearing a bright red sari and accompanied by her three children, all dressed in new clothes, saying that the elections provided the opportunity to take her children out to enjoy the day. Sursati Devi (68 years old), also of the Patel caste, arrived in a bright red sari as well, shyly explaining that she had worn what her daughter and daughter-in-law had asked her to wear, though her anklets, red bangles and look of self-satisfaction suggested that she had herself taken great pains to dress up.

 While all the Dalits of Pasiyapur and Godam patti cast their votes enthusiastically, there was also a note of disillusionment with Mayawati. Sugiya, a 62-year-old Dalit woman, said she had voted for Mayawati even though she had not done much for them: Mayawati was doing her dharma (ruling the people) while they were doing their dharma (casting vote).

'Why Do You Vote?'

Ramkishore (70 years old), a Chamar by caste, explained that because people of all castes now came to his porch stall to drink tea and eat *paan*, he felt that casteism had almost ended. However, he immediately added that he used to vote for the Congress, but after BSP came to power, he had started voting for Mayawati on the grounds of caste affinity. For Dalits like Ramkishore, casteism has two meanings: while he is happy that Brahmins now drink water from the hands of Dalits, he is also more conscious and proud of his caste identity. Nirmala Devi (52 years old) denied that women blindly follow their husbands' voting choices. The women generally vote according to their own wishes irrespective of the opinions that their husbands form after interacting with various people in the market.

 In Pasiyapur, a group of men became quiet and defensive when asked why they had voted for BSP candidate Kapil Muni Karwariya, when his father — a Brahmin mafia don of the region — had murdered seven or eight Pasis. Shyam Lal (35 years old) said that SP's Atiq Ahmed -— another mafia don, elected MP in 2004 — had killed Pasi leader Raju Pal, a BSP MLA. 'So which party was clean?', he asked, adding that even if a member of one's own family is physically or verbally challenged, the other family members feel close to him.

 It emerged that many in the Dalit hamlets did not cast their vote. After the election, they explained their impression that because all the other people of their caste were voting for the candidate, he would win anyway. Some were too busy farming to cast their vote, and some complained that unlike in previous elections BSP activists had not come to escort them to the polling booth.

Appendix K
Uttar Pradesh (West)

Researcher: Satendra Kumar

Polling Booth 294, Khanpur Village,
Sardhana AC (44), Muzaffarnagar PC (3)

Background

Khanpur is a multi-caste village in Muzaffarnagar PC and Meerut district, part of the fertile tract of Upper Doeb. The study focused on Polling Booth 294, which had a diverse caste composition, and on the Gujjar *mohalla* — the largest covered by the booth. Khanpur has few industries and is largely dependent on agriculture. Since the mid-1960s, the commercialisation of agriculture in Upper Doeb has accelerated, closely associated with the influx of Green Revolution technologies and government support for major regional crops of wheat and sugarcane. In addition, the scissors and sports goods industries of Meerut and the blanket industry of Muzaffarnagar are famous all over India.

The area is part of a larger Gujjar belt — 'Gujrat' in the local parlance — which stretches along the Ganges from Haridwar to Ghaziabad, Noida and Delhi. Independence and the subsequent abolition of the *zamindari* system benefited Gujjars, Ahirs and OBCs such as Sainis and Gaderiyas who became owners and cultivators. Khanpur became known as *Gujjro ka gaon* — a village of Gujjars.

In 2004, the village population was 2,823, distributed among 447 households. The largest group was Chamars (SC —866), followed in descending order by three OBC groups: Sainis (478), Gujjars (276) and Ahirs (252). Upper-caste Brahmins and Banias also live in the village, as do other OBC groups including Gaderiya, Dhimvar and Kumhar (Hindu); and Fakir, Nai and Lohar (Muslim). Gujjars and

Ahirs, the dominant castes, owned about 42 per cent of the agricultural land in the village. While most Chamars work as non-farm labourers outside the village, some own land ancestrally, and a few work as agricultural labourers. The shift to non-agricultural jobs and small-scale land ownership has considerably improved their economic and educational status. The numerical strength of the Chamars and the rise of the BSP in the 1990s in Uttar Pradesh provided a space for identity politics to challenge the old vertical factional politics, and has significantly weakened the political influence of the Gujjars and Ahirs in village affairs.

Muzaffarnagar PC comprises five ACs: Muzaffarnagar, Charthawal, Budhana, Khatuali, and Sardhana. The PC had an electorate of 1,370,117 distributed among approximately 800 villages. About 72 per cent of the electorate lived in villages, and the remaining 28 per cent in towns and market centres. Nearly 67 per cent were Hindus and 33 per cent Muslims.

Delimitation

The 2008 delimitation exercise shifted Khanpur from Hastinapur AC and Meerut-Mawana PC to Sardhana AC and Muzaffarnagar PC. The exercise also changed the social composition of the Muzaffarnagar PC, as a large number of Jat villages were shifted from the Kairana area to the newly-created Budhana AC, which was added to Muzaffarnagar PC. This made Muzaffarnagar PC very attractive to the incumbent MP of the Kairana PC, Anuradha Chaudhary (SP–Rashtriya Lok Dal [RLD] alliance), and she decided to contest the Muzaffarnagar seat in 2009.

Electoral History

Until 1962, the Congress dominated Muzaffarnagar. In 1967, the CPI won the seat. In the 1970s, the popularity of the Congress declined heavily, while the LD and Janata Dal (S) established their presence across the Upper Doeb. In 1984, Congress won, reflecting their gain of power in Delhi, but then lost in 1989 to Janata Dal's Mufti Mohammad Sayeed, a Kashmiri. In the 1990s, the BJP won the seat three consecutive times before Congress regained it in 1999. However, in 2004 they lost to the SP–RLD alliance, which took seven of the

13 Lok Sabha seats in western UP, largely as a result of Ch. Chaudhary Ajit Singh's MAJGR formula, which allied Muslims, Jats, Gujjars, and Rajputs. Since the 1950s, Muzaffarnagar PC has largely elected Jat and Muslim MPs.

Hastinapur AC, to which the village used to belong, had been reserved for SCs; Chamar candidates were invariably elected as MLAs. After the Bhikund incident between two rival groups of dacoits, the region's Gujjars opposed the Chamar candidate in the 1996 Vidhan Sabha election, voting in an independent candidate of the Khaitik caste, who later joined the BJP. In the 2002 assembly elections, the Gujjars of Khanpur actively supported the winning candidate Prabhudayal Valmiki (SP). In 2007, Prabhudayal Valmiki lost to Yogesh Verma (BSP), a Chamar. Gujjar votes were divided between Congress and BSP, while the BJP's traditional vote bank — the Gaderiyas — voted for the new SKP, launched by regional middle-class Gaderiya leaders.

In the 2005 Panchayat elections, the post of *pradhan* (chief) was reserved for a woman and won by an Ahir candidate. A political understanding between Gujjars and Ahirs meant that they had shared the post for much of the last 50 years but Chamars have also been able to win. While Panchayat elections had previously been fought according to vertical factions, castes and religions, villagers increasingly relate directly with political parties, and with broader regional and national identity politics.

Contest and Outcome of the 2009 Election

Though 23 candidates stood, the main contest was among the BSP (Kadir Rana — Muslim/Rajput), RLD (Anuradha Chaudhary — Hindu/Jat), SP (Sangeet Som — Hindu/Rajput) and Congress (Harindra Malik — Hindu/Jat). In RLD circles, it was alleged that the BSP candidate had paid Harindra Malik to stand in order to divide Jat votes. This allegation was refuted by Congress workers and others.

For the first time BSP won the Muzaffarnagar PC, as Kadir Rana defeated Anuradha Chaudhary of the RLD–BJP alliance. The BSP's promotion of a Dalit–Muslim alliance (DM) paved the way for this victory. Muzaffarnagar PC has 1,370,117 electors, and turnout was 54.3 per cent.

Table K1
Total Votes Polled by Each Candidate: 3-Muzaffarnagar PC

	Name of Candidate	Remarks	Party	Votes Secured	Total Electors (%)	Total Votes Polled (%)
1	Kadir Rana	M, 45	BSP	275,318	20.09	36.96
2	Dheer Singh	M, 45	CPI	3,655	0.27	0.49
3	Thakur Sangeet Singh Som	M, 29	SP	106,667	7.79	14.32
4	Harindra Singh Malik	M, 54	INC	73,848	5.39	9.91
5	Anuradha Chaudhary	F, 48	RLD	254,720	18.59	34.19
6	Abdul Aziz Ansari	M, 57	PECP	6,537	0.48	0.88
7	Ashutosh Pandey	M, 30	LD	3,781	0.28	0.51
8	Nawab Ali	M, 38	NLHP	723	0.05	0.10
9	Manish Bhai Urf Nitu	M, 35	ABHM	377	0.03	0.05
10	Satish Kumar	M, 32	JSP	710	0.05	0.10
11	Salamudeen Urf Salmu Malik	M, 45	NELU	635	0.05	0.09
12	Inderpal	M, 67	IND	1,119	0.08	0.15
13	Narendra Kumar	M, 44	IND	795	0.06	0.11
14	Parmod Pal	M, 41	IND	678	0.05	0.09
15	Bhagwat Singh	M, 66, SC	IND	694	0.05	0.09
16	Mukta Singh	F, 25	IND	3,037	0.22	0.41
17	Ranveer	M, 49	IND	3,597	0.26	0.48
18	Rajendra Singh	M, 60	IND	449	0.03	0.06
19	Reeta Urf Reeta Kashyap	F, 31	IND	1,640	0.12	0.22
20	Vijay	M, 36, SC	IND	1,296	0.09	0.17
21	Veerpal	M, 32	IND	2,242	0.16	0.30
22	Satyaveer	M, 45	IND	600	0.04	0.08
23	Salek Chaudhary	M, 37	IND	1,883	0.14	0.25
	Total			745,001		

Source: Prepared by Satendra Kumar.
Note: ABHM = Akhil Bharat Hindu Mahasabha; F = Female; IND = Independent; JSP = Jansatta Party; LD = Lok Dal; M = Male; NELU = Nelopa (United); NLHP = National Lokhind Party; PECP = Peace Party; RLD = Rashtriya Lok Dal.

Research Questions

The Campaign

During April, *karyakarta*s (activists) and local caste leaders visited the village in large cars (though without flags). Caste meetings were held almost every week in neighbouring villages or towns. Gujjar leaders tried to unite their *biradari* (caste) behind one candidate, as did the Sainis, Dhimvars and Gaderiyas, who also wanted to improve their political visibility in western UP. In Khanpur and Muzaffarnagar the election was fought on local issues.

From 22 April to 5 May (2009), Khanpur — indeed the whole of rural western UP — was stirred up by politicians, activists and newspapers: villagers could almost always be found discussing, judging and gossiping about candidates, parties, *jan sabha*s, *biradari*s, panchayats, and rallies during *hukka* sessions and card games, weekly markets and wedding ceremonies, in buses, fields, and at intersections. The village became emotionally charged, politically conscious and socially polite.

Role of the Media

Most residents of rural western UP read the *Amar Ujala* and *Dainik Jagran* — two of the region's popular vernacular newspapers — which pursued election stories with greater zeal than their metropolitan counterparts. Each day, around eight copies of *Amar Ujala* were delivered across the village. In the Gujjar *mohalla*, two copies were circulated among 35–40 readers — mainly men who read while sitting and smoking at Birma's or Sukhbeer's *baithak* (a small gathering) (women did not regularly read newspapers). Nevertheless, people maintained scepticism about newspaper reports, having more faith in radio and television. In some cases, readers concocted their own stories based on what they read. For example a report that Kadir Rana's procession had been attacked in one village was retold thus: 'He has been largely rejected by all Hindu castes. In almost 15 villages his entry is now barred. He is going to lose to Anuradha'. Visual media gained popularity in the late 1990s in rural Western UP, though scant supply of electricity has made it hard for villagers to enjoy access to it.

Language of Politics

For many villagers, political discussions were a routine, like their agricultural work. The language of democratic politics was largely borrowed from religion, the *jajmani* system, patron–client relationships, family, kinship, and marriage. Some terms also referred to mythical characters and popular culture. Old words mixed with new and several English words were accommodated in the local parlance.

While the Chamars largely set their eyes on the Delhi seat for their leader Mayawati, using the slogan: 'UP has become ours, now it is Delhi's turn', upper-castes and OBCs were anxious about her proposed land consolidation. Their buzzword throughout the village was: 'Defeat the BSP'. Muslims were not involved in this rhetoric; however, they saw themselves as voting for a brother (a Muslim) rather than for BSP. This was articulated in a popular slogan: 'first preference is given to a brother [*biradari bhai*], second, a candidate from SP, and third, one who can defeat the BJP'.

Polling Station

The school housing Polling Booths 293 and 294 was located in the Gujjar *mohalla*. One Gujjar explained that the location of the village entrance and vital government institutions in the Gujjar *mohalla* meant that, although the Chamars were emerging as a new power in the village, they could not challenge the Gujjars.

As Khanpur is not a large village, there was no need for transportation on polling day. Men dressed casually, ready to go to their fields after voting. The Lok Sabha elections were not seen as particularly important for villagers as they rarely knew the candidates, and thus 'nobody takes risks', unlike during Panchayat elections when turnout nears 100 per cent, and people are ready to die for their candidates.

Women did not appear at the polling booth until later in the day. Sarbati, a *loharin* (blacksmith), who was bathing her buffalos, gave her reasons:

> Give me some time. I have to finish my household chores, and then I will bathe and go with the other women of the *mohalla*. The men have already gone. They do not have so much work. I have to take care of kids and cattle both.

At around noon the women started pouring into the streets in groups of four to six, sometimes more, wearing new outfits and makeup. The polling station was suddenly full of colours — red, yellow, blue, orange, and green, including black *burkha*s and embroidered *chadder*s. While upper-OBC and upper-caste (Gujjar, Ahir, Brahmin) and Muslim women were accompanied by men of their households or associates of the polling agents, women from lower castes such as Chamar, Valmiki, Saini, Kumhar, and Dhimvar arrived unaccompanied. Chamar women were the most aware about the voting process. They voted openly and excitedly for Mayawati. The atmosphere of the polling booth and village was festive. Youths stood outside the school premises and went from door-to-door to give directions to women and the elderly, while chatting about who would win.

'Why Do You Vote?'

Despite widespread disappointment and anger regarding the performance of the BSP's incumbent Hastinapur MLA, people asserted that they would continue to vote: many held the opinion that it is their only right in independent India. Voting gave them the empowering feeling of being a free citizen; even one vote could change the destiny of a contesting candidate.

Voting is also popularly viewed as an important duty for a citizen. One young man, Hasim, whose family stopped sowing sugarcane in order to vote, explained how he felt everyone was doing something on Election Day (polling officers, political leaders, police, the pradhan, other villagers); voting was the greatest contribution they could make to maintaining democracy in the country, or *desh*. Neither poverty nor low literacy had dissuaded Hasim from being a politically aware citizen of India, despite living in a situation where electricity supply is erratic, children walk 5 km for schooling, and many are forced to curtail their studies owing to financial difficulties.

For many, participating in the elections was a strategy to build links with political leaders and the local officials who frequent their offices. A group of villagers explained that:

> During the elections, citizens are honoured by political parties, leaders and the government . . . It is the voters who become God and decide the fate of all leaders. At least for one day, we voters get the power to choose and reject.

Some viewed voting as a strategy to tame the state or create a moral world. In Khanpur, villagers also see their voting right as affirming the right to an equality not seen except on polling day.

Bibliography

Abeìles, Marc. 1991. *Quiet Days in Burgundy: A Study of Local Politics.* Cambridge: Cambridge University Press.

Ahuja, Amit and Pradeep Chhibber. 2009. 'Civic Duty, Empowerment and Patronage: Patterns of Political Participation in India', http://www.sscnet.ucla.edu/polisci/cpworkshop/papers/Chhibber.pdf (accessed 27 May 2012).

Amin, Shahid. 1987. 'Approver's Testimony, Judicial Discourse: The Case of Chauri Chaura', in Ranajit Guha (ed.), *Subaltern Studies: Writings on South Asian History and Society.* New Delhi: Oxford University Press.

Banerjee, Mukulika. 2001. *The Pathan Unarmed: Opposition and Memory in the North West Frontier.* Oxford: James Currey.

————. 2004. 'Populism or the Democratisation of Democracy', in Rob Jenkins (ed.), *Regional Reflections: Comparing Politics Across India's States.* New Delhi: Oxford University Press.

————. 2007. 'Sacred Elections', *Economic and Political Weekly*, 42(17): 1556–62.

————. 2008. 'Democracy, Sacred and Everyday: An Ethnographic Case from India', in Julia Paley (ed.), *Democracy: Anthropological Perspectives.* Santa Fe: School for Advanced Research Press.

————. 2010a. 'A Left Front Election', in Anthony Heath and R. Jeffery (eds), *Diversity and Change in Modern India: Economic, Social and Political Approaches.* Oxford: Oxford University Press.

————. 2010b. 'Leadership and Political Work', in Pamela Price and Arild Ruud (eds), *Power and Influence in India: Bosses, Lords, and Captains*, pp. 20–43. New Delhi: Routledge.

————. 2011. 'Elections as Communitas', *Social Research*, 78(1): 75–98.

Bardhan, Pranab. 2005. 'Democracy and Poverty: The Peculiar Case of India', in *Scarcity, Conflicts and Cooperation: Essays in Political and Institutional Economics of Development.* Cambridge MA: MIT Press.

Bate, Bernard. 2009. *Tamil Oratory and the Dravidian Aesthetic: Democratic Practice in South India.* New York: Columbia University Press.

Bear, Laura. 2001. 'Making a River of Gold: Speculative State Planning, Informality and Neoliberal Governance on the Hooghly', *Focaal*, 61: 46–60.

Béteille, André. 2008. 'Constitutional Morality', *Economic and Political Weekly*, 43(4): 35–42.

————. 2012. *Democracy and its Institutions.* New Delhi: Oxford University Press.

Bhargava, Rajeev. 2010. *The Promise of India's Secular Democracy*. New Delhi: Oxford University Press.

Bora, Banasmita. 2009. 'On the Electoral Process', *Economic and Political Weekly*, 44(39): 105–7.

Brass, Paul. 1985. *Caste, Faction and Party in Indian Politics: Election Studies*. New Delhi: Chanakya Publications.

———. 1997. *The Theft of an Idol: Text and Context in the Representations of Collective Violence*. Princeton NJ: Princeton University Press.

Breman, J. 2007. *The Poverty Regime in Village India*. New Delhi: Oxford University Press.

Butler, David; Ashok Lahiri and Prannoy Roy. 1995. *India Decides: Elections 1952–1995*. New Delhi: Books & Things.

Chakrabarty, Dipesh. 2000. *Provincializing Europe: Postcolonial Thought and Historical Difference*. Princeton NJ: Princeton University Press.

Chakrabarty, Dipesh, Rochona Majumdar and Andrew Sartori. 2007. *From the Colonial to the Postcolonial: India and Pakistan in Transition*. New Delhi: Oxford University Press.

Chakravarti, Anand. 1975. *Contradiction and Change: Emerging Patterns of Authority in a Rajasthan Village*. New Delhi: Oxford University Press.

Chandra, Kanchan. 2004. *Why Ethnic Parties Succeed: Patronage and Ethnic Head Counts in India*. New York: Cambridge University Press.

Chatterjee, Partha (ed.). 2008. *The Present History of West Bengal: Essays in Political Criticism*. New Delhi: Oxford University Press.

Chatterjee, Partha, P. K. Bose and R. Samaddar. 1997. 'Discipline and Development', in Partha Chatterjee (ed.), *The Present History of West Bengal: Essays in Political Criticism*. New Delhi: Oxford University Press.

Chhibber, Pradeep. 2001. *Democracy without Associations: Transformation of the Party System and Social Cleavages in India*. Ann Arbor: University of Michigan Press.

Coles, Kimberley. 2007. *Democratic Designs: International Intervention and Electoral Practices in Postwar Bosnia-Herzegovina*. Ann Arbor: University of Michigan Press.

Corbridge, Stuart and John Harriss. 2010. 'The Continuing Reinvention of India', in Chandan Sengupta and Stuart Corbridge (eds), *Democracy, Development and Decentralisation in India*. London: Routledge.

Corbridge, Stuart, John Harriss and Craig Jeffrey. 2013. *India Today: Economics, Politics and Society*. London: Polity Press.

Datar, Abhay. n.d. 'Annotated Bibliography on Election Studies', http://www.unipune.ac.in/dept/mental_moral_and_social_science/politics_and_public_administration/ppa_webfiles/pdf/new11/Link_AnnotatedBibliography.pdf (accessed 9 October 2010).

Dubner, Stephen J. and Steven D. Levitt. 2005. 'Why Vote?' *The New York Times*, 6 November.

Dunn, John. 1993. 'Studying Elections', unpublished paper prepared for the Social Science Research Council Asia Program on Elections in Southeast Asia, Woodrow Wilson Center, Washington DC, 16–18 September.

Falcao, Vanita. 2009. 'Urban Patterns of Voting and Party Choices', *Economic and Political Weekly*, 44(39): 99–101.

Fuller, Christopher. 1996. *Caste Today*. New Delhi: Oxford University Press.

Gilmartin, David. forthcoming. *Election Commission of India Diamond Jubilee Commemorative Volume*.

———. 2007. 'Election Law and the "People" in Colonial and Postcolonial India', in Dipesh Chakrabarty, Rochona Majumdar and Andrew Sartori (eds), *From the Colonial to the Postcolonial: India and Pakistan in Transition*. New Delhi: Oxford University Press.

———. 2009. 'One Day's Sultan: T. N. Seshan and Indian Democracy', *Contributions to Indian Sociology*, 43(2): 247–84.

Guha, Ranajit. 1983. 'The Prose of Counter-Insurgency', in *Subaltern Studies: Writings on South Asian History and Society*. New Delhi: Oxford University Press.

Guha, Ramachandra. 2010. 'Political Leadership', in Neerja Jayal and Pratap Bhanu Mehta (eds), *A Dictionary of Indian Politics*. New Delhi: Oxford University Press.

———. 2012. *Makers of Modern India*. New Delhi: Penguin.

Gupta, Akhil. 1988. *Postcolonial Developments: Agriculture in the Making of Modern India*. Delhi: Oxford University Press.

———. 2008. 'Literacy, Bureaucratic Domination, and Democracy', in Julia Paley (ed.), *Democracy: Anthropological Perspectives*. Santa Fe: School for Advanced Research Press.

Gupta, Akhil and K. Sivaramakrishnan (eds). 2011. *The State in India after Liberalization: Interdisciplinary Perspectives*. London and New York: Routledge.

Hansen, Thomas Blom, 1988. 'The Ethics of Hindutva and the Spirit of Capitalism', in Thomas Blom Hansen and Christophe Jaffrelot (eds), *Compulsions of Politics: BJP and Competitive Politics in India*. Delhi: Oxford University Press.

Harriss, John. 1986. 'The Working Poor and the Labour Aristocracy in a South Indian City: A Descriptive and Analytical Account', *Modern Asian Studies*, 20(2): 231–83.

———. 2005. 'Political Participation, Representation and the Urban Poor: Findings from Research in Delhi', *Economic and Political Weekly*, 40(11): 1041–54.

Hasan, Zoya. 2010. 'Political Parties', in Neerja Jayal and Pratap Bhanu Mehta (eds), *The Oxford Companion to Politics in India*. Delhi: Oxford University Press.

Hauser, Walter and W. Singer. 2001.'The Democratic Rite: Celebration and Participation in the Indian Elections', in Neerja Jayal (ed.), *Democracy in India*. New Delhi: Oxford University Press.

Holston, James. 2008. *Insurgent Citizenship: Disjunctions of Democracy and Modernity in Brazil.* Princeton NJ: Princeton University Press.

Jaffrelot, Christophe. 2003. *India's Silent Revolution: The Rise of the Lower Castes in North India.* London: Hurst & Company.

———. 2005. *Dr Ambedkar and Untouchability: Analysing and Fighting Caste.* New Delhi: Permanent Black.

———. 2006. 'Voting in India: Electoral Symbolism the Party System and the Collective Citizen', in Romain Bertrand, Jean-Louis Briquet and Peter Pels (eds), *The Hidden History of the Secret Ballot.* Bloomington and Indianapolis: Indiana University Press.

———. 2008. 'Why Should We Vote?', in Christophe Jaffrelot and Peter van der Veer (eds), *Patterns of Middle Class Consumption in India and China.* New Delhi: Sage.

Jayal, Neerja and Pratap Bhanu Mehta (eds). 2010. *The Oxford Companion to Politics in India.* New Delhi: Oxford University Press.

Jeffrey, Craig. 2009. *Timepass: Youth, Class, and the Politics of Waiting in India.* Stanford: Stanford University Press.

Jenkins, Rob. 2004. *Regional Reflections: Comparing Politics across India's States.* New Delhi: Oxford University Press.

Jodhka, Surinder. 2012. 'The Problem', *Seminar*, 633.

Kapur, Devesh and Pratap Bhanu Mehta. 2005. *Public Institutions in India: Performance and Design.* New Delhi: Oxford University Press.

Katju, Manjari. 2006. 'Election Commission and Functioning of Democracy in India', *Economic and Political Weekly*, 41(17): 1635–40.

Kaviraj, Sudipta. 2003. 'On the Crisis of Political Institutions in India', *Contributions to Indian Sociology*, 18(2): 223–43.

———. 2011a. 'Indian Politics', Lecture, University of Pavia, May.

———. 2011b. 'On the Enchantment of the State: Indian Thought on the Role of the State in the Narrative of Modernity', in Akhil Gupta and K. Sivaramakrishnan (eds), *The State in India after Liberalization: Interdisciplinary Perspectives.* London and New York: Routledge.

Kohli, Atul. 1988. *India's Democracy: An Analysis of Changing State–Society Relations.* Princeton, New Jersey: Princeton University Press.

Kothari, Rajni. 1970. *Caste in Indian Politics.* New Delhi: Orient Longman.

Krishna, Anirudh. 2010. 'Local Politics', in Neerja Jayal and Pratap Bhanu Mehta (eds), *The Oxford Companion to Politics in India.* New Delhi: Oxford University Press.

Kumar, B. Venkatesh. 2009. *Electoral Reforms in India: Current Discourses.* New Delhi: Rawat Publications.

Kumar, Sanjay. 2009. 'Patterns of Political Participation: Trends and Perspective', *Economic and Political Weekly*, 44(39): 47–51.

Kumar, Sanjay and Praveen Rai. 2013. *Measuring Voting Behaviour in India.* New Delhi: Sage.

Lama-Rewal, Stephanie Tawa. 2009. 'Studying Elections in India: Scientific and Political Debates', *South Asia Multidisciplinary Academic Journal*, 3, http://samaj.revues.org/index2784.html (accessed 24 January 2012).

Lokniti. 2008. *State of Democracy in South Asia*. New Delhi: Centre for the Study of Developing Societies and Oxford University Press.

Macmillan, Alistair. 2010. 'The Election Commission', in Neerja Jayal and Pratap Bhanu Mehta (eds), *A Dictionary of Indian Politics*. New Delhi: Oxford University Press.

Manor, Jim. 2012. 'Did Poverty Initiatives Help Re-Election?' in Lawrence Saez and Gurharpal Singh (eds), *New Dimensions of Politics in India*. London: Routledge.

Mehta, Pratap. 2003. *The Burden of Democracy*. New York, Penguin.

Mehta, Uday. 2007. 'Indian Constitutionalism: The Articulation of a Political Vision', in Dipesh Chakrabarty, Rochona Majumdar and Andrew Sartori (eds), *From the Colonial to the Postcolonial: India and Pakistan in Transition*. New Delhi: Oxford University Press.

Michelutti, Lucia. 2008. *The Vernacularisation of Democracy: Politics, Caste and Religion in India*. New Delhi and London: Routledge.

Miller, Daniel. 1997. *Capitalism: An Ethnographic Approach*. Oxford: Berg Publishers.

Mosse, David. 1994. 'Idioms of Subordination and Styles of Protest among Christian and Hindu Harijan Castes in Tamil Nadu', *Contributions to Indian Sociology*, 28(1): 67–106.

Narain, Iqbal, K. C. Pande, M. L. Sharma, and Hansa Rajpal. 1978. *Election Studies in India: An Evaluation*. New Delhi: Allied Publishers.

Norval, Aletta J. 2006. 'Democratic Identification: A Wittgensteinian Approach', *Political Theory*, 34(2): 229–55.

Oldenberg, Philip. 1999. 'The Thirteenth Election in India's Lok Sabha (House of the People)'. http://www.asiasoc.org/publications/Indian_elections.13.a.html (accessed 6 November 2013).

Ong, Aihwa. 1987. *Spirit of Resistance and Capitalist Discipline: Factory Women in Malaysia*. New York: State University of New York Press.

Paley, Julia. 2002. 'Toward an Anthropology of Democracy', *Annual Review of Anthropology*, 31:469–96.

———(ed.). 2008. *Democracy: Anthropological Perspectives*. Santa Fe: School for Advanced Research Press.

Palshikar, Suhas. 2007. 'The Imagined Debate between Pollsters and Ethnographers', *Economic and Political Weekly*, 42(43): 24–28.

Parry, Jonathan. 1989. *Death in Banaras*. Cambridge: Cambridge University Press.

Parry, Jonathan and Maurice Bloch (eds). 1989. *Money and the Morality of Exchange*. Cambridge: Cambridge University Press.

Raza, Danish. 2012. 'Move Over Pundits, Detectives Help Parties Choose Candidates'. *First Post*, 12 April, http://www.firstpost.com/politics/move-over-pundits-detectives-help-parties-choose-candidates-273471.html?utm_source=ref_article (accessed 7 October 2013).

Reddy, Sanjay. 2005. 'A Rising Tide of Demands: India's Public Institutions and the Democratic Revolution', in Devesh Kapur and Pratap Bhanu

Mehta (eds), *Public Institutions in India: Performance and Design*, pp. 457–75. New Delhi: Oxford University Press.

Runciman, David. 2008. 'Why Not Eat an Eclair?' *London Review of Books*, 30(19): 11–14.

Ruparelia, Sanjay. 2008. 'How the Politics of Recognition Enabled India's Democratic Exceptionalism', *International Journal of Politics, Culture and Society*, 21(1–4): 39–56.

———. 2011. 'Expanding Indian Democracy: The Paradox of the Third Force', in Sanjay Ruparelia, Sanjay Reddy, John Harriss, and Stuart Corbridge (eds), *Understanding India's New Political Economy: A Great Transformation?* pp. 186–203. London: Routledge.

Schaffer, Frederic Charles. 1998. *Democracy in Translation: Understanding Politics in an Unfamiliar Culture*. Ithaca and London: Cornell University Press.

——— (ed.). 2007. *Elections for Sale: The Causes and Consequences of Vote Buying*. Boulder, Colorado: Lynne Rienner Publishers.

Shah, A. M. (ed.). 2007. *The Grassroots of Democracy: Field Studies of Indian Elections*. Delhi: Permanent Black.

Shah, Ghanshyam. 1975. *Caste Association and Political Process in Gujarat: A study of Gujarat Kshatriya Sabha*. Bombay: Popular Prakashan.

Shastri, Sandeep, K. C. Suri and Yogendra Yadav. 2009. *Electoral Politics in Indian States: Lok Sabha Elections in 2004 and Beyond*. New Delhi: Oxford University Press.

Shils, Edward. 1997. *The Virtue of Civility: Selected Essays on Liberalism, Tradition, and Civil Society*. Indianapolis: Liberty Fund.

Snelling, Jonathan. 2002. *Stranger than the Bullet: An Unconventional History of the Vote*. London: Robson Books.

Suri, K. C. 2009. 'The Economy and Voting in the 15th Lok Sabha Elections', *Economic and Political Weekly*, 44(39): 64–70.

Taussig, Michael. 1980. *The Devil and Commodity Fetishism in South America*. Chapel Hill: University of North Carolina Press.

Taylor, Charles. 2004. *Modern Social Imaginaries*. Durham: Duke University Press.

———. 2007. 'Cultures of Democracy and Citizen Efficacy', *Public Culture*, 19(1): 117–50.

Tocqueville, Alexis de. 1945. *Democracy in America*, vol. 2. New York: Alfred A. Knopf.

Turner, Victor. 1969. *The Ritual Process*. London: Penguin.

———. 1974. *Dramas, Fields, and Metaphors: Symbolic Action in Human Society*. Ithaca: Cornell University Press.

Varshney, Ashutosh. 2002. *Ethnic Conflict and Civic Life: Hindus and Muslims in India*. New Haven: Yale University Press.

Verba, Sidney, Norman H. Nie and Jae-On Kim. 1971. *The Modes of Democratic Participation: A Cross-National Comparison*. Beverly Hills CA: Sage.

Weiner, Myron. 1957. *Party Politics in India: The Development of a Multi-Party System*. Princeton NJ: Princeton University Press.
———(ed.). 1968. *State Politics in India*. Princeton NJ: Princeton University Press.
Wilkinson, Steven. 2004. *Votes and Violence: Electoral Competition and Ethnic Riots in India*. Cambridge: Cambridge University Press.
Yadav, Yogendra. forthcoming. *Election Commission of India Diamond Jubilee Commemorative Volume*.
———. 2007. 'Epilogue: Invitation to a Dialogue: What Work Does "Fieldwork" Do in the Field of Elections?' in A. M. Shah (ed.), *The Grassroots of Democracy: Field Studies of Indian Elections*. Delhi: Permanent Black.
———. 2010. 'Political Representation', in Neerja Jayal and Pratap Bhanu Mehta, *A Dictionary of Indian Politics*. New Delhi: Oxford University Press.
Yadav, Yogendra and Suhas Palshikar. 2009. 'Between Fortuna and Virtu: Explaining the Congress' Ambiguous Victory in 2009', *Economic and Political Weekly*, 44(39): 33–46.

Field Reports (Unpublished)

Carswell, Grace and Geert De Neve. 2009. 'Allapuram Election Report, Tamil Nadu'.
Chakrabarty, Dolonchampa. 2009. 'Report on West Bengal: Parliamentary Election 2009'.
Datar, Abhay. 2009. 'Comparative Electoral Ethnographies — Report, Maharashtra'.
Falcao Vanita. 2009. 'CEE Report, Rajasthan'.
Goldy M. George. 2009. 'A Research of Chotte Katekoni village of Jangir–Champa in Chattisgarh'.
Jani, Mahashweta. 2009. 'An Ethnographical Study of Elections '09 in Modasa — Gujarat'.
Krishnamurthy, Mekhala. 2009. 'CEE Report: Harda'.
Kumar, Satendra. 2009. 'Report Prepared for the Comparative Electoral Ethnographies Project, UP'.
Narayan, Badri. 2009. 'Sawaa Lakh ki Baat (Worth a Lakh and a Quarter): An Election in a Village, Uttar Pradesh'.
Nasir Rosina. 2009. 'Comparative Electoral Ethnography, Delhi'.
Singh, Priyadarshini. 2009. 'Comparative Electoral Ethnography: Bihar'.

Film

Slumdog Millionaire. Dir. Danny Boyle. Christian Colson, 2008.

About the Author

Mukulika Banerjee is Associate Professor, Department of Anthropology, London School of Economics and Political Science. She was educated at the Universities of Delhi and Oxford and has previously held appointments at Wolfson College, Oxford, and University College London. Her publications include *The Pathan Unarmed: Opposition and Memory in the North West Frontier* (2001), *The Sari* (2003, co-authored with Daniel Miller) and *Muslim Portraits: Everyday Lives in India* (2008, edited). She is also the editor of the Routledge book series 'Exploring the Political in South Asia'.

Index

of, 18; public deliberation and
(peaceful) protest, 19
demonic nature of political discourse, 105–13
dharma to vote, 99–100, 140, 263
door-to-door campaigning, 56–60
Dravida Munnetra Kazhagam
(DMK), 52–53, 65, 123, 126,
129
Dunn, John, 30, 172
duty to vote, 9, 38, 78, 91–92, 99–100,
114, 140, 162, 164–65

ek din ka sultan, 83, 140
election campaign, description of,
40; announcement of candidates, 40, 45–47; candidate's
good oratorical style, 71; electoral alliances, role of, 77–80;
Gujarat constituency, case example, 46–47; importance of
'being seen', 71–75, 179; Lalu
Prasad's rally, 68–69; local party
machines campaigning, 75–77;
Mayawati's rally, 70; Narendra
Modi's rally, 70–71; nomination
sabha, 45–47; North-East Delhi
constituency, case example,
44–45; organising, 47–48; party
workers, political work of, 40,
43, 47–71; politeness, norms
of, 83–86; pre-nomination
work, 43–45; Rahul Gandhi's
public meeting, 67–68, 92;
Shahnawaz Hussain's campaign
(BJP–JD[U]), 61–62; show of
strength, 46; threat of violence
during, 80–81, 83–86. *See also*
party workers, political work
of; promotions, campaign
Election Commission of India
(ECI), 10–11, 119–21; constitutional authority, 117; role in
Indian public life, 54–55

election day, 127–38; aged voters,
plight of, 132–33; atmosphere
of polling stations, 133; casting
of vote, 134–35; *chunav samagri*
(election materials), 122; day
before, 122–27; paperwork, 138;
presence of 'micro observers',
137; *samagri vitaran* (distribution of materials), 122; sealing
process, 127; 'Vote Puja' (vote
worship), 138–40; voters, preparation of, 127–28
election duty, 116–17, 122–23, 138,
206, 222, 237, 247, 270
election officials: Annual Confidential Report (ACR), 117;
chunav samagri, 122; division
of labour between, 118; duty of,
116; election duty as 'serving the
nation' *(desh seva)*, 117; essential supplies to, 122–23; food,
137; honoraria given to, 126; at
local level, 116; marking on left
index finger, 121–22; procedure
for recording essential information, 118; procedures to handle
problematic situations, 118;
process of 'randomisation', 116;
samagri vitaran, 122; sealing
process, 127; stress and tension,
116–17; training sessions, 118
elections: anthropology and, 22–26;
as carnivals, 3, 10–16, 80–83;
2009 comparative electoral
ethnographies (CEE) project,
31–39; definition, 172–73; election officials, duty of, 116–18;
ethnographic perspective on,
6–7, 26–31; 1962 General
Elections, 120–21; as 'great
festival' *(chunavi mahaparv)*,
117; history of, 119–22; Indian
election studies, 19–22; as a key
indicator of democracy, 16–19;

contact with individual voters, 56–59; *Jan sabhas*, 60; large rallies, 65–71; last minute preparations, 126; lunch and dinner gatherings, 61–65; *nukkad* meetings, 60; organised youth meetings, 60–61; organising campaigns, 47–48; *padyatras*, 60; pit-stop tours, 63; as a polling booth agent, 128; at polling booths, 128; producing and distributing promotional material, 49–56; public meetings, 59–71; transportation of voters, 131; venues for meetings, choosing, 66

Pattali Makkal Katchi (PMK), 78

permanent displays, 50, 89

pit-stop tours, 63

politeness, norms during elections, 83–86

political language, 40; bilingualism in, 91–92; caste-based, 94–96; corrupting nature of politics, ways of explaining, 109–12; demonic nature of, 105–13; Dravidian political rhetoric, case of, 101; English words, use of, 88–91; illiterate voters and, 93; jokes, 100–1; names and acronyms, 92–94; neologisms, 100–1; and perceptions of politicians, 106–7; political rhetoric, 101–5; popularly-used terms relating to politics, 91; 'vote', 89–90; 'vote bank', 91; UPA government, parody for, 100; use of euphemism and analogy, 96–98; use of marriage-related metaphors, 97–98; vernacular alternatives for English word, 90–91; *matdan*, 98–100

political music, 54

political representation in India, 175–76

political rhetoric, 101–5

political work, 40, 43, 47–71. *See also* party workers, political work of

polling booth, culture of, 40–41; booths designated as 'sensitive" 125–26; making arrangements, 124–25; research site in Meerut district, 124; school buildings as polling stations, 124–25; sealing process, 127; Sector Magistrate (SM), visit of, 126; security personnel and mobile police teams, role of, 125

polling officials (PO), 118, 137

popular political understandings, 11

popular sovereignty, 3, 140

postal voting, 142, 158

posters, 49

'predicting' election results, 21

pre-nomination work, 43–45

presiding officer (PRO), 118, 127

Prevention of Atrocities Act, 153

promotions, campaign, 49–56; bottles of liquor, free distribution of, 50; campaign vehicles, 51; employment opportunity and, 50; flags, 49; giant cutouts, 50, 89; handbills, 49; *Jan sabhas*, 60; merchandise, 51; murals or wall paintings, 49, 87–88; Narendra Modi's TV appearances, 50; *nukkad* meetings, 60; organised youth meetings, 60–61; *padyatras*, 60; paid news, 51–52; pamphlets, 49; permanent displays, 50, 89; political music, 54; posters, 49; street theatre, 49; text messages, 52–53; TV appearances, 50; vans with loud-hailers, 49–50, 90